DATE DUE

ANIMAL ACTS

ANIMAL ACTS

Configuring the Human in Western History

Edited by
Jennifer Ham and Matthew Senior

ROUTLEDGE
New York & London

Published in 1997 by
Routledge
29 West 35th Street
New York, NY 10001

Published in Great Britain by
Routledge
11 New Fetter Lane
London EC4P 4EE

Library of Congress Cataloging-in-Publication Data

Animal acts : configuring the human in western history / edited by
  Jennifer Ham and Matthew Senior.
      p.   cm.
  Includes bibliographical references and index.
  ISBN 0-415-91609-7. — ISBN 0-415-91610-0 (pbk.)
    1. Human beings—Animal nature.   2. Philosophical anthropology.
  3. Human beings in literature.   I. Ham, Jennifer.
  II. Senior, Matthew.
  GN280.7.A55   1996
  128—dc20   96-38517
                                                                  CIP

Contents

Contributors

Karla Armbruster is Assistant Professor of American Studies at the University of Colorado–Boulder. She is presently completing a book on environmental advocacy in American literature and culture.

James W. Armstrong is Visiting Assistant Professor of English at Northwestern University. He is the coauthor of *Country Survey*, and his poems and essays have appeared in *Riverwatch, Snowy Egret, Orion Magazine,* and *TriQuarterly.*

David Clark is Associate Professor of English and Co-Director of the Plurality and Alterité Interdisciplinary Research Group at McMaster University. He is coeditor and has contributed essays to *Intersections: Nineteenth-Century Philosophy and Contemporary Theory* and *New Romanticisms: Theory and Critical Practice.* He has also contributed articles to *Monster Theory: Reading Culture* and *Freakery: Cultural Spectacles of the Extraordinary Body.*

Tom Conley is Professor of French at Harvard University. His recent work includes *Film Hieroglyphs: Ruptures in Classical Cinema; The Graphic Unconscious in Early Modern French Writing; The Self-Made Map: Cartographic Writing in Early Modern France;* and translations of *The Fold* by Gilles Deleuze and *The Year of Passages* by Réda Bensmaïa.

Paul H. Fry is William Lampson Professor of English and Master of Ezra Stiles College at Yale University. He is the author of *The Reach of Criticism: Method and Perception in Literary Theory; The Poet's Calling in the English Ode;* and *A Defense of Poetry: Reflections on the Occasion of Writing.*

Jennifer Ham is Assistant Professor of German and Humanistic Studies at the University of Wisconsin–Green Bay. She has published on nineteenth- and twentieth-century German culture and film and is presently completing a book entitled *Urban Amusements: Wedekind, Physicality and Popular Entertainment at the Turn of the Century.*

Marie-Hélène Huet is Frederick Huetwell Professor of Romance Languages at the University of Michigan. She is the author of *L'Histoire des voyages extraordinaires; Le Heros et son double; Rehearsing the Revolution: The Staging of Marat's Death 1793–1797; Monstrous Imagination;* and *Mourning Glory: The Will of the French Revolution.*

Charles D. Minahen is Associate Professor of French at Ohio State University. He is the author of *Vortex/t: The Poetics of Turbulence;* the editor of *Figuring Things: Char, Ponge, and Poetry in the Twentieth Century;* and the coeditor of *Situating Sartre in Twentieth-Century Thought and Culture* (forthcoming).

Joyce E. Salisbury is Frankenthal Professor of History at the University of Wisconsin–Green Bay. Her most recent books include *Church Fathers, Independent Virgins; The Beast Within: Animals in the Middle Ages;* and *Perpetua's Passion: A Study of Martyrdom and Memory.* She is also series editor for the Garland Medieval Casebook series.

Marian Scholtmeijer teaches in the English and First Nations Studies Program at the University of Northern British Columbia. She is the author of *Animal Victims in Modern Fiction: From Sanctity to Sacrifice* and has contributed articles to *Animals and Women: Feminist Theoretical Perspectives; Environmental Ethics;* and *Women and the Canadian Environment* (forthcoming).

Matthew Senior is Assistant Professor of French at the University of Minnesota–Morris. He is the author of *In the Grip of Minos: Confessional Discourse in Dante, Corneille, and Racine.* "When the Beasts Spoke" is part of a work in progress entitled *Orpheus and Linnaeus: Naming Animals in Classical France.*

Gregory B. Stone is Associate Professor of French, Italian, and Comparative Literature at Louisiana State University. He is the author of *The Death of the Troubadour: The Late Medieval Resistance to the Renaissance.* He is presently finishing a book, tentatively entitled *Boccaccio and the Ethics of Nature.*

Illustrations

Acknowledgments

Both of us are grateful to the following individuals and institutions for the intellectual stimulation, material support, and collegial solidarity they extended to us during different stages of this project: The Institute for Research in the Humanities at the University of Wisconsin–Madison, and in particular its director, Paul Boyer, and assistant administrator, Loretta Freiling; the National Endowment for the Humanities, Anton Kaes, and the fellows of the NEH seminar at the Stanford Center in Berlin; the McKnight Arts and Humanities Endowment of the University of Minnesota; and the Research Councils of the University of New Orleans and the University of Wisconsin–Green Bay.

This project emerged from conference panels on the subject of animality, presented at the Modern Language Association Convention in Chicago and at the University of Kentucky Foreign Language Conference in Lexington, and from the inspiration of our friend and colleague Joyce Salisbury, whose work introduced us to the historicity of animals. We would also like to express our appreciation to Tom and Verena Conley, whose ongoing advice, example, and encouragement have been vital to us over the years and whose hospitality is remembered most fondly. Thanks also to Wolfgang Natter of the University of Kentucky, Maggie Von Hellwig of the University of Minnesota–Morris Library, and Karen Deaver, who carefully read the draft of the entire manuscript and prepared it for publication.

We sincerely thank our families and friends for their patience, love, and good humor and are particularly grateful to have shared vicariously in the animal experiences, compassion, and courage of two astute horsewomen: Gretchen Ham and Fran Senior.

Introduction

We must become beasts to become wise.

—Montaigne, *Apology of Raymond Sebond*

Would that you were as perfect as animals at least! But animals have innocence.

—Nietzsche, *Thus Spoke Zarathustra*

Animal acts: amusing spectacles with animal and human protagonists, a form of popular entertainment with a long history in the West, from the bull acrobats of Crete to the Roman circus, the Renaissance carnival, and the turn-of-the-century variety show.[1] According to the superstitions of the theater, it is unwise to follow animals or children onto the stage, as if animal or child mimesis provoked a catharsis that nullifies the ego identifications and discursive logic of serious adult theater, as if the spectacle of animals and humans performing together called the spectator to other self-recognitions than that of the responsible citizen of the *polis* or the autonomous subject of philosophy and ethics. The animal act configures the human in the company, in the obscure language and thought, of the animal. Animal vitality and consciousness are vicariously restored to the human being, allowing for conceptual breakthroughs and flights of fancy. Men and women participate in the dignity and splendor, the Nietzschean "innocence" and eternal truthfulness of the animal; the living creature, for its part, performs with humans, is metamorphosed, *becomes* human.[2]

The comic, light-hearted animal act of today is a vestige of other activities that humans have engaged in throughout history with and as animals to define themselves as humans: sacrifices, beast mummeries, divinations; metamorphoses, transmigrations, fables; hunting, zoos, circuses; dissections, ape projects, natural histories. In these various animal acts, whether chance

1

encounters or structured performances, the human shares space and consciousness with the beast; deep identifications and violent denegations are acted out. According to the unpredictable logic of the event and according to the rhetoric of the text that records the event, zones of contact between the human and the animal are established, and continuums or gaps in the scale of nature are defined.

The project of Western philosophy has always been to find what is exclusively human in the human animal: man is the rational, speaking, bipedal, tool-making, history-possessing, incest-prohibited, fire-discovering animal. The project of the animal act, on the other hand, is to *con-figure* the human with the animal, to write zoomorphically and anthropomorphically, to define zones of animality in the human and zones of humanity in the animal. In its essence the animal act is a flight from the humanistic definition of man, a descent through the body *out* of the subject/object world of metaphysics, a quest for another kind of language which merges with the sounds and gestures of animals, a pre-philosophical, pre-humanistic language from "the dawn of thinking" which lets nature speak for itself.[3]

We have chosen the word *configure* to characterize the animal act, advisedly. According to its Latin etymology, the word means "to form together, to dispose in a certain form, figure or shape." The first English usages of the word occur in seventeenth-century treatises on astronomy and astrology, where configuration means "the position of the stars in regard to each other" or "the face of the horoscope according to the relative positions of the planets at any time."[4] Currently, the word most frequently refers to computer applications: "the way the constituent parts of a computer system are chosen or interconnected in order to suit it for a particular task or use."[5] In a general sense, configuring evokes the technological mastery of the material and natural world through the deciphering and replication of molecular and biological codes, the reduction of all human and natural signs to the binary code of the computer. Configuration is one translation of *Ge-stell*, Heidegger's term for the exploitive, instrumental representation at the core of technology, the "enframing" of nature as a vast reservoir of energy to be stockpiled and spent.[6]

To speak of animal configuration, however, is to go against the grain of technological reason and question whether computer writing is a universal model of figuration applicable to inorganic, organic, and cognitive processes. Animal sounds, signs, and consciousness are raised as a countermodel to scientific denotation. The animal is called upon as a witness to the primordial truth of poetry and philosophy, the immanent intuition of the being of the world which Rilke describes in one of his letters:

You must understand the concept of the "Open," which I have tried to propose in the elegy, in such a way that the animal's degree of consciousness sets
it into the world without the animal's placing the world over against itself at
every moment (as we do); the animal is *in* the world; we stand *before it* by
virtue of that peculiar turn and intensification which our consciousness has
taken. By the "Open," therefore, I do not mean sky, air, and space; *they*, too,
are "object" and thus "opaque" and closed to the man who observes and
judges. The animal, the flower, presumably *is* all that, without accounting to
itself, and therefore has before itself and above itself that indescribably open
freedom which perhaps has its (extremely fleeting) equivalents among us
only in those first moments of love when one human being sees his own vast-
ness in another, his beloved, and in man's elevation toward God.[7]

Thus the word *configuration*, which in our culture evokes instrumental,
technological *Ge-stell*, could also be applied to the poetic, animalistic representation that Rilke describes here. The word can house within itself the tension
between scientific and poetic attempts to configure humans and animals.
"Apes are apes, apes are not humans; but because of the very close genetic
similarity which they share (>98% shared DNA), there are neurobiological
grounds to anticipate some degree of similarity in their psychology."[8] This is
the scientific configuration of humans and animals, the quantifiable, codifiable
specification of what is common to both species, to which might be opposed
La Fontaine's myth of the original configuration of man and beast: "When
Prometheus wanted to form man, he took the dominant quality of each beast;
from these different pieces he composed our species; he made that work
which is called the *little world*, the microcosm;"[9] or we could ponder
Shakespeare's more succinct statement in *Midsummer Night's Dream* that
"man is but an ass" (4.1, 206).[10]

From the objective distance of the computer terminal and the laboratory, the
scientist configures with bytes and DNA. Thrown into the phenomenal world of
passing shapes and fleeting sounds, the poet and the philosopher configure man
in the signs and monstrous apparitions that Alonso describes in *The Tempest*:
"Such shapes, such gesture, and such sound expressing / (Although they want
the use of tongue) a kind / Of excellent dumb discourse" (3.3, 37–39).[11]

It is this "excellent dumb discourse" which is the subject of the present study,
a configuration which leads back to the confused origin of humans and animals,
not to the installation of man the decoder and programmer of nature.
Configuration orignally had an astrological meaning in the English language; it
bespoke a world in which the arrangement of the stars was a destiny for man, a
sacred language to be read, not an electronic code to be imposed on the universe.

To open the question and begin to describe the obscure figural ground that humans share with animals, we will make the following observations: animals exhibit *behavior;* they have degrees of consciousness and *language;* their behavior and signifying practices are evolutionarily linked to ours; they apprehend reality, and they apprehend us; at such moments we are phenomenalized by the animal gaze. Perhaps such animal thoughts are radically untranslatable into human language and consciousness, but perhaps such thoughts are the essential ground upon which human rationality emerges. The primordial revelation of the human, the most essential calling to consciousness of man, whether religious conversion, humanistic discovery of desire, philosophical *Dasein,* or ethical imperative, has something to do with this moment of estrangement when the human being catches sight of itself in the eyes of the animal or sees other human beings as animals. As an ethical, linguistic, philosophical, and psychological entity, the human being is that animal which first walks on four feet, then two, and finally three.

The consciousness and language of the animal may mean absolutely nothing and represent for us the core of meaninglessness and the lure of the void which inhabit all thought, communication, and social life. The Heideggerian abyss which separates us from animals may be the void of meaninglessness. The animal may be continually signifying nothing—but so might we. The sacrifice of the animal may be a sacrifice of or to this meaninglessness.[12]

Until we have more solid evidence of what animal consciousness is, we should perhaps refrain from anthropomorphic and zoomorphic fantasy. We should patiently await the experiments of those who study animal consciousness or calculate the percent of DNA that humans share with apes. To do so, however, is to follow a scientific prejudice. The game has already begun; historically and conceptually we are already on Prospero's island. To encounter, to play and act with animals begs the question: we are already thrown into the zoomorphic circle where humans communicate and emote with animals.

Throughout Western history, the significance of such moments of play and performance has been variously received. The transcendental and metaphysical tradition of philosophy in the West (Aristotle, Augustine, Aquinas, Descartes, Hegel) has rejected or considered as a primitive mode of thought the mixing of human and animal traits; essentialist philosophies of Being and Logos have dismissed the signs and behavior of animals as insignificant chatter or mechanical mimicry.[13] A theriophilic ("animal loving"), Orphic line of thinkers (Aesop, Plato, Ovid, Lucretius, the Medieval fablists, Rabelais, Montaigne, La Fontaine, Darwin, Nietzsche) has affirmed the ineradicable and salutary animality of man.[14] This tradition of thought, whatever its local investments in the history of philosophy, has been attentive to animal creativity and exemplarity, sometimes comparing animals favorably to vain and cruel humans, sometimes choosing the very opaqueness and simplicity of animal conscious-ness as a metaphor for the radical otherness of nature within and without man.

Starting with Nietzsche and Heidegger and continuing into the present, ani-mality has become a major issue in contemporary philosophy. Nietzsche's rejection of dualism ("Body I am *entirely*"[15]) involved a deliberate use of animal voices to articulate his philosophy. In his attempt to recover the original sense of Being in the *Dasein*, Heidegger moved human thought close to and then decisively away from animal consciousness.[16] Contemporary post-humanist thinkers and artists have continued to rethink the animal/human border. Gilles Deleuze advocates becoming-animal as a liberating experiment in nomadic thought; he sees a parallel between his work and the striking representations of animal carcasses in the work of Francis Bacon.[17] Jacques Derrida has described animality as a realm of pure difference without distinction.[18] In Jean Baudrillard's writings, the exile and rational analysis of animal behavior signi-fies the triumph of Enlightenment ideology and the loss of symbolic exchange while, at another level, the persistent fascination with animals is an instance of *seduction* and the disintegration of the sign into meaninglessness.[19] In the phi-losophy of Emmanuel Levinas, the foundational ethical moment involves an apprehension of the other as animal.[20]

At times in history, the irreducible animality of man has seemed, paradoxi-cally, to be the only human instinct left on the planet capable of saving man from the excesses of his "humanity." The essays assembled here show that the artistic and historic reinvention of humanness has often involved a return to animality. To invent new languages and civilizations it was necessary to give animal voices to political, philosophical, and moral actors. Marie de France, Boccaccio, and Rabelais used animals to create national literatures and define philosophical epochs; the irrational force of the French Revolution could only be figured as an animal myth by its historians; modernity, in Flaubert, Nietzsche, Wedekind, and Kafka, is expressed by metamorphosis and the con-fusion of human and animal traits; Dian Fossey's experiences with gorillas raise most of the fundamental issues of our age: nationalism, the environment, gen-der, race; the style and intelligibility of the English language itself are discussed from a zoomorphic perspective by E. B. White.

In the most extreme example of salutary animality discussed in this volume, the French philosopher Emmanuel Levinas describes his encounter with the dog Bobby in Concentration Camp 1492. The animal's recognition of the Jewish prisoners as humans, in the most desultory and inhuman landscape of the twentieth century, somehow makes it possible to continue to philosophize on the basis of this fundamental ethical intuition.

In the final animal act of this volume, a comic farce after the atrocities of history, all of the pathos and stupidity, the grandeur and *bêtise*, of the American fifties appears to us in Gary Larson's cartoons. From the darkest depths of the Holocaust to the comically absurd present, the tale of the twentieth century can be told as an animal act.

Notes

1. On the history of animal acts, see Gustave Loisel, *Histoire des ménageries de l'antiquité à nos jours* (Paris: Doin, 1912); Roland Auget, *Les Jeux Romains* (Paris: Flammarion, 1970) and *Histoire et légendes du cirque* (Paris: Flammarion, 1974); Pascal Jacob, *La Grande Parade du cirque* (Paris: Gallimard, 1992).

2. The notion of *becoming*, as a transformative exchange of human and animal traits, is outlined by Gilles Deleuze and Félix Guattari in *A Thousand Plateaus: Capitalism and Schizophrenia*, trans. Brian Massumi (Minneapolis: University of Minnesota Press, 1987), 26–38, 232–309. See also Tom Conley's essay in the present volume.

3. The phrase is taken from Heidegger's "Letter on Humanism," *Martin Heidegger Basic Writings*, trans. David Krell (San Francisco: Harper Collins, 1993), 251. Heidegger, along with Nietzsche and Gilles Deleuze, would have to be considered a major philosophical reference for a theory of the animal act: the *Dasein* is close to animal consciousness in its pure apprehension of Being. Heidegger specifically refers to animals in his essay on Rilke, "What Are Poets For?" *Poetry, Language, Thought*, trans. Albert Hofstadter (New York: Harper & Row, 1971), where he explores the convergence of the poet's and the animal's intuition of Being. In the "Letter on Humanism," the author of *Sein und Zeit* argues that animals are "in a certain way most closely akin to us." And yet, crucially, Heidegger insists that they are "at the same time separated from our ek-sistent essence by an abyss" (230).

4. *Webster's New Twentieth-Century Dictionary*, 2nd. ed., "configure."

5. *Oxford English Dictionary*, "configuration."

6. *The Question Concerning Technology*, trans. William Lovitt (New York: Harper & Row, 1977), 19.

7. Cited by Heidegger in "What Are Poets For?" *Poetry, Language, Thought*, trans. Albert Hofstadter, (New York: Harper & Row, 1971), 108.

8. Duane Rumbaugh, "Primate Language and Cognition: Common Ground," *Social Research* 62 (1995), 713.

9. Jean de La Fontaine, preface to *Les Fables, Oeuvres complètes*, ed. Jean-Pierre Collinet, 2 vols. (Paris: Gallimard, 1991) vol. 1, 8.

10. *The Riverside Shakespeare* (New York: Houghton Mifflin, 1974), 241.

11. Ibid., 1627.

12. On animal sacrifice and its social implications, see Marcel Detienne, *The Cuisine of Sacrifice Among the Greeks*, trans. Paula Wissing (Chicago: University of Chicago Press, 1989); Marcel Mauss, *The Gift: The Form and Reason of Exchange in the*

Archaic Societies, trans. W. D. Halls (New York: Routledge, 1990); Georges Bataille, *The Accursed Share*, trans. Robert Hurley (New York: Zone, 1991); and Jean Baudrillard, *Symbolic Exchange and Death*, trans. Iain Grant (London: Sage, 1993).

13. On animals in the ancient world, see Richard Sorabji, *Animal Minds and Human Morals* (New York: Cornell University Press, 1993). For the medieval period: Joyce Salisbury, *The Beast Within: Animals in the Middle Ages* (New York: Routledge, 1994). For the Renaissance and after: Keith Thomas, *Man and the Natural World* (New York: Pantheon, 1983); Ernst Mayr, *The Growth of Biological Thought: Diversity, Evolution, and Inheritance* (Cambridge: Harvard University Press, 1982); and Harriet Ritvo, *The Animal Estate: The English and Other Creatures in the Victorian Age* (Cambridge: Harvard University Press, 1987). Also see "Zoological Taxonomy and Real Life," *Realism and Representation: Essays on the Problem of Realism in Relation to Science, Literature, and Culture*, ed. George Levine (Madison: University of Wisconsin Press, 1993), 235–254; "Barring the Cross: Miscegenation and Purity in Eighteenth- and Nineteenth-Century Britain," *Human, All Too Human*, ed. Diana Fuss (New York: Routledge, 1994); "Border Trouble: Shifting the Line between People and Other Animals," *Social Research* 62 (1995), 481–500. On Descartes, see Leonora Rosenfield, *From Beast Machine to Man Machine: The Theme of the Animal Soul in French Letters from Descartes to La Mettrie* (New York: Oxford University Press, 1940); and Bruce Mazlish, *The Fourth Discontinuity: The Co-Evolution of Humans and Machines* (New Haven: Yale University Press, 1993). Hegel discusses animality in "the "artificer" section of the *Phenomenology of Spirit*, trans. J. N. Findly (Oxford: Clarendon Press, 1977), 421–424. For a general discussion of animality and philosophy, see J. B. Pontalis, ed. *De la Bêtise et des bêtes* (Paris: Gallimard, 1988); James Sheehan and Morton Sosna, eds. *The Boundaries of Humanity: Humans, Animals, Machines* (Berkeley: University of California Press, 1991); Jean-Yves Goffi, *Le Philosophe et ses animaux* (Nîmes: Jacqueline Chambon, 1994); and Diana Fuss, ed. *Human, All Too Human* (New York: Routledge, 1996).

14. On the thereophilic tradition, see George Boas, *The Happy Beast in French Thought of the Seventeenth Century* (Baltimore: Johns Hopkins Univeristy Press, 1933).

15. Friedrich Nietzsche, *Thus Spoke Zarathustra* in *The Portable Nietzsche*, trans. Walter Kaufmann (New York: Viking, 1963), 146.

16. See note 3.

17. *A Thousand Plateaus*, op. cit.; *Francis Bacon: logique de la sensation*, 2 vols. Paris: Editions de la Différence, 1994.

18. Jacques Derrida, "On Reading Heidegger: An Outline of Remarks to the Essex Colloquium," *Research in Phenomenology* 17 (1987): 171–188. See David Clark's essay in the present volume for a complete citation and discussion of this passage.

19. Jean Baudrillard, *Symbolic Exchange and Death*, 166–177; *Seduction*, trans. Brian Singer (New York: St. Martin's, 1990), 88–89.

20. Emmanuel Levinas, *Difficult Freedom: Essays on Judaism*, trans. Sean Hand (London: Athlone, 1990), 153.

1 ❧

Human Beasts and Bestial Humans in the Middle Ages

Joyce E. Salisbury

One of the major ways people define their identity is in relation to what they are not. Questions of the definition of humanity have frequently formed the basis for our reflections on animals. As Keith Thomas, in his study on man and the natural world, observed: ". . . it is impossible to disentangle what the people of the past thought about plants and animals from what they thought about themselves."[1] This is certainly true; as we study people's views of animals, we learn their perceptions of humanity. In this essay, I shall analyze medieval explorations of human identity that were shaped by people's definition of animality. Medieval thinkers repeatedly defined humanity by trying to establish a clear boundary between humans and animals. By focusing our attention on this interspecies border, we can learn much about animals, people, and human identity.

Medieval ideas were significantly shaped by Christian thinkers in the early centuries after the birth of Jesus. Among other topics, Church Fathers considered the relationship between humans and animals and decided the two had nothing in common. Animals had no souls; they could look forward to no afterlife; they existed only to serve human needs. The boundaries between human and animal were wide, and theologians believed there was no possibility for transition between the species. St. Augustine can speak for the position of the early Church when he wrote: "And so I should not believe, on any consideration, that the body—to say nothing of the soul—can be converted into the limbs and features of animals. . . ."[2] Classical tales of metamorphosis were declared impossible, and the permeable boundary that seemed to exist between people and animals in Greco-Roman times was sealed.

In the twelfth century, this belief in the dramatic difference between humans and animals began to change. Due probably to the repopularization of some classical texts, people again began to be portrayed along a continuum with animals, sharing many bestial traits.[3] In medieval literature from the twelfth century to the end of the Middle Ages, we see a growing preoccupation with human/animal hybrids and a growing credulity with regard to such creatures. In striking contrast to Augustine, the early-thirteenth-century chronicler Gerald of Wales told the following tale:

> One evening . . . he happened to meet a girl whom he had loved for a long time. . . . He was enjoying himself in her arms and tasting her delights, when suddenly, instead of the beautiful girl, he found in his embrace a hairy creature, rough and shaggy, and indeed, repulsive beyond words. As he stared at the monster his wits deserted him and he became quite mad.[4]

The transition from the confident articulation of separation of species to the bewildering blurring of boundaries described by Gerald may be seen in a number of sources, from scientific to literary. One way to study the edges of the human and animal worlds is to look at creatures that were believed to occupy a borderline region between the species. People defined their humanity as they thought about half-human creatures that increasingly populated art and literature after the twelfth century.

Literature and art increasingly portrayed borderline creatures like apes, centaurs, wild people, and even whole "races" that seemed to combine features of humans and animals. Descriptions of most of these creatures had been inherited from classical texts, but most of the early medieval texts either ignored or expressed skepticism about their existence. Augustine can again serve to represent the early Christian position:

> This assumes, of course, the truth of their stories about the divergent features of those races, and their great difference from one another and from us. The definition is important; for if we did not know that monkeys, long-tailed apes and chimpanzees are not men but animals, those natural historians . . . might pass them off on us as races of men, and get away with such nonsense.[5]

After the twelfth century, skepticism seems to have been cast away, and exotic creatures from hybrids to monstrous races captured the medieval imagination.[6] Many of the creatures were included in the thirteenth-century

Figure 1. Manticore. Bodleian Library, University of Oxford. MS. Bodl. 764, fol. 25r.

bestiaries, and the entries in these "scientific" works reveal the extent to which people could imagine the blurring of the species.

One popular example in the bestiary is the manticore, shown here in Figure 1. The manticore was described as having the head of a man, the body of a lion, and a tail with the sting of a scorpion.[7] This creature literally embodied the hybridization that people's imaginations created on the border of the species. The question, for the scientific bestiary (and its readers), was whether this creature was human or animal. The face is visually a defining feature, marking a creature as human. The face was thought to reveal intellect ("reason" in medieval terminology) which was the *sine qua non* of humanity. So, with a human face, the manticore might rightfully be considered human in spite of the bestial body. However, the manticore's behavior marked it as animal. The bestiary gave the manticore characteristics that would define it as vicious—an animal quality: it had a triple row of teeth and blood-red eyes.

Descriptions of teeth and blood in the eyes revealed a vicious, passionate nature. By locating these characteristics in the humanlike face, the reader was cued to see the beast in the visage of the man. Finally, the bestiary tells us that the manticore had an insatiable taste for human flesh.[8] The manticore in Figure 1 is shown indulging this taste. Perhaps more than any other behavior, the taste for human flesh defined creatures as bestial in the medieval mind. Humans eat animals; animals eat humans. Therefore, if something eats humans, it is an animal. In spite of his human face, the manticore happily chewing on a human leg was an animal.

The manticore might have been seen as purely an animal that only appeared to resemble a human. This would have followed the analysis of Augustine: they were animals which the uninformed saw as human. However, the texts show that people were not only concerned with surface characteristics that seemed to blend species. Sometimes their descriptions showed concern for a mixing of the actual essence of human and animal. For example, the bestiary says of centaurs that ". . . the nature of men and horses can be mixed."[9] If the actual nature of humans and animals could be mixed, then increasingly the only way to sort out the difference was by behavior, as we saw in the manticore. His eating habits definitively defined him as animal.

The concern for ambiguous species extended well beyond the scientific bestiaries. We can also trace the increasing popularity of borderline creatures in late medieval travel literature. The fourth-century *Life of Alexander* was translated into vernacular languages after the twelfth century and spread widely,[10] no doubt fascinating readers with tales of Alexander's encounter with Amazons, "dog-headed men and men without heads who had eyes and mouths in their chests."[11] Another extremely popular travel story was *Mandeville's Travels*, which was written in French in about 1360, then translated quickly into every major European language.[12] Mandeville's work is rich in detail drawn from many earlier medieval sources and represents almost a compendium of exotic creatures that inhabited late medieval imaginations. All the monstrous races, from dog-headed cynocephali to giants, to sciopods (creatures with one giant foot) appear in the travelogue, and many of the creatures are described with the kind of detail designed to accent their bestiality. For example, the cynocephali, giants, and other monsters were described as cannibals, attributing to them, like the manticore, the quality that most defined animals, the desire to eat humans.[13] The popularity of *Mandeville's Travels* expresses the late medieval preoccupation with creatures on the border of humanity, and literature like this probably also served to increase the fascination.

The proliferation in literature and art of such creatures on the edges between humans and animals reveals the change in mind-set that began to return medieval Europe closer to the classical view that saw humans and animals along a continuum. This trend culminated in treatment of metamorphosis— the shape-shifting between human and animal.

Pagan literature (both classical and Germanic) offered many tales of meta- morphosis. These stories show an awareness of animal qualities within each of us, and in the stories people are usually transformed when they are indulging in practices usually defined as bestial. For example, in an Irish myth a man changes into a swan to possess a woman he desires.[14] This transformation links the human and animal world at a moment of sexuality, a time when people imagined the animal side emerged. Sometimes animal traits were undesirable ones: lust, cannibalism, or violence. At other times, however, animal traits, like strength or cunning, were sought out. In the *Volsunga Saga* two men put on wolfskins to take on the fierceness and invincibility of that animal.[15]

Whether people were trying to mimic good or bad animal qualities, pagan metamorphosis myths expressed the emergence of animal traits at the expense of human ones. This perception required a belief in humans as a mingling of both animal and human, a belief in a continuum of life that linked human and animal. When confronted by such tales, early Church Fathers rejected them as impossible.[16] This ecclesiastical position influenced religious and secular law, such as the Norwegian law code which stated: "No man shall utter slan- der . . . or tell impossible tales about another. Impossible is that which cannot be true . . . like calling him a werewolf. . . ."[17] However, the early medieval paradigm of the separation of humans from animals did not last.

In the twelfth century we may see a significant turning point in medieval perceptions of metamorphosis. One measure of such change may be seen in the fortunes of Ovid's book, *Metamorphosis*, devoted to the subject of transfor- mations. Before the twelfth century, there were very few copies made of this text. Between the twelfth and the fourteenth centuries, there was an explosion of popularity of it, shown in the numbers of new manuscripts, but also in the many commentaries on the work.[18]

Furthermore, from the twelfth century to the end of the Middle Ages there were increasing references in the literature to people changing into animals. In addition to the shape-shifting woman described above, Gerald of Wales described old women in Wales, Scotland, and Ireland who changed themselves into hares so they could steal people's milk by sucking the teats of cows.[19]

Among the most influential works with this theme is Marie of France's *Lais*, in which she popularized a number of folk tales. In one, she told of a were- wolf called Bisclavret. Marie tells us that "people used to say—and it often actually happened—that some men turned into werewolves and lived in the woods."[20] Marie then proceeds to tell the tale of one such werewolf, and her

story is instructive, for it sheds a good deal of light on medieval views of metamorphosis.

Marie tells the tale of a man who was condemned to become a wolf and
spend three days of every week in the woods. This unhappy man confessed his
plight to his beloved bride. The faithless woman could not accept the beast
within her husband: "She never wanted to sleep with him again."[21] She
revealed the secret to a knight who wished to be her lover. The two stole the
man's clothing, which was the mechanism of his conversion back to human
form, so condemning the man to remain a wolf. While in the woods, the wolf
was befriended by a king, who noticed the animal's exceptional abilities and
said, "It has the mind of a man. . . . This beast is rational—he has a mind."[22]
Unlike the faithless wife who could not see beyond the beast in the man, the
wise king could see the man within the beast.

The wolf's human qualities were confirmed when he attacked the knight
who had taken his wife, clothing, and humanity, and when he attacked his
vain wife and bit off her nose. The king forced the wife to restore the wolf's
clothing. The wolf became a man again, the wife was banished (to bear nose-
less daughters), and the friendship with the king continued.

Marie concluded her tale saying that the lay ". . . was made so it would be
remembered forever."[23] What morals were implicit here that should be
remembered? There was the obvious, of course, that one had better select
one's wife wisely and perhaps not trust a woman with a secret. Beyond this,
however, we learn something about Marie's views of humans and animals. The
man, as sympathetically as he was portrayed, had a beast within him.[24] Half
the time he was an animal before his wife was involved. In this we see most
clearly the beginnings of the twelfth-century acceptance of an animal side of
people. The animal side consumed the human through the agency of a
woman, more carnal and closer to animals than even the half-wolf man.
Through the woman, he lost almost all trace of his humanity, actually and
symbolically, because of the loss of his clothing. However, consistent with
Christian belief, the wolf retained his humanity within, for he did not lose his
rational, human thought. Finally, he was restored to humanity again through
the agency of a friend and lord, a higher spiritual being. Marie shows us that
we are all subject to a loss of humanity if we focus on the wrong things. Faith
in one's lord, a spiritual tie, should be placed above carnal attraction.

The blurring of the boundaries between human and animal led, perhaps
inevitably, to reflections upon what it meant to be human. These reflections
led writers to define "humanity" on the basis of behavior, not simply species.
Like the manticore and the werewolf, one is human if one acts so, and is bes-

tial in other cases. Humanity became defined by such things as wearing clothing, eating in certain ways, and generally acting with reason (rather than
passion). As people began to define humanity by behavior, it seems to have
opened the possibility for redefining people who had previously been accepted
as human. Early Christian thinkers had categorically stated that all people
were human. However, by the late Middle Ages some groups of people
seemed to be less human than others. During the early Middle Ages, the poor
and women may have been considered lesser humans, but by the late Middle
Ages, they were considered closer to animals. As the boundaries between
humans and animals became increasingly blurred, marginalized groups seemed
to slip below the human boundary.

For example, Marie of France's influential twelfth-century fable collection
shows an increasing bestialization of the poor. To the traditional collection of
animal fables, Marie added stories with a folk tradition, and many of these stories featured people, mostly peasants. She has fourteen peasants in her tales
and only four "rich men." The rich men were usually portrayed sympathetically, but the peasants were uniformly shown as stupid. A male peasant foolishly
believes he can give birth, and peasant husbands believe the most transparent
excuses given them by their adulterous wives.[25] One of the defining qualities of
animals in the Middle Ages was their irrationality. Humans had reason, animals did not. By showing peasants as uniformly stupid and irrational within a
context of animal fables, Marie subtly, yet powerfully, reduced their status to
the borders of the bestial.

Peasants were also defined as bestial by their sexual habits, which were designated by the elite as animal-like,[26] and even by elements of their diet. A loaf
called "horsebread" was baked out of the less desirable grains, and this was prepared for consumption by horses, dogs, and paupers.[27] While this practice may
seem a practical way of cheaply feeding the poor, and indeed may have begun
as such, nevertheless the association between paupers and animals would not
have been lost on people who believed profoundly in the notion that you are
what you eat.

Women, too, were increasingly portrayed as bestial. A good example of this
trend is in the fourteenth-century Spanish *Book of Good Love* by Juan Ruiz,
which further developed the comparisons between women and animals in
order to explain how one should treat women. Women were like horses, so
they should be forced into sexual intercourse; women were like hares, who get
confused when hunted.[28] Ruiz went even further in his description of bestial
women. He described a "mare-girl" in detail, and his description shows the
blending of human and animal that characterized this lower-class woman:

> Her ears were greater than the ones that from a donkey sprout;
> Her neck was black, thick-set, and short, and hairy all about;
> Her nose was beaked and longer than the great flamingo's snout; . . .
> Her mouth was fashioned like a hound's with muzzle thick and short;
> With long and narrow horse's teeth of every crooked sort; . . .
> And like a yearling heifer's, great big ankles you would see.[29]

His description continued along those lines until every part of the woman was equated with an animal. He was obviously playing with the notion that intercourse with this creature was bestiality, and he showed how quickly and easily women could be reduced to the animal world.

Images of "wild people" in art and literature reflect another place where preoccupation with what is humanity appears. As David Sprunger notes: "As a group, the wild folk represent at one time both the animal and the human."[30] In these portrayals, men and women were shown covered with body hair and living in an "uncivilized" way with primitive tools and food. The excess bodily hair on these creatures with human faces was similar to the animal body of the manticore; it signaled the bestial. The hairy women were particularly remarkable, since it was considered a characteristic of women that they were not covered with hair. Thus, a woman portrayed as covered with hair was even more striking, more bestial than a man. Hairiness on the body further signaled that wild women were highly sexual,[31] an animal trait, and it seemed to show how close all women were to the bestial.

The increasingly frequent portrayal of women as animal-like can be also seen in stories of sanctity. One example is the metamorphosis of the story of St. Agnes the martyr (portrayed in Figure 2). Agnes was martyred in 304 A.D. under the persecutions of Diocletian. The early versions of the martyrdom tell of a young virgin who was arrested for her belief in Christianity. The Roman prosecutor threatened to place her in a brothel so she would lose her virginity before her death. When she was exposed naked to the crowd, a lustful young man was struck blind for gazing at the virgin. This miracle defeated the governor's intention to have the maiden violated, so he simply sent the executioner to behead her. The martyr died and ascended into heaven with her purity intact.[32]

By the thirteenth century, this fairly straightforward martyr story was dramatically changed. In the famous collection, *The Golden Legend*, Agnes' virginity was saved by a sudden miraculous growth of golden hair that covered her body.[33] This transformation in the story serves to change the role (and image) of the woman. She is made more passive: instead of her power striking her observers blind, her suitors reject her for her furry, bestial appearance.

Figure 2. St. Agnes, from the *Belles Heures of Jean, Duke of Berry*, fol. 178. All Rights Reserved, The Metropolitan Museum of Art, New York.

Figure 2 is from the *Belles Heures of Jean, Duke of Berry*, and dates from the fifteenth century, at the end of the Middle Ages. The figure portrays St. Agnes based on the later version of the tale. Here we see her at the moment of the miracle that saved her virginity. The representation is rare,[34] and the artist's portrayal is remarkably like the images of wild women in the art of the period. Without advance knowledge of her sanctity, one would imagine her as bestial.

We may contrast this portrayal with other, more common images of "hairy anchorites," in which hairiness is a mark of holy people leaving civilization. One such example of a longhaired holy woman was Mary of Egypt, who lived so long in the desert that her hair grew to cover her modestly when her clothes had worn away.[35] Mary did not depart much from the expected portrayal of a modest woman. Her hair stayed on her head in a human fashion and simply served as clothing, the wearing of which was another human characteristic. The contrast between these two images of saints is further evidence that a change was taking place in the late Middle Ages. By then women, even saintly ones, were very close to the animal world. The bestialization of women in the late Middle Ages was one more example of a general blurring of lines between humans and animals.

This general survey of some of the ambiguous creatures in medieval imagination reveals that late medieval thinkers became increasingly concerned with the question: What is a human? Once the clear distinctions between the species had blurred, humanity became not what you are, but how you act. These medieval thinkers defined humanity as the rational, the logical, and the compassionate. Whenever we transcend our animal inclinations—our appetites, our passions—then we embrace what was defined in the Middle Ages as the human. By exploring humanlike animals and bestial humans that seemed to exist on the borders of humanity, we can see the growing ambiguity between the species. By the late Middle Ages the animal that prowls within each of us had become increasingly evident. Thinkers moved toward the Greco-Roman view that saw humans along a continuum with animals, with the potential of lowering themselves to the bestial level by their actions. This view that we can see emerging in the twelfth century dominated Renaissance thought.[36] Beginning in the twelfth century, the metaphors people used to understand themselves and their actions caused them to link themselves with animals in their own imaginations. In the Middle Ages, this did not lead to any particular compassion for animals; that would have to wait until the nineteenth century. However, if Marie of France's sympathetic portrayal of the werewolf is any indication, the changing view of animals perhaps led to more compassion for the animal part within us all.

Notes

1. Keith Thomas, *Man and the Natural World* (New York: Pantheon, 1983), 16. See also, Linzey, Andrew A. and T. Regan, *Animals and Christianity: A Book of Readings* (New York: Crossroad, 1988), xiii, for the same recognition: ". . . the path to self-understanding must proceed through an understanding of 'the other,' even when the other is not human."

2. Augustine, *City of God* (Middlesex: Penguin, 1972), xviii, 18, 783.

3. See J. E. Salisbury, *The Beast Within* (New York: Routledge, 1994) for a full development of this argument.

4. Gerald of Wales, *The Journey through Wales/The Description of Wales* (New York: Penguin, 1988), 116.

5. Augustine, *City of God*, 662–663.

6. J. B. Friedman, *The Monstrous Races in Medieval Art and Thought* (Cambridge, MA: Harvard University Press, 1981), 4.

7. T. H. White, *The Bestiary: A Book of Beasts* (New York: Putnam, 1960), 51.

8. White, 51.

9. White, 51, 86.

10. Callisthenes (Pseudo), *Alexander of Macedon*, trans. Elizabeth H. Haight (New York: Longmans, Green, 1955), 8–9.

11. Callisthenes, 117–119, 122.

12. M. Letts, trans., *Mandeville's Travels* (Nendeln/Liechtenstein: Kraus Reprint, 1967), xxvii–xxxviii. See J. W. Bennett, *The Rediscovery of Sir John Mandeville* (New York: Modern Language Association, 1954), 1. See also pages 219–243 for the immediate and extraordinary influence of the work.

13. Letts, *Mandeville's Travels*, 138, 141–143, 199.

14. J. Gantz, *Early Irish Myths and Sagas* (New York: Penguin, 1981), 111–112.

15. Salisbury, *Beast Within*, 160.

16. Tertullian, "On the Soul" in *Tertullian: Apologetical Works and Minucius Felix Octavius*, trans. Edwin A. Quain (New York: Fathers of the Church, 1950), 255. Ambrose, "On Faith in the Resurrection," *Funeral Orations by Saint Gregory Nazianzen and Saint Ambrose*, trans. L. P. McCauley, et al. (Washington: Catholic University of America, 1953), 256–257.

17. L. M. Larson, *The Earliest Norwegian Laws: Being the Gulathing Law and the Frostating Law* (New York: Columbia University Press, 1935), 123.

18. L. Barkan, Leonard, *The Gods Made Flesh: Metamorphosis and the Pursuit of Paganism* (New Haven: Yale University Press, 1986), 104, 308 n. 17.

19. Gerald of Wales, "History and Topography of Ireland," in *The Historical Works of Giraldus Cambrensis*, ed. Thomas Wright (London: George Bell, 1887), 83.

20. Marie of France, "Bisclavret," in R. Hanning and J. Ferrante, eds., *The Lais of Marie de France*, (Durham, NC: Labyrinth Press, 1978), 92.

21. Marie de France, "Bisclavret," 94.

22. Marie of France, "Bisclavret," 96.

23. Marie of France, "Bisclavret," 100.

24. Hanning and Ferrante point out that the whole lay is a ". . . parable about the forces of bestiality that exist within human nature and how they should (and should not) be confronted, used, or transcended." *Lais of Marie de France*, 101.

25. Harriet Spiegel, ed. and trans., *Marie de France: Fables* (Toronto: University of Toronto Press, 1987), 135–140.

26. Andreas Capellanus, *Art of Courtly Love*, trans. John J. Perry (New York: W. W. Norton, 1969), 149.

27. C. Dyer, *Standards of Living in the Later Middle Ages* (Cambridge: Cambridge University Press, 1989), 57.

28. Juan Ruiz, *The Book of Good Love*, trans. E. K. Kane (Chapel Hill: University of North Carolina Press, 1968), 93, 120.

29. Juan Ruiz, *The Book of Good Love*, 145–146.

30. David A. Sprunger, "Wild Folk and Lunatics in Medieval Romance," in *The Medieval World of Nature*, ed. J. Salisbury (New York: Garland, 1993), 145. The best summary of the wild folk remains R. Bernheimer, *Wild Men in the Middle Ages: A Study in Art, Sentiment, and Demonology* (Cambridge: Harvard University Press, 1952).

31. Joan Cadden, *Meanings of Sex Difference in the Middle Ages* (Cambridge: Cambridge University Press, 1993), 181–182.

32. Prudentius, "The Martyrs' Crown," in *The Poems of Prudentius*, trans. M. C. Eagan, (Washington, DC: Catholic University Press, 1962), 274–280. See also Butler's summary of the accounts of Prudentius and Ambrose, in A. Butler, *The Lives of the Fathers, Martyrs, and other Principal Saints* (New York, n.d), 82–83.

33. Jacobus de Voragine, *The Golden Legend*, trans. G. Ryan and H. Ripperger (New York, 1969), 111.

34. *The Belles Heures of Jean, Duke of Berry*, eds. M. Meiss and E. Beatson (New York: G. Braziller, 1974), 263.

35. J. E. Salisbury, *Church Fathers, Independent Virgins* (London: Verso, 1991), 70.

36. See, for example, G. C. Taylor, "Shakespeare's Use of the Idea of the Beast in Man," *Studies in Philology* 42 (1945), 530–543.

Bibliography

Ambrose. "On Faith in the Resurrection," *Funeral Orations by Saint Gregory Nazianzen and Saint Ambrose*, trans. L. P. McCauley, et al. Washington, DC: Catholic University Press, 1953.

Augustine. *City of God*. Middlesex: Penguin, 1972.

Barkan, Leonard. *The Gods Made Flesh: Metamorphosis and the Pursuit of Paganism*. New Haven: Yale University Press, 1986.

The Belles Heures of Jean, Duke of Berry, eds. M. Meiss and E. Beatson. New York: G. Braziller, 1974.

Bennett, J. W. *The Rediscovery of Sir John Mandeville*. New York: Modern Language Association, 1954.

Bernheimer, R. *Wild Men in the Middle Ages: A Study in Art, Sentiment, and Demonology*. Cambridge: Harvard University Press, 1952.

Butler, A. *The Lives of the Fathers, Martyrs, and Other Principal Saints*. New York, n.d.

Cadden, Joan. *Meanings of Sex Difference in the Middle Ages*. Cambridge: Cambridge University Press, 1993.

Callisthenes (Pseudo). *Alexander of Macedon*, trans. Elizabeth H. Haight. New York: Longmans, Green, 1955.

Capellanus, Andreas. *Art of Courtly Love*, trans. John J. Perry. New York: W.W. Norton, 1969.

Dyer, C. *Standards of Living in the Later Middle Ages*. Cambridge: Cambridge University Press, 1989.

Friedmann, John Block. *The Monstrous Races in Medieval Art and Thought*. Cambridge: Harvard University Press, 1981.

Gantz, J. *Early Irish Myths and Sagas*. New York: Penguin, 1981.

Gerald of Wales. "History and Topography of Ireland," in *The Historical Works of Giraldus Cambrensis*, ed. Thomas Wright. London: George Bell, 1887.

———. *The Journey through Wales/The Description of Wales*. New York: Penguin, 1988.

Jacobus de Voragine. *The Golden Legend*, trans. G. Ryan and H. Ripperger, New York, 1969.

Larson, L. M. *The Earliest Norwegian Laws: Being the Gulathing Law and the Frostating Law*. New York: Columbia University Press, 1935.

Letts, M., trans. *Mandeville's Travels*. Nendeln/Liechtenstein: Kraus Reprint, 1967.

Linzey, Andrew and Tom Regan. *Animals and Christianity: A Book of Readings*. New York: Crossroad, 1988.

Marie of France. "Bisclavret," in R. Hanning and J. Ferrante, eds. *The Lais of Marie de France*. Durham, NC: Labyrinth Press, 1978.

Prudentius. "The Martyrs' Crown," in *The Poems of Prudentius*, trans. M. C. Eagan. Washington, DC: Catholic University Press, 1962.

Ruiz, Juan. *The Book of Good Love*, trans. E. K. Kane. Chapel Hill: University of North Carolina Press, 1968.

Salisbury, Joyce E. *The Beast Within: Animals in the Middle Ages*. New York: Routledge, 1994.

———. *Church Fathers, Independent Virgins*. London: Verso, 1991.

Spiegel, Harriet, ed. and trans. *Marie de France: Fables*. Toronto: University of Toronto, 1987.

Sprunger, David A. "Wild Folk and Lunatics in Medieval Romance," in *The Medieval World of Nature*, ed. J. Salisbury. New York: Garland, 1993.

Taylor, G. C. "Shakespeare's Use of the Idea of the Beast in Man," in *Studies in Philology* 42 (1945), 530–543.

Tertullian. "On the Soul," in *Tertullian: Apologetical Works and Minucius Felix Octavius*, trans. Edwin A. Quain. New York: Fathers of the Church, 1950.

Thomas, Keith. *Man and the Natural World*. New York: Pantheon Books, 1983.

White, T. H. *The Bestiary: A Book of Beasts*. New York: Putnam, 1960.

2 🦎

The Philosophical Beast
On Boccaccio's Tale of Cimone

Gregory B. Stone

> But it is the knowledge of necessary and eternal truths which distinguishes us
> from mere animals, and gives us reason and the sciences, raising us to knowl-
> edge of ourselves and of God. It is this in us which we call the rational soul
> or mind.
>
> —Leibniz, *Monadology*

> It is probably of more advantage to the animal to have his mind filled with
> pleasing and encouraging visions, independently of their truth.
> —Charles Sanders Peirce, "The Fixation of Belief"

One of the tales of the *Decameron* recounts the history of a young Greek
nicknamed Cimone, a nickname that signifies, says Boccaccio, "Brute
Beast."[1] Although the son of a noble aristocrat, Cimone is born and remains an
animalistic idiot—until the day that he chances to catch sight of a most beautiful woman, whereupon he is almost instantly transformed into a brilliant
philosopher and man of letters, a godlike sage. The first half of the tale
recounts Cimone's sudden rise from the depths of bestiality to the heights of
human perfection. He has become a metaphysician, one who "deems divine
things more worthy of reverence than worldly ones."[2] Now, if the tale ended
there, it would be a rather unexceptional Platonizing insistence that love, trig-
gered by the sight of physical beauty, can ennoble the human soul, can deliver
the lover from animality to divinity, can end up as *theoria*, as the rational

vision of eternal, metaphysical truth. But the tale does *not* end there, for, even after becoming "wise" (*savio*) and "most eminent among philosophizers,"[3] Cimone never stops being Cimone. That is, the idiot-turned-philosopher stubbornly refuses to be designated by his actual given name (Galeso) and insists that he still be called "Brute Beast." And this persistence of Cimone's animality, even after he has attained the heights of metaphysical wisdom, is not merely a nominal matter, for the rest of the tale tells of the ferocious philosopher, "fierce as a lion,"[4] perpetrating a terrible spree of kidnapping, murder, and pillage for the sole purpose of achieving his own private, selfish, and worldly desires. My aim in this essay is to consider the following question: what is signified by the philosopher Cimone's *failure to become other than beast?* And here, at the outset, I shall intimate my response: Boccaccio's primary task in writing the tale of Cimone is to reinvent the very essence and purpose of philosophy.

This notion that the philosopher cannot escape animality was greatly pleasing to certain medieval audiences, if we can judge by the tremendous popularity of a legendary episode in the life of Aristotle, a thinker whose authoritative status in the later Middle Ages was such that he was often simply called The Philosopher. According to the thirteenth-century Old French *Lai d'Aristote*, for example, Aristotle, after having exhorted his pupil Alexander the Great not to waste his time loving a certain beautiful young woman, is himself seduced by and enamored with this very same woman. In the end Aristotle is forced to "become beast," as the woman makes him perform a curious sort of foreplay, makes him prance around on all fours, horselike, while she is mounted in a saddle on his back. Aristotle is turned into a horse, a traditional symbol (since at least the time that Plato wrote in the *Phaedrus* of "the wanton horse of the lover's soul") for that part of us that turns against our higher otherworldly metaphysical salvation in favor of this worldly satisfaction.[5]

There is in Boccaccio's tale of Cimone a significant trace of this legendary account of Aristotle's animality. For Cimone's father, who cannot bear the sight of his idiotic son and will have nothing to do with him until after he has been turned from a beast into a philosopher (or, in the father's words, "from a donkey into a man"[6]), is named Aristippo. This name names an indivisible conjunction of philosophy and bestiality, for it is formed by the combination of The Philosopher and the horse (in Greek, *hippo*): Arist[otle] + [h]ippo = Aristippo. Cimone's father's horror at the sight of his animalistic son is thus not the philosopher's horror at what is completely alien or other but, rather, is the philosopher's repression of his own animality, his refusal to acknowledge the latent horseness made manifest, like a neurotic symptom, in the letters of his own name. In naming Cimone's father Aristippo, Boccaccio suggests that the son's persistent animality is not an aberration, that insofar as he is both philosopher and beast he is more like his father than unlike him, that the philosopher is always in some sense an animal. And this shall be the question that guides us for the rest of this essay: *in what sense is the philosopher an animal?*

In the tradition exemplified by the *Lai d'Aristote*, animality is an *ethical failure*. Aristotle knows what a perfect human should do, knows what is morally right, yet he is unable to act in accord with this knowledge. This is clear at the end of the *lai*, where Aristotle argues that the lesson to be drawn from his "becoming beast" is that the temptation to do wrong is so powerful that even the world's greatest philosopher cannot refrain, and hence Alexander should try even harder than ever to keep traveling on the right road of moral rectitude. Animality in this perspective is a failure of one's will to match the perfection of one's knowledge: Aristotle is knowledgeable, but not wise, since *wisdom* (and humanity, as opposed to animality) *is doing the right things*.

This notion that true philosophical wisdom is a primarily a matter of *ethics* is characteristic of the "early" or "Augustinian" period of medieval philosophy. In the *Confessions*, Augustine *knows* the truth of Christianity well before he is able to *will, desire, or enact* his conversion. Knowing the truth but unwilling to act in accordance with it, the preconversion Augustine has the right *theoria* but does not engage in the right *praxis*. For Augustine, wisdom (that which he gains after his conversion) is proper *praxis*, the regulation of one's will, the capacity to act in a way that conforms to what one already knows to be true, the capacity to do the right things. Reiterating the Platonic notion that all knowledge is recollection, remembrance of what one always already innately knows, Augustine suggests that knowledge is in itself not especially problematic, not hard to come by, since all human beings naturally know what is universally true. What *is* hard to come by is the proper disposition of one's will, the proper control of one's desire. Hence, in the earlier medieval period, to be an intellectual or a philosopher (one who knows) is nothing special or extraordinary, is not an especially meritorious distinction (since everyone always already knows). The perfectly wise human, the real sage, in the early Middle Ages is not the one who knows but the one who *acts* properly—that is to say, not the philosopher but the *saint*. In the *Confessions*, this perfect human is Monica, Augustine's unlearned and unlettered mother, who, in matters of the intellect, is the polar opposite of the great philosopher. Saints, the great heroes and heroines of the early Middle Ages, are proclaimed worthy on account of their ethical practices, not on account of their theoretical or metaphysical knowledge. In this early medieval tradition, animality's opposite is saintliness, and animality itself is synonymous, as it is for Boethius, with "wickedness."[7]

But there was also a "late," "Aristotelian," or "scholastic" period of medieval philosophy that insisted that wisdom is primarily a matter of *knowledge*, and that animality is an *epistemological failure*. In this tradition, animality's opposite is philosophy: the philosopher is the one and only type of human who is not an animal, and to be fully human, to transcend animality, is simply identical to being a theorizing metaphysician. This is the era of the birth of the modern university, of the glorification of the "intellectual" as a superior type, the only truly human human being, the only real sage.[8] Late medieval philosophy inverts the Augustinian subordination of knowledge to ethics—or, perhaps more precisely, it collapses these two alternatives into one imperative: to have the right theory *is* the most perfect human practice, to know truth *is* the supreme ethical activity. This difference in priority is clear in the famous opening sentence of Aristotle's *Metaphysics* (a sentence cited by Dante in the opening sentence of his philosophical manifesto, the *Convivio*): "All men naturally desire to know." For Aristotle, what is innate, an unproblematic and wholly untroubling matter of native instinct, universally common to all humans, is desire, one and the same desire to know what is true—whereas what is problematic, a task to be mastered, is the acquisition of the knowledge of truth. Augustine's position is just the reverse: knowledge of truth is innate, universally common to all humans—whereas the task to be mastered is to acquire the right desire, the will to act in accord with one's knowledge. For Augustine, the whole aim or *telos* of human existence is achieved when we desire what we ought to desire; for Aristotle, the whole aim or telos of human existence is achieved when we know truth. In this scholastic tradition, *wisdom is knowing the truth*.[9] In the later Middle Ages the intellectual replaces the saint as the figure upon whom the collective hopes of humanity are pinned. And within this tradition, to suggest, as Boccaccio's tale of Cimone suggests, that the philosopher remains an animal is tantamount to calling him a nonphilosopher and is to deny that he has acquired knowledge of truth.

This scholastic notion that animality's opposite is philosophy or the rational knowledge of truth has its roots in Aristotle's *De Anima*. For Aristotle, animality is, most generally, the mark of anything living, of anything animated by soul (*anima*). But there is, for Aristotle and for the scholastics, another, restricted sense of "animal," closer to our modern-day understanding of the term. This restricted sense of animality is established in Aristotle's tripartite hierarchy of the faculties of soul. There are, for Aristotle, three faculties of soul: (1) the vegetative or nutritive; (2) the sensitive or imaginative; (3) the rational or intellective. All living creatures possess at least the first faculty of soul, the capacity to generate and grow; plants and other low-level organisms possess *only* this first faculty. The second faculty of soul is the capacity to perceive sensations and images; those creatures that we nowadays call "animals" possess this second faculty in addition to the first one. Only humankind among living creatures possesses, in addition to the first two, the third faculty, the capacity to exercise reason in order to know and understand the unseen, universal, disembodied truth behind sensations or appearances, to know the invisible causes of visible perceptions. The difference between animals and humans, in sum, is that whereas animals perceive without understanding, humans are sometimes able to understand what they perceive, to know the truth behind visible appearances. As Aristotle states: "it is, however, clear that perceiving and understanding are *not* the same. For while all animals have a share of the former, only a few have a share of the latter."[10] I presume that by "only a few" Aristotle means "only humans"—or at least this is what he was taken to mean in the late Middle Ages. Hugh of St. Victor, for instance, says that this power of "understanding things absent . . . belongs to humankind alone."[11] Animals dwell in the ignorance of what is true, in error, which Aristotle calls "a peculiar feature of animals"; humans, though also often dwelling in error, can, unlike animals, sometimes attain what Aristotle calls "true knowledge."[12]

As I have suggested, in the scholastic period of medieval philosophy the definition of the dividing line between animality and humanity is rendered quite specific: animals, says Ulrich of Strassburg, differ from humans in that *animals cannot have knowledge of cause and effect.*[13] Now, in the discourse of late medieval philosophy, "knowledge of cause and effect" is another way to say "metaphysics." The difference between animals and humans is that *animals cannot do metaphysics*, cannot participate in the science of cause and effect, cannot contemplate the hidden, unseen Cause (Being or God) that transcends and governs the material world of transitory becoming, of sensations, perceptions, images.

In late medieval philosophy, philosophical wisdom is primarily the knowledge of causes. Real causes, such as the First Cause or Uncaused Cause, are unseen causes, immaterial, invisible, imperceptible to the senses or the imagination. Knowledge of such causes can be gained only through abstract reasoning, logic. This kind of knowledge, which does not depend on images or sense perceptions, and which can be acquired only by creatures who possess the rational faculty of soul, is called *theoria*. In fact *theoria* or "theoretical science" is, for Aquinas, just synonymous with "philosophy," and its distinguishing mark is its "not relying on imagination."[14] Humans differ from animals in that humans can participate in a science, known as "philosophy" or "theory," that does not depend upon images, sensations, material signifiers. Humans transcend their animality only insofar as they participate in that science. In brief, of all humans, *only the theorist is not a beast.*

Late medieval philosophers engage in an orgy of narcissistic self-congratulation, insisting time and again that philosophers are the best, if not the only, human beings (in this respect they are quite faithful to Aristotle, who, in his *Nicomachean Ethics*, calls contemplative reason "the most nearly divine element in us" and asserts that the philosophical life "will be man's complete happiness"[15]). Echoes of this Aristotelian aggrandizement of the philosopher are ubiquitous in the late Middle Ages. Boethius of Dacia, for instance, in his treatise *On the Highest Good or the Philosophical Life*, praises the philosopher as "a man who lives according to the genuine natural order and who has achieved the best and most elevated aim of human life."[16] This extreme exaltation of philosophy and the philosopher leads Dante to proclaim in the *Convivio* (a work whose relentless purpose is to celebrate *theoria* as the supreme human endeavor, as that which allows us to approach divinity, to escape animality by achieving the specifically human *telos*) that the philosopher is "almost another God incarnate."[17] But the award for the most outrageous self-complacency must go to Jean de Jandun, who writes that "not to be in Paris [that is, not to study philosophy] is to be half human."[18] Here we have a clear indication of what it means to be a *beast* in the late medieval discourse of philosophy: if your life is not spent in the pursuit of *theoria*, then you are little or no better than an animal.

An aspect of Boccaccio's aim in writing the tale of Cimone, a philosopher who yet remains a beast and whose father's name names the inseparability of philosophy and animality, is simply and obviously to undermine scholasticism's glorification of the philosopher as the only truly nonanimalistic, the only truly human, human being. Boccaccio ridicules Dante's notion (a notion writ large throughout the *Convivio*) that philosophers are the only perfectly achieved humans, that theorists transcend animality, that perfect knowledge automatically and mechanically entails ethical perfection. Boccaccio mocks the idea, one that still persists today and remains just as ridiculous as ever, that someone who possesses the right theory and who knows the truth will necessarily do the right things, that humanity's knowledge of objective truth will lead to the founding of the correct political and social order. From one perspective, then, Cimone is like a preconversion Augustine (although much more atrociously immoral): he is a philosopher, but his being a philosopher does not keep him from behaving in a manner that humans call "animalistic," does not keep him from abducting an innocent woman against her will and from slaughtering everyone who tries to stand in his way. Cimone ascends to the heights of metaphysical knowledge, but this knowledge does him no good in matters of ethics or morality. Animality's opposite is not *theoria*, as the scholastics and Dante insist that it is, but rather is again, as in the earlier Middle Ages, saintliness.

There is something to be said in favor of this "Augustinian" reading of Boccaccio's tale of Cimone, and indeed this is the sort of reading that dominates recent criticism of the tale.[19] But I shall suggest that Boccaccio's real aim is something more complicated than a simple return to Augustine's insistence that philosophical wisdom is right ethical *praxis*. For Boccaccio takes seriously the scholastic view that knowledge of what is right must be acquired, is problematic, not just given to or naturally known by all humans everywhere at all times. So before we dismiss Boccaccio's representation of a bestial philosopher as a mere imitation of Augustine's representation of his preconversion self, we must press onward, beginning with a slightly closer look at the idea of philosophy that prevailed in Boccaccio's age.

Boccaccio's inherited idea of philosophy (the idea that he wholly rejects by writing the tale of Cimone) was shaped by his reading of Dante's philosophical treatises, the *Convivio* and *De Monarchia*. Although Dante recognizes that the history of philosophy may be divided into both theoretical and practical sciences, he is unequivocal in his insistence that the only philosophical study truly worthy of the name is that whose object is *theoria* and not *praxis* (this would explain why only the theoretical parts of these treatises are complete, while the promised practical parts are left unfinished—since, in Dante's view, once you know the right theory, the right practice follows as a matter of course). For Dante, the theorist's primary task is to attain true rational knowledge of the "first guiding truth," the foundational truth that guarantees that everything logically derived from it is itself also true:

> Since every non-original truth is always revealed on the basis of a first guiding truth, it is inevitable that every investigation should arrive at the cognition of this first truth and should refer to it analytically, in order to attain certainty about all the assertions that have their roots in it.[20]

Dante anticipates the geometric method of Cartesian rationalism, insisting that anything logically linked to an absolutely certain foundation of truth is itself absolutely certain, and that the philosopher's goal is to find such a foundation.

For Dante, "philosophy" or *theoria* means all of the following: (1) certain knowledge of the foundational truth, the truth that anchors and guarantees all other truths; (2) knowledge gained by the rational faculty of soul, "not relying on the imagination"; (3) knowledge of objective truth, truth that is not man-made, that exists prior to and outside of human beings; (4) knowledge that is valued for its own sake, not for its practical benefits.[21]

Dante was craftily able to maintain this fourth criterion while at the same time asserting that *theoria* is the very foundation of all right *praxis*. That is,

Dante's insistence on the superiority of theory to praxis is not by any means an asceticism, not a renunciation of the secular, ethical, political life. On the contrary, theoretical knowledge is our salvation not only in and of itself (the theorist is virtually a divine being, nearly another Christ, "almost another God incarnate") but also insofar as such knowledge provides the ground or foundation for all ethical practices, establishes the right moral and political order for *this* world. Dante was greatly interested in instituting on earth the perfect political system, and he espoused his views concerning such a system in the *De Monarchia*. Dante asserts that the power to govern the social and political order, the power to legislate and enforce morality, should rest entirely in the hands of a single individual—the emperor. This emperor should be absolutely powerful and absolutely wealthy—so powerful and so wealthy that he lacks, and hence desires, nothing other than what he already has. Only such a person can make decisions and judgments that are always in the universal or common interest of humankind, never in his own self-interest. The emperor, having everything and desiring nothing, never acts out of personal or partisan desire for gain or privilege. But how does the emperor know what is in the universal and common interest of humankind? Such knowledge is to be found in *theoria*, in philosophy. The emperor, says Dante, must be a student of Aristotle. The emperor's role is to put into practice the universal truths that are known by philosophers. Theory or philosophical knowledge, then, is our salvation. Theory is the keystone on which the *praxis* of a just society is founded. Without theory, without the certain knowledge of a universal foundational truth that is not contingent but necessary, not historical or manmade but eternal, not subject to the influence of partisan interests and desires but beneficial for the totality of humankind, there can be no just moral order.

But Dante, unlike Plato, does not wed the emperor and the philosopher into a single "philosopher-king." The theorist is perfectly content in beholding universal truths, the emperor perfectly content in governing practical life according to the truths beheld by the theorist. Dante maintains a clear distinction between philosopher and emperor because he wishes to suggest that theory governs practice *from the outside*, that theory does not belong to the order of practical life but rather to a higher, more divine, more universal and transcendent order. The perfect philosopher and the perfect emperor are alike in one respect: *neither has any desire*—and hence neither can be accused of promulgating truths or laws that stem from his own self-interests or desires, neither can be accused of arbitrarily imposing an imaginary order whose *telos* is his own pleasure or satisfaction. There is nothing historically or culturally contingent about the truths or laws found by the philosopher and the emperor.

Moreover, Dante maintains the distinction between philosopher and emperor in order to suggest that, in the final analysis, the philosopher is a more perfect human being than the emperor. Pure theory without regard to practice, the rational intellect's imageless contemplation of truth for its own sake, is humanity's ultimate achievement, the farthest we can ever get from animality.

All of this optimistic glorification of philosophy as the key to the ethical perfection and salvation of both individuals and society Boccaccio undoubtedly encountered in reading Dante's philosophical works. But there was also in Boccaccio's cultural milieu a significant variation on philosophy's self-conception, a pessimistic, skeptical one—and one whose central claim was that the human *anima* is inescapably "animal." I am referring to the lyric poetry of Guido Cavalcanti, the brilliant Florentine who was once Dante's best friend and of whom Boccaccio says, in a tale in the *Decameron* in which Cavalcanti is the protagonist: "he was one of the best logicians in the world and an excellent natural philosopher."[22] Here Boccaccio's phrasing is extremely important, indicating a profound understanding of Cavalcanti's poetic project. For by insisting that Cavalcanti was a "natural philosopher" Boccaccio is also insisting that Cavalcanti was *not* a "first philosopher," theorist, or metaphysician. As Aquinas says, to study metaphysics is to graduate from the study of a lesser but chronologically prior study, natural philosophy or physics; it is to graduate from the study of material signifiers to the study of immaterial signifieds:

> Some objects of our speculation, then, depend on matter for their existence, unable to exist except in matter. . . . Such things are studied by *physics*, or *natural science*. . . . Then there are other objects of speculation which don't depend for their existence on matter and are able to exist out of matter. . . . All such things are studied by *theology*—science of the divine—so-called because God is its prime object of study. But it is also called *metaphysics*— "after physics"—because *we learn it after physics, only able to reach what can't be sensed through what can* [emphasis added]. And again it is called *first philosophy*, since all other sciences come after it in the sense of deriving their first principles from it.[23]

Boccaccio, by calling Cavalcanti an excellent physicist but failing to mention any distinction he may have won in the field of metaphysics, suggests that Cavalcanti was never able to "reach what can't be sensed through what can," never able to graduate from the science of the signifier to the science of the signified, from the visible to the invisible, from determinate materiality to universal immateriality. And indeed, as we shall see momentarily, this animal-like failure to achieve *theoria*, this failure to bridge the gulf between perceptible image and imperceptible thought, is precisely the obsessive preoccupation of Cavalcanti's lyric poetry. And if, as Boccaccio suggests, Cavalcanti's science does not reach to the realm of "first philosophy," then Cavalcanti can have no knowledge of the "first guiding principle," no certain foundation for any other knowledge. Lacking any certain foundation, Cavalcanti opts for nihilistic despair, melancholy meditations on his own intellectual impotence and his impending death.[24]

Dante and Cavalcanti make up the nucleus of that handful of Italian poets whom Dante called, and whom literary historians still call, the poets of the *dolce stil nuovo* ("sweet new style"). These *stilnovisti*, as they are also called, wrote lyric love poetry in the tradition of the Provençal troubadours: the poet or "I" sings his desire for a lady who is difficult or impossible to possess. What is *new* about the "new style" is that love lyric has become a thoroughly *philosophical* discourse: the poet or "I" is not just anybody, but is a would-be philosopher, and the desired lady is no lady, but rather is Lady Philosophy, Truth, *Theoria*. On this score, at least, Dante and Cavalcanti are in perfect accord: their love poems are not so much about lovers attempting to love as they are about philosophers attempting to philosophize, theorists attempting to theorize. But Dante and Cavalcanti apparently had a somewhat bitter parting of ways—the most likely cause being that Dante was, as we have seen, extremely optimistic in his view of philosophy, whereas Cavalcanti was, as we are about to see, extremely pessimistic.

Cavalcanti's lyric poetry is saturated with the doctrines of what the orthodox medieval establishment treated as an outlaw philosophy, the teaching of which was banned in Paris in the late thirteenth century—a philosophy known nowadays as "Latin Averroism" or "Radical Aristotelianism." This "Averroism," which was in vogue, especially in Italy, in the last few decades of the thirteenth and the first few decades of the fourteenth centuries, was an elaboration of certain ideas put forth by Averroes (Ibn Rushd), the great twelfth-century Arabic philosopher.[25] In his commentary on Aristotle's *De Anima*, Averroes suggested a certain interpretation of a highly obscure passage concerning the rational or intellective faculty of the soul, and the implications of Averroes' interpretation led, in the works of the Latin Averroists, to certain extreme, radical, unequivocably heretical conclusions. Averroes insisted (and here I am simplifying a great deal, since the issues involved are quite technical and complicated) that Aristotle was saying that only the rational faculty of the soul is immortal *and* that there is, for the whole collection of all individuals of the human species, *only one rational soul*. To repeat: for the entire human species, one and only one soul is rational and immortal. The heresy of Averroism is obvious: our individual souls do not survive the death of our bodies. Moreover, Averroism denies to individual humans the very thing that, according to the kind of Aristotelianism endorsed by Dante and by late medieval philosophy in general, makes us human and not animal—namely, that third and highest faculty of soul, the rational or intellective. Averroes insists that individual humans never attain universal knowledge, since our knowledge can never be purely immaterial or abstract, and always remains dependent on "phantasms" (images and sense perceptions).[26] In Cavalcanti's Averroist scheme of things, *human beings are, epistemologically speaking, in no way superior to animals*. We can never really have true theoretical knowledge, knowledge of hidden, unseen, invisible, or divine realities, knowledge of that foundation or "first guiding truth," because we are always, like animals, condemned to think through the apprehension and manipulation of images, sensations, physical or material signifiers. Like animals, our highest apprehension of reality is never more than imaginative, never truly rational or theoretical. Apparent "truths" derived from images cannot lead to *theoria*, to objective knowledge of a truth that is not of our own making. As the twelfth-century Jewish philosopher Maimonides, a contemporary of Averroes, wrote in his *Guide of the Perplexed* (a book that rejects the possibility that we can ever have any knowledge of metaphysical truth):

> Matter is a strong veil preventing the apprehension of that which is separate from matter as it truly is. . . . Hence whenever our intellect aspires to apprehend the Deity or one of the intellects, there subsists this great veil interposed between the two.[27]

Averroists like Cavalcanti are philosophical pessimists who insist that our thinking is inescapably material, that we never achieve "true knowledge" or *theoria*, never attain a purely abstract, rational vision of the unseen, never attain that "power of understanding things absent" that Hugh of St. Victor says distinguishes us from animals. They emphasize "this great veil," this radical gulf between our imaginations, on the one hand, and true knowledge of reality, on the other. Our thinking is always, as Aristotle says of animals, "in error," more a matter of perception than of understanding.

Cavalcanti's lyric poetry is obsessed with the prospect of the human soul's mortality. For instance, the following lines from "O tu, *che porti nelli occhi sovente*" lament the fact that there is no salvation, no afterlife for the human *anima*:

> O you, who in your eyes often contain
> Love holding three arrows in hand,

> This spirit of mine that comes from afar
> Commends to you the grieving *anima*
>
> Which the Syrian archer has already
> Wounded in the mind with two arrows;
> He bends the bow for the third, but so gently
> That, being present with you, it does not reach me:
> For it would be the salvation of the soul
> That lies, as it were, among the limbs, dead. . . .[28]

Here the human soul is dead, has no hope of salvation, precisely because the third of three arrows shot at the *anima* from on high has not reached its destination. I take this third arrow to signify the third and highest of the three faculties of soul according to Aristotle's tripartite scheme in *De Anima*. That is, this poem is above all an assertion that humankind does not possess the capacity for truly rational, truly intellectual thinking. Note that Cavalcanti represents two arrows (the first and second faculties of soul) as having indeed reached the human *anima*—which is to suggest that the human soul is, with respect to its possession of faculties, in no way distinct from the souls of all other animals: humans, *just like all other animals*, possess the first two but not the third faculty of soul. And as it is for all other animals, so our human souls are mortal. There is, in Cavalcanti's pessimistic philosophy, no philosophical salvation. In fact, for Cavalcanti, we never really philosophize, insofar as to philosophize is to think rationally, theoretically, to think thoughts totally free from an animal-like dependence on images, perceptions, material signifiers. Cavalcanti's poetry is a philosophical longing for true philosophical knowledge, yet at the same time a grim and unfaltering insistence that such knowledge is never possible. Cavalcanti is a philosopher who incessantly laments the fact that he is not truly a philosopher.

Still, Calvalcanti's philosophy is just a variation of Dante's (it is not, as Boccaccio's is, a radical rediscovery of ancient antifoundational pragmatism). Cavalcanti still shares with Dante the same essential definition: wisdom or philosophy is theoretical knowledge, contemplation of universal truth. The only dispute between Cavalcanti and Dante concerns whether such knowledge is ever really possible: Dante is pretty sure that we can achieve *theoria* or at least get sufficiently close to found the whole political, social, and moral order on what knowledge we do achieve; Cavalcanti is pretty sure that we can never get very close to *theoria*, and he hence renounces any hope of political reform, instead turning inward to self-pity, mournful despair, suicidal melancholy.

Cavalcanti's problem is that he cannot imagine any definition of wisdom or philosophy other than the dominant late medieval one. Thus, even though he repeatedly insists that the philosopher's vision is at best indirect or fleeting, that metaphysical knowledge is impossible, still Cavalcanti never renounces the abstract vision of the invisible, knowledge, *theoria*, as the supreme human aim, as that for which he is hopelessly longing. For instance, in the following stanzas from "*Chi è questa che vèn, ch' ogn' om la mira*" the poet desperately desires to see Truth or Lady Philosophy, wants to achieve theoretical knowledge:

> O God, what she looks like [*sembra*] when she turns her eyes
> Let Love say, for I could not describe it.
> To me she seems [*pare*] so much a lady of good will
> That any other, in comparison with her, I call vexation.
>
> One could not describe her gracefulness,
> For every noble virtue inclines toward her
> And beauty displays her as its goddess.
>
> Our mind [*mente*] was never so lofty
> And never was such salvation granted us
> That we could really have *knowledge* [*canoscenza*] of her.[29]

For Cavalcanti, knowledge or *theoria* is not our salvation, if only because we never really do have knowledge. What is recounted here is a fleeting and oblique glance, a momentary glimpse which instills in the poet-philosopher a desire for true *canoscenza*, for true knowledge, for a face-to-face, permanent, theoretical view of Being. What the poet experiences is not real *theoria* but rather a desire for real *theoria*: he wants to gaze upon, to behold, to contemplate, to know the Lady (Truth), but she is already gone. The poet can sense or perceive images, can behold semblances and apparitions (as suggested by the verbs *sembra* and *pare*), but he cannot have rational knowledge, true knowledge of the invisible. Again, the key references here are to Aristotle's *De Anima*: the human *mente* ("mind," which is, in medieval Aristotelianism, the equivalent of *anima*) is not "high" or "lofty" enough to achieve rational knowledge, knowledge of absent, universal, unseen, eternal truths. The highest faculty of the human mind is the faculty to sense or perceive visible images, material signifiers—and hence the gist of this poem is, again, that we are, epistemologically speaking, in no way superior to animals. Cavalcanti's whole position can be summed up in the following paraphrase: "I would, if I could, like to know—but I'm afraid that I can't ever really know, and this destroys me." What Cavalcanti lacks is an alternative conception of philosophy, the sort of alternative formulated by Boccaccio in the tale of Cimone: a pragmatic conception according to which it is perfectly possible to philosophize without knowing, without seeing, without *theoria*, without metaphysics, without foundations, without good reason.

I have just indicated what I take to be the essence of Boccaccio's reinvention of philosophy. To say, as Boccaccio says, that the philosopher is an animal is to say, following Cavalcanti, that humankind can never achieve rational certainty, objective knowledge of foundational truth, that humans do not possess that third and highest faculty of soul. But Boccaccio makes a turn that Cavalcanti failed to negotiate, dares to assert that philosophy can survive the confession of its irrational animality, can be an adventure on (to borrow a phrase from Boccaccio's close friend and intellectual colleague Petrarch) "an unfounded sea."[30] For Boccaccio's Cimone, giving up the hope of *theoria* (which is what he does when he refuses his real name, Galeso, in favor of the name that means "Brute Beast"),[31] giving up the hope of finding the "first guiding truth," is not counsel to despair but rather an affirmative call to unfounded *praxis*. That is, Cimone's reaffirmation of his native animality does not disqualify him from remaining a philosopher, nor does his initial "becoming philosopher" mean that he is ever anything other than an animal. Contradicting the whole medieval tradition (which, in both its "early" and "late" periods, regards wisdom and animality as opposites), Boccaccio insists that wisdom and animality are inseparable, the two sides of the same coin. After Boccaccio's Cimone, it is possible to conceive of the philosopher as a paragon of *both* wisdom and animality.

I have no space remaining in the present essay to demonstrate in a detailed manner my reading of Boccaccio's tale—though I plan to do so elsewhere.[32] In what little space is left, I shall perform one brief foray into Boccaccio's text, followed by some assertions concerning Boccaccio's reinvention of antifoundational pragmatism.

Boccaccio's new definition of wisdom or philosophy is formulated right at the start, in the very first phrase of the tale's rubric (that little heading or plot summary that Boccaccio inscribes before the beginning of each tale): *Cimone amando divien savio ed Efigenia sua donna rapisce in mare*. This phrase may be very literally translated as "Cimone loving becomes wise and abducts his woman Efigenia to the sea." But there is a problem posed by the phrase, both for translators and interpreters alike—and that is whether there should be some punctuation, perhaps a pause or a full stop, after the word *savio* ("wise") and before the word *ed* ("and"). That is, is the bestial act of kidnapping an unwilling woman something that happens *after* Cimone becomes a philosopher, or is it something that is simultaneous with his becoming a philosopher? The currently most popular English translation, G. H. McWilliam's Penguin Classics version, suggests the former alternative, that *first* Cimone becomes wise *and then* he kidnaps the woman whom he desires: "Cymon acquires wisdom through falling in love with Iphigenia, whom he *later* [emphasis added] abducts on the high seas." The problem with this translation is not just that it adds things to the text that are not there, but moreover that it too easily serves the interests of the "Augustinian" interpretation. From such a translation one can get the idea (an idea frequently endorsed by recent critics) that the tale is divided into two movements: first, a classic fable of stilnovistic or Platonic love, of love resulting in metaphysical wisdom ("Cimone, loving, becomes wise"); secondly, a denial of stilnovism, a deflation of the value of such wisdom if it is not accompanied by ethical goodness ("Later he abducts his woman to the high seas"). Such a translation lends credence to the view that Boccaccio's whole point is moralistic, that Boccaccio is saying that even if you know as much as Plato, such knowledge means nothing without a perfect will, since you are still not immune from animalistic wickedness.

There is an alternate translation, one that I consider more faithful to Boccaccio's aim, one according to which Cimone's becoming wise just *is* his becoming beast: "Cimone, loving, *wises up and abducts*, etc. . . . ." In this view, Cimone's wisdom is his renunciation of the hope of foundational *theoria* in favor of the enactment of unfounded *praxis*. Cimone's wisdom is his instituting, his actualizing a state of affairs that is founded upon nothing more universal and objective, nothing more rational, than his own desire.[33]

If in the early medieval period philosophical wisdom means *doing the right things* and in the later medieval period philosophical wisdom means *knowing the right things*, in the period that is inaugurated by Cimone, the period that we call the Renaissance, philosophical wisdom means *doing desired things*. After Cimone, philosophy means instituting or legislating a state of affairs *for no good reason* other than the fact that such a state of affairs is encouraging, pleasing, satisfying, or desirable. Wisdom is renouncing the prerequisite that the political, social, moral order must be founded upon a rational knowledge of absolute truth, of what is universally right. For, whatever we might think of Cimone's abducting an unwilling woman and his slaughtering everyone who would stand in his way, there is no way that we can construe those actions as "right." And that is precisely Boccaccio's point: the philosopher is no longer one who obeys a preestablished, universally valid, and objective moral order, but rather is now one who commands the creation of a contingent social order through the imposition of a personal, partisan, slanted, subjective vision of an encouraging and pleasing possible future. The philosopher is no better than everyone else, either ethically or epistemologically. The only thing that makes the philosopher wise (better) is that admitting that he is no better and knows no more than everyone else does not stop him from legislating his own *ethos*, a pleasing society. Boccaccio's philosopher does not shrink back from the world like Cavalcanti, waiting for death, but rather he rushes headlong into a high-seas adventure. The philosopher is he who takes measures to institute his will on the basis of no good universally acceptable reason. Philosophy is the legislation of a desirable, but not necessarily a true or rational, social order. As Deleuze says, commenting on a passage in Nietzsche that asserts that real philosophizing begins *where reason is lacking* (isn't this just what Boccaccio is saying to Cavalcanti—that just because we are never rational, just because we are only animals, does not mean that we cannot philosophize?):

> It is not that the philosopher must add the activity of the legislator to his other activities because he is in the best position to do this—as if his own subjection to wisdom qualified him to discover the best possible laws to which men in their turn ought to be subjected. The point is a completely different one: that the philosopher, as philosopher, *is not* a sage, that the philosopher, as philosopher, ceases to obey, that he replaces the old wisdom by command, that he destroys the old values and creates new ones, that the whole of his science is legislative in this sense.[34]

Boccaccio's Cimone fulfills Dante's dream that the philosopher will be the ultimate legislator of the world. Yet at the same time this philosophical beast, this precursor of Nietzsche, radically undermines Dante's rationalism through his animality, his lack of any reasonable foundation for the institutions, for the world, that he inaugurates. Cimone is the first Renaissance man—Renaissance man, Brute Beast, he whose essence is his animality. And if Cimone ever does become, as he suggests that he will, "more glorious than any god,"[35] this is because, as Socrates says of the gods, "the holy is what pleases them."[36]

Notes

1. *"Cimone, il che nella lor lingua sonava quanto nella nostra bestione."* Giovanni Boccaccio, *Decameron*, ed. Cesare Segre (Milano: Mursia, 1966), 321–322.

2. *"egli giudicava le divine cose esser di piú reverenza degne che le mondane,"* ibid., 322.

3. *"valorosissimo tra' filosofanti,"* ibid., 323.

4. *"fiero come un leone,"* ibid., 325.

5. *Le Lai d'Aristote*, ed. Maurice Delbouille (Paris: Bibliothèque de la Faculté de Philosophie et Lettres de l'Université de Liège, 1951). For a different perspective on the *Lai d'Aristote*, see my *The Death of the Troubadour: The Late Medieval Resistance to the Renaissance* (University of Pennsylvania Press, 1994), chap. 3.

6. *"di montone fatto tornare un uomo,"* *Decameron*, 324.

7. In Boethius' *Consolation of Philosophy*, it is Lady Philosophy herself who unequivocally expresses the early medieval definition of animality as *wickedness:* "The
   result is that you cannot think of anyone as human whom you see transformed by
   wickedness. You could say that someone who robs with violence and burns with
   greed is like a wolf. A wild and restless man who is forever exercising his tongue
   in lawsuits could be compared to a dog yapping. A man whose habit is to lie hidden in an ambush and steal by trapping people would be likened to a fox. A man
   of quick temper has only to roar to gain the reputation of a lion-heart. The timid
   coward who is terrified when there is nothing to fear is thought to be like the
   hind. The man who is lazy, dull, and stupid, lives an ass's life. A man of whimsy
   and fickleness who is forever changing his interests is just like a bird. And a man
   wallowing in foul and impure lusts is occupied by the filthy pleasures of a sow. So
   what happens is that when a man abandons goodness and ceases to be human,
   being unable to rise to a divine condition, he sinks to the level of being an animal. . . ." *The Consolation of Philosophy*, trans. V. E. Watts (Penguin Books, 1969),
   125.

8. On the rise of the intellectual in the later Middle Ages, see Alain de Libera, *Penser
   au moyen âge* (Paris: Seuil, 1991).

9. As Aristotle says in the *Nicomachean Ethics*, "the wise man must not only know
   what follows from the first principles, but must also possess truth about those
   principles." From *Aristotle's Ethics*, ed. and trans. John Warrington (London: J. M.
   Dent, 1963).

10. *De Anima* III, 3; trans. Hugh Lawson-Tancred (Penguin Books, 1986), 197.

11. *The Didascalicon of Hugh of St. Victor*, trans. Jerome Taylor (New York: Columbia
    University Press, 1961), I, 3, 49.

12. *De Anima*, III, 3.

13. See Alain de Libera, *Introduction à la mystique rhénane: d'Albert le Grand à Maître
    Eckhart* (Paris: O.E.I.L., 1984), 107.

14. Thomas Aquinas, *Selected Philosophical Writings*, trans. Timothy McDermott
    (Oxford University Press, 1993), 3 and 5.

15. Aristotle, *Nicomachean Ethics*, 228 and 229.

16. Cited in Alain de Libera, *Penser au moyen âge*, 177.

17. *Convivio* (Milan: Garzanti, 1980) IV, xxi, 10.

18. Cited in Alain de Libera, *Penser au moyen âge*, 136.

19. See, for instance, Millicent Marcus, "The Sweet New Style Reconsidered: A Gloss
    on the Tale of Cimone (*Decameron* V, 1)," *Italian Quarterly* (1980), 5–16.

20. *De Monarchia*, I, 2. English translation from *Ernes to Grassi, Renaissance
    Humanism: Studies in Philosophy and Poetics* (Medieval and Renaissance Texts and
    Studies: Binghamton, NY, 1988), 5.

21. On these definitions of *theoria*, see Thomas Aquinas, op. cit., 3–10.

22. *Decameron* VI, 9 (402).

23. Aquinas, *op. cit.*, 8.

24. My understanding of Cavalcanti is greatly indebted to Robert Pogue Harrison, *The
    Body of Beatrice* (Baltimore: The Johns Hopkins University Press, 1988), chap. 4.

25. For an account of Averroes' influence on Dante's theory of literary meaning, see my "Dante's Averroistic Hermeneutics: On 'Meaning' in the *Vita Nuova*," *Dante Studies* (1994).

26. See Richard C. Dales, *The Problem of the Rational Soul in the Thirteenth Century* (Leiden and New York: E. J. Brill, 1995), 113–117. As Dales suggests, Averroism is in part the claim that the sort of knowledge possessed by individual humans can never transcend the specific and determinate material circumstances from which it arises, can never be abstract or universal: "Because the possible intellect is by nature continuous with the phantasms, it can communicate this understanding to each individual *respecting only his phantasms*, for it is a process or activity, not, prior to receiving forms from the phantasms, a repository of known objects. Hence *the knowledge of each man is his own*, and it is this individual body of understanding that constitutes the speculative intellect, which, *since it depends on the sense knowledge provided by the body*, is perishable" [emphasis added]. Averroism was considered to be, in short, the claim that the human species is not rational, that humans are just animals and not rational animals; Dales (131) cites the following remark by the thirteenth-century scholastic John Pecham: "[According to Averroes], reason does not place man in his species, nor is it his perfection in first being. From this it follows that man is not to be defined through [the] rational. . . . [This position] destroys the foundations of nature, as well as merits and rewards. . . . Therefore this heresy is to be repudiated. No one assents to it but a pernicious heretic, and no one defends it as probable but a madman."

27. *Guide of the Perplexed*, trans. S. Pines (Chicago: University of Chicago Press, 1963), III, 9, 436–437.

28. Translation (slightly modified) from *The Poetry of Guido Cavalcanti*, ed. and trans. Lowry Nelson, Jr. (New York: Garland, 1986), 29.

29. Translation (slightly modified) from Nelson, *op. cit.*, 7.

30. "I swim through a sea that has no floor [*fondo*] or shore/I plow the waves and found [*fondo*] my house on sand and write on the wind." From *Petrarch's Lyric Poems*, trans. Robert M. Durling (Harvard University Press, 1976), 366 (song 212).

31. In a more detailed reading of Boccaccio's tale of Cimone, one that I hope to publish in the future, I will show that the name "Galeso" signifies, through an allusion to a certain passage in Dante's *Convivio, theoria*.

32. See previous note.

33. I am arguing that the new philosophy of Boccaccio's Cimone is something akin to the "neopragmatism" of Richard Rorty. See especially the two volumes of Rorty's *Philosophical Papers, Objectivity, Relativism, and Truth* and *Essays on Heidegger and Others* (New York: Cambridge University Press, 1991).

34. *Nietzsche and Philosophy*, trans. Hugh Tomlinson (New York: Columbia University Press, 1983), 92.

35. "*più glorioso che alcuno iddio*," *Decameron*, 324.

36. Socrates makes this remark in Plato's *Euthyphro*; citation from *The Collected Dialogues of Plato*, ed. Hamilton and Cairns (Princeton University Press, 1961), 184.

Bibliography

Alighieri, Dante. *Convivio*. Milan: Garzanti, 1980.

Aquinas, Thomas. *Selected Philosophical Writings*, trans. Timothy McDermott. Oxford University Press, 1993.

Aristotle. *De Anima*, trans. Hugh Lawson-Tancred. Penguin Books, 1986.

———. *Aristotle's Ethics*, ed. and trans. John Warrington. London: J. M. Dent, 1963.

Boccaccio, Giovanni. *Decameron*, ed. Cesare Segre. Milano: Mursia, 1966.

Cavalcanti, Guido. *The Poetry of Guido Cavalcanti*, ed. and trans. Lowry Nelson, Jr. New York: Garland, 1986.

Dales, Richard C. *The Problem of the Rational Soul in the Thirteenth Century*. Leiden and New York: E. J. Brill, 1995.

Deleuze, Gilles. *Nietzsche and Philosophy*, trans. Hugh Tomlinson. New York: Columbia University Press, 1983.

de Libera, Alain. *Penser au moyen âge*. Paris: Seuil, 1991.

Harrison, Robert Pogue. *The Body of Beatrice*. Baltimore: The John Hopkins University Press, 1988.

Le Lai d'Aristote, ed. Maurice Delbouille. Paris: Bibliothèque de la Faculté de Philosophie et Lettres de l'Université de Liège, 1951.

Rorty, Richard. *Philosophical Papers*, Volumes 1 and 2, *Objectivity, Relativism, and Truth* and *Essays on Heidegger and Others*. Cambridge University Press, 1991.

Stone, Gregory B. *The Death of the Troubadour: The Late Medieval Resistance to the Renaissance*. Philadelphia: University of Pennsylvania Press, 1994.

3

Pantagruel-Animal

Tom Conley

> *Un jour Pantagruel se pourmenant hors de la ville vers l'abbaye sainct Antoine, devisant et philosophant avecques ses gens et aulcuns escholiers, rencontra un homme beau de stature et élégant en tous linéamens du corps, mais pitoyablement navré en divers lieux et tant mal en ordre qu'il sembloit estre eschappé ès chiens; ou mieulx ressembloit un cueilleur de pommes du païs du Perche.*[1]

[One day Pantagruel, taking a walk outside of the city in the direction of Saint Martin's Abbey, chatting and philosophizing with his friends and a few students, met a man handsome of stature and elegant in all bodily features, but pitifully pocked in many different places and so unkempt he was more like a refugee of the dogs; or better, he looked like an applepicker from the country of Perche.]

The words describing the irruption of a sudden event, the initial meeting of Pantagruel with Panurge on the outskirts of Paris, are engraved in the memory of every reader of Rabelais. Their attraction seems timeless in the way they stage an encounter with alterity. For the purpose of exploring the theme that in this collection of essays Jennifer Ham and Matthew Senior call the *animal act*, I would like to return to this moment in *Pantagruel* (1532) in order to see to what role animals (especially dogs) play in early modern constructions of things uncanny. The episode that Rabelais relates of a giant's encounter with a singular other broaches a quasi-total "social fact" touching on our relation with the unknown.[2] The latter, the basis for much of our experience of life in general, acquires an animalistic aura. If its presence is more strongly felt in the copious body of Renaissance literature confined to rare-book rooms in university libraries, it may be because we live in them in order to imagine that the human subject of that era—figures we assume to be like Pantagruel or Panurge—inhabited a world in which the unknown was felt more intensely and immediately than now.

Readers of early modern literature would like to believe that the horizons west and east, expanded drastically by oceanic voyages undertaken by Portuguese, Spanish, and French sailors, rolled back *terrae incognitae* but also brought closer to home the wonder and fear aroused by new islands and their inhabitants. Because of the history of conceptual structures determining our time, we cannot avoid inflecting the idea of consciousness of everyday life in the Renaissance with the Freudian sense of the uncanny. No doubt we also tend to believe that the meeting with a figure as strange as Panurge, who comes both from home (the Touraine) and the limits of known lands and languages (Turkey and the Aegean archipelago), would have been more disquieting in the early 1500s than now, when we relive our originary encounter of his person and body.

In what follows I do not want to posit that the renascent sensorium held a relation with the unknown that was more intense than it is today. Rather, it might be more fitting to speculate that its expressive force is due to the articulation of the unknown with familiar figures drawn from plant and animal kingdoms. In much of the vernacular writings we inherit from early modern France, the unknown is, foremost, invented through a *spatialization* of language and experience that is defined in proximity with lines that are at once drawn and dissolved between the realms of the human and things animal and vegetal. Space allows the writer to project human or socially coded—recognizable, familiar, everyday, or "canny"—activity into the workings of flora and fauna.[3] In turn, the latter offer an immediately palpable sense of unnameable ways of living and of feeling the environing world by allowing us to fancy becoming shapes that are both familiar and strange. The unknown is tested in the age of discovery by dint of a desire to make consciousness coextensive with space, but also, and no less, to project consciousness into areas that allow the imagination to be identified with the expanding array of animals and plants inhabiting a growing number of printed bestiaries and cosmographies.

Scholarship inflected by anthropology would remark that Panurge resembles the trickster, a figure living in the liminal areas of a society, who serves to define its limits by transgression or passage through them. The attractiveness of the category of the trickster results not merely from a sociological function that tampers with codes of conduct in order better to define them, but also to our desire to enact the violence on our own world in the way that these figures

do upon theirs.[4] Panurge inspires the imagination of an unnameable, instinctual energy approximated by the actions of fellow animals. No less, the trickster
is also the figure (in North American Indian literature often assuming the guise
of a coyote) endowed with a monstrous eros that is ultimately sterile. He for-
nicates but cannot engenger. His phallus is so long that it needs to wrap about
his body or be carried in a rucksack. A totemic figure (thus affiliated with the
animalcules that populate literature of French Humanism), the trickster also
conduces to the ideology of Erasmian reform that played an increasingly
prominent role in political spheres in the age of Francis I and Charles V.

Yet, in this episode and its echoes elsewhere in the work, what we see of
Panurge exceeds the limits of humanism and even constructive trickery.[5]
Arguably, the history of the creation of the character-as-animal might in fact
obfuscate the relation with the unknown (or space outside of human ken) that
enters into the ninth chapter of *Pantagruel*. To determine why, it may be useful, first, to review the relation that Panurge holds as "animal" with the literal
space of *Pantagruel*, and then, second, to consider that relation in light of the
political ethnography of Gilles Deleuze and Felix Guattari in *1000 plateaux*, in
which they formulate the concept of *becoming-animal*. Thus, in the first section of this study, emphasis will be placed on the way that Panurge emerges
into the Rabelaisian world with bestial trappings, while in the second section,
a greater risk will be taken by affiliating the figure with a concept not easily
extrapolated from its source or applied to other works to any efficacious
degree. In the comparison of the presentation of Panurge in *Pantagruel* to the
figure that becomes "other," some principles of the animal act, it is hoped, will
be delineated.

The Panurgic Creature

Panurge is initially described as a lean figure, of an elegance that has been
marred by quirks of fate and history. Pocked and scarred by the dogs that had
bitten him when he escaped the clutches of Turkish infidels, he simply
appears, without rhyme or reason, on the road to Paris. We soon learn that he
had escaped from the *paillards Turcqs* who had been roasting him over a fire.
But in the initial meeting with Pantagruel, he utters his name at the end of a
barrage of more than a dozen real and imaginary languages in which he begs
for food to fill an empty stomach. Before he is "baptized" as Panurge in the
Rabelaisian novel, the figure has already been compared to a dog, the attributes of which will mark the character, six chapters later, who barks, growls, yaps,
sniffs, saunters, ferrets, struts, and pisses about the streets of Paris. The gentle

giant and his entourage seem to amble with ease about the city, while Panurge scampers about them. Panurge's nostrils absorb the odors of the city so well that in the space of a few days *"il sceut toutes les rues, ruelles et traverses de Paris comme son Deus det"* (238) [he knew all the streets and crossing of Paris as well as his *Deus det*].

In chapter 9 the crafty, street-smart character staggers into the Rabelaisian world. He disappears shortly and then, suddenly, five chapters later, returns. He is uncanny. He finds his way in the midst of the princely characters who greet him with charity, but he also initiates regress and violence that capture their fancy and fondest affection. In the ninth chapter, the tenor of his communication with Pantagruel inverts the recently failed encounter with the Limousin student who had counterfeited French by "skinning" Latin (192) two chapters before. In that bungled meeting, the event of a singular encounter was signalled by the same deictic formulas that describe the meeting of Pantagruel and Panurge. *"Quelque jour, je ne sçay quand, Pantagruel se pourmenoit avecques ses compaignons par la porte dont l'on va a Paris. Là rencontra un escholier tout joliet qui venoit par icelluy chemin"* (190) [One day, I can't remember when, Pantagruel was walking with his companions by the portal that leads to Paris. There he met a very comely student who was coming along the same road]. The promise to engage with the other fails for reasons that are apparent in the spatial register of the narrative, in which the Limousin embodies a non-place in an area that should otherwise be—if we are to use clear and common French—France itself. Disgusted by the Limousin's Latinate speech (or perhaps projecting onto the Limousin his own feeling of failure at being unable to comprehend what his interlocutor is saying), Pantagruel threatens to force the stranger to puke good French: *"Tu escorches le latin; par Saint Jan, je te feray escorcher le renard, car je te escorcheray tout vif"* (193) [You're skinning Latin; by Saint Jean, I'll make you skin the fox, because I'm going to skin you alive]. He suggests that the Limousin's body will be turned inside out in the way that the hides of animals are cut from their bodies to obtain their pelts. The narrative does exactly that—in its inversion of its own linguistic components—when, two chapters below, a similar incipit leads to the opposite outcome. In the passage of time and space of the Librairie de Saint-Victor (chapter 7) and the letter from Gargantua (chapter 8) a sentimental and an academic education have been gained. Most important, and no less miraculously, an ability to welcome the arrival of the other has been mastered.

Panurge originates in part from the spatial opposition of the episodes, from a palinodic narrative of reversals and rewritings. The traits that are shared between the one chapter (6) and the other (9) include the Limousin's school Latin that resembles one of Panurge's discourses; a propensity for coprophilia, in the remark that the Limousin "*conchiot toutes ses chemises*" (193) [was shitting all of his garments] as soon as Pantagruel took him by his neck, which Panurge will share with his companions once he gets his stomach filled; comparisons to animals describing the personage and his Limousin counterpart. The latter is a fox that will be skinned alive. His breeches are sewn in the style of a codfish's forked tail. Panurge has escaped from the dogs (207) and will go to bed with the hens (213).

In the antithetical structure, underscored at once by the similarity of the staging and the gap inserted between each of the episodes, the beginning of an "animal act" can be discerned. Regression initiates the arrival of Panurge, who embodies the world and a desire to eat it too. His appearance forces recall of the Limousin, who had rabidly foamed Latin at the mouth: he and his friends, he says in response to Pantagruel's inquiry about their *habitus*, "*nous despumons la verbocination latiale*" ["we spew latinate verbocination"].[6] The staggered plan is underscored again, in the gap between the end of the ninth chapter and the beginning of the fourteenth, when suddenly again, after disappearing in the Baisecul-Humevesne debates (chapters 10 to 13, 213–226), Panurge returns with the composite trappings of a fish and a feline. Shrivelled like a smoked herring and pitter-pattering as might an emaciated cat on a floor strewn with shucked oysters, he enters the stage to drink like a sparrow in spring and spin his yarn about how he escaped from the jaws of the evil *bashatz*.[7]

The tale establishes a spatial articulation that locks into the staggered pattern of the earlier episodes, extending the paratactic organization of the novel and, no less, conferring it with an abrupt effusion of animality. The fourteenth chapter picks up where the ninth abruptly ended. After sketching out his "map" of language to Pantagruel and his companions, Panurge admits that he has come from Turkey, "where I was a prisoner," resulting from a botched French expedition sailed to Lesbos "*en la male heure*" (212–213) [in 1502, as history books report], to regain the Holy Land. Panurge's association with the fabled island recalls a moment in the chronicle of French relations with the Ottoman Empire, to be sure, but it also underscores the double valence of his own character. The story ascribes a geographic cause for his trickery and ambivalence.[8] The tale of his pursuit by Turkish curs completes the geography, but only such that the attitudes of the infidels are mirrored in the trickster's own character. As he tells his story, Panurge is "*eximé comme un hareng soret*" [shrivelled as a smoked herring], but in his escape he roasts one of his enemies "*comme on fait les harens soretz à la cheminée*" (230) [the way herrings are smoked in a fireplace]. He sets the Turkish city aflame and is doused by the charitable public before he almost wets and dirties his own breeches, "*dont je fuz tant aise que je me cuydé conchier de joye*" (231) [for I was so happy I thought I was incontinent with joy]. Pursued by the enemy, he tosses bacon strips to the dogs that curry on his heels. The tale is told, it seems, to round out and to explain why he is so *"pitoyablement navré"* when he first encounters Pantagruel. The incipit to the chapter that follows the account of the dogs' pursuit clarifies the point before new details are appended: *"Pantagruel, quelque jour, pour se recréer de son estude, se pourmenoit vers les faulxbours sainct Marceau, voulant veoir la follie Goubelin. Panurge estoit avecques luy, ayant tousjours le flacon soubz sa robbe et quelque morceau de jambon"* (232) [One day, in order to take a break from his studies, Pantagruel was walking toward the outskirts of Saint Marceau, intending to visit the Gobelin dyeworks. Panurge was by his side, always with a flagon and some piece of ham under his cape].

It quickly becomes evident that Panurge has not surrendered his means of escape from the Turks, and that he is ready to evade whatever dogs might ambush him in the confines of Paris.[9] The goal of visiting the Gobelin works foreshadows the episode of canine micturition that will follow in chapter 22 (inverting his being drenched in Turkey), when Panurge will play a dirty trick on the haughty Parisian lady who rejected his seductive entreaties. In revenge Panurge sprinkles the hems of the woman's dress with a magic drug that attracts all the dogs of Paris, which urinate on her. "*C'estoit la plus grande villanie du monde*" (206) [It was the greatest villany of the world]. Whereas Panurge took flight from Lesbos and the Orient, pursued by a pack of "more than 1,311" dogs, he now causes "more than 6,014" dogs to prance and spray over the lady. The urine was so copious that it became the river that passes by Saint-Victor, "*auquel Guobelin tainct l'escarlatte, pour la vertu spécifique de ces pisse-chiens. . . .*" (267) [where the Gobelin works dye in scarlet because of the specific virtue of these dog-pissers].

The tale sums up the touristic venture, begun in chapter 15, by mythifying the site of the Gobelin industry. At the Bièvre River in Paris, the alum salts that passed through the tincture baths were said to have left all about the area a pervasive stench of stale urine. In the comic epic, the origin of the molecular properties of the site are, the text implies, better explained through the tale of a gigantic canine *compisserie* than by chemical analysis. A "toponymical story" *par excellence*, the anecdote also connects the spatial points of chapters 15 and 22 to the animal kingdom with which Panurge is affiliated.[10] We learn during the promenade *en route* to the Gobelins that Panurge has an idea for an organic refortification of the city's walls. It accompanies his delirious story of the symbiotic relation of a lion and a fox who collaborate in a tail-wagging venture that wipes clean and deodorizes an old lady's *callibistry*. The story is prefaced by the *aparté* to the effect that the event took place *"Au temps que les bestes parloyent (il n'y a pas troys jours) . . . par la forest de Bièvre"* (234) [In the days when animals used to talk (not more than three days ago) . . . in the Bièvre forest]. The Bièvre becomes an aromatically charged site where animals and humans are identical. It is as if the olfactive areas of space and language at these three junctures were also promising the revival of instinctual drives. A confusion of sensation, odor, and discourse prevails. The aroma that enhances the amphibious play of language seems based on an identity of animal and human drives.

Here is where we begin to see the emergence of the "Pantagruel-Animal," and where an anthropological interpretation of the work coexists with the humanistic, Christian, and historical levels that recent scholarship has studied so carefully.[11] Here, too, is where the "animal" and "vegetable" properties of the text, cued by the olfactive and spatial signs, endow the writing with a force that exceeds any containing frame of interpretation, and where, too, its "animal acts" can be viewed in light of the concept and practice of "becoming-animal."[12] To this side we can now turn.

Devenir–animal

In *1000 plateaux*, a polemical treatment of capitalism and schizophrenia, Gilles Deleuze and Félix Guattari hypothesize that any life that is worth living must be lived affirmatively, generously, and intensively. A spirited attack on psychiatrics based on principles of castration, loss, and estrangement, their work appeals to literature, cinema, and the arts to expand the range of sensation that can be obtained through an art of the practice of philosophy, and to promote, as a general and enduring cause, affective agency. Among its many agendas count the concerns for ways that humans can intensify experience—to savor, extend, proliferate, and cultivate it—by way of "becoming-other." In a central chapter (in fact at a vanishing point of the volume), the theme of "becoming-intense" is studied as a function of "becoming-animal" and "becoming-imperceptible," along with "becoming-woman," "becoming-child," and "becoming-molecular." We can achieve a totalizing sense of *Einfühlung* (a term Deleuze and Guattari borrow from Wilhelm Worringer's work on the affective force of tracery and lines in Gothic ornament) or a benevolent empathy, they say, that refuses to capture or retain the essence of things and bodies that are other, even though we seem to metamorphose into them.

In a broad sense, the enterprise of *1000 plateaux* radicalizes the evangelical mission of *caritas* that was current in the circles of Erasmian humanism in the 1530s, but in the way Deleuze and Guattari treat the theme, it is freed of the redemptive ideology that (as Marcel Mauss has implied) can make Christian goodness so obnoxious or poisonous. Literature, they argue, affords its readers a chance to engage in totalizing processes of transformation. Certain texts, such as Kafka's journals and stories, Melville's novels, and so on, rank among the most exemplary models of becoming-other and becoming-animal. They write:

> *Il s'agit de faire corps avec l'animal, un corps sans organes définis par des zones d'intensité ou de voisinage. . . . Par exemple: non pas imiter le chien, mais composer son organisme avec autre chose, de telle manière qu'on fasse sortir de l'ensemble ainsi composé, des particules qui seront canines, en fonction du rapport de mouvement et de repos, ou du voisinage moléculaire dans lequel elles entrent. Il est entendu que cette autre chose peut être très variée, et tenir plus ou moins directement à l'animal en question: ce peut être l'aliment naturel de l'animal (la terre et le ver), ce peut être ses relations extérieures avec d'autres animaux (on deviendra chien avec des chats, on deviendra singe avec un cheval), ce peut être un appareil ou prothèse que l'homme lui fait subir (muselière, rennes, etc.), ce peut être quelque chose qui n'a même plus de rapport avec l'animal considéré.*[13]

> [It means being embodied with the animal, an organless body defined by zones of intensity or proximity. . . . For example: not imitating the dog, but putting together its organism with *something other*, so that from the composite whole particles will be emitted that are canine, as a function of the relation of movement and rest, or of the molecular proximity in which they enter. It goes without saying that this something other can vary a great deal and be more or less directly tied to the animal in question: it can be the animal's natural diet (the earth and the worm), it can be its outer relations with other animals (one becomes a dog in the midst of cats, or a monkey with a horse), it can be a machine or a prosthesis that the human straps about the animal (a muzzle, reins, etc.), it can be something that really has nothing to do with the animal in question.]

A welter of forces and lines of thinking are summed up here. Before relating it to the animicular qualities of Panurge, we can trace several lines of force that define what it means to "become-animal."

Foremost is a continuous process of transformation that pertains to the infinitive function of *devenir*. *Devenir-animal*, the composite noun Guattari and Deleuze coin and use in different contexts, suggests that a processual, active force of change continues to exert influence on a species or an object; that it turns it into an animal; and that, too, the action is so infinite in extension that the perception of time becomes equivalent to that of space (space becomes active because it is infinitely durative).[14] Implied, too, is that the operation does not follow a regressive itinerary which might treat alterity in a romantic way of dualism and complementarity (in a Jekyll-Hyde condition), nor that something atavistic or recidivistic is at stake or "unleashed" when a human "reverts" to becoming a dog. Second, if there is regression, it moves along an infinite trajectory in which originarity has no single or privileged point: becoming has nothing to do with a substitutive process by which, through the transcending miracle of metaphor, a subject approximates or becomes "like" an animal, "miming" or "representing" its salient traits.

For the authors of *1000 plateaux*, becoming-animal is therefore not an activity that moves through metaphor. To show how, the authors specify how *devenir-animal* has variants such as *devenir-chien*, *devenir-enfant*, and *devenir-fleur* that are isomorphic with *devenir-femme*. The latter category, the subject of extensive debate among readers of Deleuze and Guattari, concerns the subjacent category of things molar (that tend to be inflected as masculine) and molecular (which are generally feminine).[15] Becoming is a molecular process, and the subject who becomes an animal, a flower, or a stone diffuses masses of particles so as to create new spaces and relations that confuse organic and inorganic realms. Whoever becomes-animal does not necessarily resemble the molar or aggregated traits of the animal in question, although imitation or metaphor may be catalysts for the operation. The authors thus state:

> *Nous voulons seulement dire que les aspects inséparables du devenir-femme doivent d'abord se comprendre en fonction d'autre chose: ni imiter ni prendre la forme féminine, mais émettre des particules qui entrent dans le rapport de mouvement et de repos, ou dans la zone du voisinage de micro-femininité, c'est-à-dire produire en nous-mêmes une femme moléculaire, créer la femme moléculaire. Nous ne voulons pas dire qu'une belle création soit l'apanage de l'homme, mais, au contraire, que la femme comme entité molaire a à devenir femme, pour que l'homme aussi le devienne ou puisse le devenir.* (338)

> [We are only stating that the inseparable aspects of becoming-woman must first be understood as functions of other things: neither to imitate nor to assume feminine form, but to emit particles that enter into a relation of movement and rest, or the proximitous zone of micro-femininity, in other words, that produce in ourselves a molecular woman, create the molecular woman. We do not mean that a handsome creation is under the aegis of man but, to the contrary, that the woman as molar entity has to *become woman* if the man can also or even become woman.]

Hence, in order to become other—and elsewhere in the context are implied the variants of becoming minoritarian, of becoming man, woman, calf, wolf, tick, orchid, morel, chanterelle, dog, and so on—it suffices to engage a *double* movement by which two materially composed, self-cohering chemical bodies ionize themselves, radiate molecules, or disperse their surfaces into each other's direction so that the identity of the one is diffused into zones or neighboring areas that are then recombined. Through molecular action there takes place an intensification of the experience of space and corporal extension.

It might be added that the dialectics of a "self" and an "other" or a traditional staging of a meeting with alterity might be too clumsy or too simple a model for the kind of exchange that Deleuze and Guattari are describing. When "surfaces," "folds," "molecular swarms," "convections," and other terms borrowed from atomistic traditions describe the process of encountering and becoming other, new relations with alterity are engaged. The two writers appeal to the idioms of chemistry, of Lucretian philosophy, of biology, and Leibnizian monadology to show how intensities, how myriad forms and contents of expressivity, or how *zones* of variously perceived relations of identity are summoned when the event of an encounter takes place.

What subsumes the action of becoming-animal is not binary, it is not just digital communication, nor can it be mapped on a grid of Saussurean oppositions of language: signifiers and signifieds are not exchanged in a dialectic where the self would sublate the other (for example, "self + other = negation of the other as negation," which would be tantamount to meaning, in our context: "Pantagruel + Panurge = negation of Panurge as negation") in order to reconfigure his or her being.[16] Becoming-animal can be sensed in a tonal fashion, in ways that are both digital and analogue, such that, assigned to the field of *sensation*, they become a perception of form *and* an expression of signifiers, the infinite sum being the form *and* expression of their effects. The form *and* expression of their meaning meld to the degree that their signs are emitted and then swirl, fold, and create zones of interprenetration that color or give various chromatic and olfactive charges to their apprehension of each other. This is not to say that the meeting of Panurge and Pantagruel could be charted according to an affective register that has the vibratory intensity of what we experience when we retrace the famous meetings in French literature and cinema (say, of Proust's Jupien and Charlus, Gide's Michel and Moktir, Renoir's Lestingois and Boudu, Céline's Bardamu and Robinson, or, again, Renoir's Marceau and La Chesnaye), but that the affective zones of the meeting are rich in sensation.

The reader of *Pantagruel* undoubtedly feels that the encounter of the two figures establishes a zone of *affective emission*, in which a nearly mystical latency is discerned, in which we witness a Pantagruel on the threshold of a *devenir-Panurge* by mere contrast with the bungled meeting that had begun with the same phatic gestures in both the narration, the setting, the deictic markers, the tempo, and the very form of the staging of the encounter. In the first meeting, when the Limousin is seen, the time is so vague and ill-marked that it needs to be wasted or thrashed with the same violence Pantagruel applies when he squeezes the pretentious student's gullet.[17] The Limousin's seductive allure, a boy *tout jolliet*, threatens the zone of self-possession in the space defined by Pantagruel and his companions. The *escholier*'s linguistic emissions carry no aroma that Pantagruel can sniff or imbibe in his nostrils or mouth. Nothing caresses the skin or eroticizes the act of salutation. No animal orders pierce through the language, even though the adolescent's description of what he and his friends like to touch and taste would otherwise be redolent with aroma, food, and flesh.

> *Nous . . . captons la benévolence de l'omnijuge, omniforme et omnigène sexe feminin. . . , inculcons nos veretres ès penitissimes recesses des pudendes de ces meritricules amicabillissimes; puis cauponizons ès tabernes méritoires de la Pomme de pin, du Castel, de la Magdaleine et de la Mulle, belles spatules vervecines performanimés de petrosil.* (191)

> [We capture the benvolence of the omnipotent, omniform, and omnigenous feminine sex . . . we inculcate our members into the penitissimous recesses of the pudenda of these amicalissimous ladies, then we cauponize in the meritorious taverns of the Pinecone, the Castle, the Magdalene, and the Mule, spatulated fries perforaminated with parsley.]

Amid the olfactive and carnal joy in the description, nothing—at least at this point in the comic epic—is released from the discourse that would caress the skin or eroticize the decisive act of salutation.

In the second meeting, the encounter avers that it is the event signaled by the sign of its coming in the figure of Limousin, but now the languages themselves become what *molecularize* the simple request for a piece of bread. The *escholier* who was repelled and thrashed (virtually mugged, it might be implied, by a homophobe Pantagruel who possibly fears himself in congress with his Limousin other . . .) has suddenly and miraculously, as if cannibalized with pleasure, been absorbed into the speech of his interlocutor. Now, on a single occasion, a unique moment—"*un jour*"—Pantagruel ventures outside a familiar zone, "*se pourmenant hors de la ville . . . devisant et philosophant avecques ses gens et aucuns escholiers*" (207). The body of the yet-unnamed figure is of attractive demeanor, not just because he bears a nobleman's stature, but because the body is in fact already a diffusive, molecular condition that has *become-other* in its tattered and motley aspect, spotted with scabs and scars that, because our eyes are drawn to them through the narrative filter, are imbued with erotic force.

Where the body is *"pitoyablement navré en divers lieux,"* it delights and arouses, it evokes in the beholder—in ourselves, in Pantagruel, in the other *escholiers*—our desire to see and smell the traces where it remains animal: as the emanation of a dog, the body that *"sembloit estre eschappé ès chiens"* in fact is punctured too with the residual odor that spells (and smells) out the presence of the Limousin *escholier*. The riddled figure that is ready to be atomized, or to bark volleys of language and gibberish, is first seen as a point emanating from a vanishing perspective. His description in the voice of Pantagruel emits the visible particles, or characters of the man-dog, seen as a speck in the distance on the road that draws the eye into the periphery of the horizon of Paris. *"De tant loing que le* vit *Pantagruel, il dist ès assistans, voyez-vous cest homme qui vient par le chemin de Pont Charenton?"* (207, stress added) [From as far as Pantagruel saw him, he said to those in his midst, do you see this man coming down the road from the Charenton Bridge?]. In the ocular field of the description we have *already* run our eyes over the body, we have *already* palpated its bare spots and fingered the tatters of cloth that hide and reveal its muscular lines and seductive disorder *before* Pantagruel glimpses the figure in the distance.

If Deleuze's rhetoric of cinema can be marshaled to convey the construction of the meeting, we can observe, contrary to all classical practices of film editing or screenwriting, that an *affect-image* precedes the *perception-image* usually used to establish the visual boundaries at the beginning of a sequence of narrative.[18] The narrative trait that would bring into view the invention of space and visibility itself and then demarcate their frame is the "long" or "establishing" shot. It is the descriptive, even phatic element that invents the visible field before its components are adumbrated. Here, however, the perception-image *comes after* the description of detail. Conveyed is a selective and highly charged relation of intimacy, the narrative of a rush of desire, of a bodily contact so phantasized that it erases all delineations of subject and object or self and other. The attention drawn to the pocked body of the man-animal precedes its articulation as a vanishing point in a perspectival view in the narrative picture.

These *"zones d'intensité ou du voisinage"* of which Deleuze and Guattari speak in the section of becoming-animal in *1000 plateaux* depend on the emission of affective sensation wherever coded perspectival relations are intensified through sudden optical shifts. They are confirmed and crystallized at the end of the ninth chapter of *Pantagruel*. When Panurge is described affectively before being planted in Pantagruel's field of vision, the figure floats in—and hence brings into visibility—a spatially but actively indeterminate zone. The languages he broadcasts throughout most of the chapter often obfuscate the history he tells of his origins at the end. Focal and narrative inversions are identical. "*Seigneur, dist le compaignon, mon vray et propre nom de baptesme est Panurge, et à présent viens de Turquie, où je fuz mené prisonnier lorsqu'on alla à Metelin en la male heure*" (213) [Milord, said the companion, my true and proper baptismal name is Panurge, and presently I come from Turkey, where I was taken prisoner when they went to Metellin at a bad moment]. Panurge originates from a land of oddities, from the strange flora and fauna desribed in *isolarii*, recent island books (by Bartolommeo da Sonetti in 1485 and Benedetto Bordone in 1529) that had staked out ways of marking many limits of gender and of belief, and that had also brought deterritorialized spaces into the field of the known lands—including the island of "*Metelin en la male heure*"—and sea of the Aegean.

With the memory of chapter 14 in mind, we can affirm that the initial description of Panurge as a human resembling a dog, a migrant worker, an itinerant, and a nomad who "*mieulx ressembloit un cueilleur de pommes du païs de Perche*" (207) [better resembled an apple picker from the land of Perche] has a "molecular" way of announcing the coming of the tale recounting how he "escaped from the hands of the Turks" five chapters later.[19] The narration in the chapter of the encounter accounts for the antagonist's being larded and skewered on a spit in a fireplace like a roasted *connil* from Lesbos. It explains why he implored God to be free of his suffering: "*Seigneur Dieu, oste-moy de ce torment auquel ces traistres chiens me détiennent pour la maintenance de ta loy*" (228) [Dear Lord, free me of the torment in which these treacherous dogs are holding me in order to maintain your law]. It also shows that his pocked aspect smells of the bacon strips he used to divert and enrage the mastiffs that chase on his heels. "*Par ce moyen me laissèrent et je les laissé aussi pelaudans l'un l'autre. Ainsi eschappé gaillard et de hayt, et vive la roustisserie!*" (231) [That is how they left me and I left them jumping all over each other. Thus I escaped fine and dandy, and long live the barbecue!].

Although the narrative defines its spatial perimeter and is concatenated by connecting Panurge's last remark with the title ("*Comment Panurge racompte la manière comment il eschappa de la main des Turcqs*") [How Panurge told how he escaped from the hands of the Turks], that in turn is linked to and identifies the initial affect-image offered in the first glimpse of the character, roughly twenty pages above—the "molecular," emissive, intensive, zonal qualities of the *homme-chien* are continually held in view. Panurge is *already* assimilated into the dogs that he eludes. He takes the road toward the limit of the city that bears vague resemblance to the site of the meeting of the Limousin and Pantagruel; inversely, but also identical to what is emitted in the Limousin episode, the force of the affective sensations almost inspire Panurge to dirty his breeches, *les conchier de joye*. The descriptives contain the fur of the dogs that almost bit him: Panurge escapes from the hounds because their flair and aroma suffuse the very signs that he emits.

In view of the molecular qualities of the Rabelaisian style, it would be reductive to thematize the inital presentation of Panurge as a crafty canine merely because he is a trickster or a liminary figure, a variant of Hermes, used as a buffer to designate the lines separating belief and gender (because he simply collapses them); to recast these episodes into a redemptive story that parallels the Bible and thus awards us an aura of "truth" (because *Pantagruel* is saturated with a *politics*, not an essence, of Evangelical iconography); to offer a Christian allegory of Panurge and the New Testament for the sake of interpretive "damage control" protecting Rabelais from charges of sexism or misogyny (because the Baroque style of the Bible, an erotic text in its own right, is what Rabelais futher complicates in his rewriting).[20] To argue, too, that historical and ideological struggle must be taken up if we are to make sense of Panurge's canine demeanor does not suffice as a conclusion, either, because the fact of becoming-animal works against the language that would domesticate the concept.

Instead of patterning a summary along these lines, for the sake of defining an animal act we might note that the the meeting of Panurge and Pantagruel can qualify as an *event* in which a becoming-animal takes place. Conceived in the way it is offered through the encounter of the protagonist and his *agon* in the comic epic, the event is hardly something that can be set into a chronicle said to mediate history and the literary imagination. It is the advent of an animal act. We can conclude by recalling how, in *Le pli*, Deleuze rehearses one of the crucial questions subtending all of his writings and those coauthored with Félix Guattari: "What is an event?" An event is an atomizing, multiplying, emissive occurrence, an intense awareness or a perception of something that turns into a becoming-other, a becoming-animal, that somehow takes place in a swarm of sensations, in a nexus of "prehensions of prehensions."[21] The meeeting of Pantagruel and Panurge seems to be just that: it "prehends" the entire work in the ways its own zones of expression turn the characters and, ourselves, their prehenders, into Pantagruel-animals.

Notes

1. *Pantagruel*, in François Rabelais, *Oeuvres complètes*, ed. Jacques Boulenger (Paris: Gallimard/Pléiade, 1955), 207. The text reproduces the so-called "definitive" edition of 1542. The text is not greatly altered from its first edition, in 1531–1532, in this part of the chapter. (Translations that follow the French of this passage and other quoted material are mine.)

2. For the concept of the "relation with the unknown," I rely on Guy Rosolato, *La relation d'inconnu* (Paris: Gallimard, 1978), especially 254–279.

3. In *The Self-Made Map: Cartographic Writing in Early Modern France* (Minneapolis: University of Minnesota Press, 1996), 141–148, I have tried to analyse the spatial components of the adventure of alterity in this episode of *Pantagruel* and its rewriting in *Gargantua* (chap. 17). Emphasis here will be placed less on space than on the affiliation of the comic personage with areas that are demarcated and defined as powerfully (and attractively) bestial.

4. Paul Radin, *The Trickster: A Study in American Indian Mythology* (London: Routledge & Kegan Paul, 1955); Emiko Ohnuki-Tierney, *The Monkey as Mirror: Symbolic Transformations in Japanese History and Ritual* (Princeton: Princeton University Press, 1987); Michael P. Carroll, "The Trickster as Selfish-Buffoon and Culture Hero," *Ethos* 12.2 (1984), 105–131; Norman O. Brown, *Hermes the Thief: The Evolution of a Myth* (New York: Vintage, 1969); Victor Turner, *The Ritual Process: Structure and Anti-Structure* (Chicago: Aldine, 1967). See also Jerome Schwartz's keen reading of Panurge as trickster in *Irony and Ideology in Rabelais: Structures of Subversion* (Cambridge: Cambridge University Press, 1990).

5. On the strategies of totemism in evangelical literature, Jacques Berchtold makes a convincing case for Marot in "Le poète-rat," *Bibliothèque d'Humanisme et Renaissance* 50 (1988). In a decisive study of Panurge and his escape from the Turks, in "'Turkish Dogs': Rabelais, Erasmus, and the rhetoric of Alterity," *Representations* 41 (Winter 1993), 58–82, Timothy Hampton shows that humanistic, homiletic, or "redemptive" readings of *Pantagruel* often fall short of the political condition that informs the relation with alterity in the 1530s.

6. Terence Cave alertly remarks that although the two chapters are frequently contrasted, as in François Bon, *La folie Rabelais* (Paris: Minuit, 1990), the meeting with Panurge emerges from the Limousin encounter as "one of a series of recurrent episodes featuring travel and the figure of the traveller," and "an encounter with a disconcerting stranger, an alien, who proves by a reversal of perspective to be reassuringly familiar." In "Travelers and Others: Cultural Connections in the Works of Rabelais," in Jean-Claude Carron, ed., *François Rabelais: Critical Assessments* (Baltimore and London: The Johns Hopkins University Press, 1995), 45.

7. At the tavern Panurge retorts to a spectator making fun of his demeanor, "*Tu n'as pas trouvé tes petitz beuvreaux de Paris, qui ne beuvent en plus q'un pinson et ne prenent leur béchée sinon qu'on leur tape la queue à la mode des passereaux*" (227) [You can't find your little Parisian tipplebirds who drink less than a titmouse and only take a beakerful when they get their tails ruffled like sparrows]. In the dazzling flicker of obscenity (in the congress of "qu'on *leur tape la* queue.") Panurge implies that he is a bird, at least if a proverb, recorded by Randle Cotgrave in his *Dictionarie of the French and English Tongues* of 1611, was current in 1531: "*Passereaux, & moineaux sont de faux reseaux. Cockes, Sparrowes & (young) monkes are (much of a disposition) shrewd lechers.*"

8. It would not be wrong to see in the island of Lesbos and the figure of the Turk not just a space "outside" Christendom but also a doubly bound figure of admiration and repulsion. Frank Lestringant notes that the Western obsession with Turkey in the sixteenth century is couched in contradiction. The Turks are a "savage and

cruel" people, but at the same time, "esteemed for their great civility and for a sense of very rare equity. . . . Equally, a model and a foil, an institutional idea and a caricature of the 'republic,' the Ottoman Empire will be, for example, the ambiguous point of reference to the extremes of all political description." "*Guillaume Postel et l'obsession turque*," in *Ecrire le monde à la Renaissance: Quinze études sur Rabelais, Postel, Bodin, et la littérature géographique* (Caen: Editions Paradigme, 1993), 189.

9. See Hampton's remarks, *op. cit.*, 73–75, on the "bacon-bits" that are taken to be a "literal sign of alterity" (73) in the episode. Bacon and ham also have military trappings insofar as they afford a Parthian strategy of diversion for the user who survives on wit and a pair of fast legs. They also are akin to forms of *acharnement* (the term is taken from falconry), or simulacra that "bait" or madden the figure under whose nose and eyes they are placed.

10. In "*Le récit toponymique*" (reprinted in *Ecrire le monde à la Renaissance*, 109–128), Frank Lestringant has shown how many of the stories in *Pantagruel* and *Gargantua* are "toponymical" insofar as they turn on a place name that becomes the site of a dialogue which confers its origin with a myth. The *modus vivendi*, it can be emphasized, is *amphibology*, or aromatic wordplay (Victor Hugo called it "*la fiente de l'esprit qui vole*," that is, "the turd of flying wit") that generates the spatial narrative by confusing different registers (proper and common names) and in that way an *amphibious* play of forms conflating land and sea, fish and fowl, and also animal and human differences.

11. Among others, see Gérard Defaux's notes and references to his own work in his annotations to the writings of Rabelais, *Les Cinq Livres*, edited by Michel Simonin (Paris: Livre de Poche, 1994); Edwin Duval, *The Design of Rabelais's "Pantagruel"* (New Haven: Yale University Press, 1991); M. A. Screech, *Rabelais* (London: Duckworth, 1979).

12. The latter might be consigned to the realm of the "reader" and to his or her "responses" that would convey a desire to imagine "becoming-animal" through the mere pleasure of glossing the Rabelaisian text. Inasmuch as all four books of *Pantagruel* and *Gargantua* attest to a highly weakened deixis, it might be prudent to heed Walter Benjamin's warning, uttered in the first sentence of the "Task of the Translator" (in *Illuminations*), that in the consideration of any work of art or literature the presence of the spectator or the reader is immaterial. To posit the existence of the reader is tantamount to depriving the work of its violence, and also to *domesticating* it for narrow and self-serving ends.

13. Gilles Deleuze and Félix Guattari, *1000 plateaux* (Paris: Minuit, 1980), 334–335.

14. The task of reclassifying space as an *active* force that is not a background for history or discourse figures in the politics of postmodernism but, as usual, finds its keenest expression in texts that have nothing to do with its prevailing themes. The activation of space and a force producing events, I would like to argue below, has much to do with the Rabelaisian becoming-animal. The classical treatments of space as force include Edward Soja, *Postmodern Geographies: The Reassertion of Space in Critical Social Theory* (London: Verso, 1989 and 1995 rprt.); Michel de Certeau, *L'invention du quotidien* (Paris: Gallimard, 1990 rprt.).

15. Some writers, notes Judith Butler, "have argued that a rethinking of 'nature' as a set of dynamic interrelations suits both feminism and ecological aims (and has for

some produced an otherwise unlikely alliance with the work of Gilles Deleuze),"
in *Bodies that Matter* (New York: Routledge, 1993), 4. In *Oedipus and the Devil*
(London: Routledge, 1992), Lyndal Roper offers a more nuanced view of nature,
biology, femininity, and the body in early modern Europe. "Bodies are not creations of discourse" (15); the body, rather is conceived "as a kind of vessel barely
able to contain the forces inside it, all of which are imagined in highly active
terms as physical activities: gluttony, fighting, fornicating, blaspheming" (24).

16. In *Poésie et onomastie: L'exemple de la Renaissance* (Genève: Droz, 1978), François
    Rigolot remarks tersely that in the graphic register of his name *Pantagruel* equals
    Panurge + alt. Pantagruel would thus become other through addition or multipli-
    cation, but his *alterity* would forever be within him, in the genetic code of his
    anthroponym.

17. In the literature of humanism, writers regale in murdering wasted time. The
    attraction of immediate, instantaneous gloss replaces, Michel Jeanneret has argued,
    the labor of patient erudition (in *"Du mystère à la mystification: Le sens caché à la
    Renaissance et dans Rabelais,"* Versants 2 (1981–1982), 31–49). Through an
    appeal to Proust, Alfred Glauser notes that the two educations in the early chap-
    ters of *Gargantua*—clearly rehearsed in the two encounters above—effect a
    movement that goes from time lost to time regained, in *Rabelais créateur* (Paris:
    Nizet, 1966). In any event, the text evinces a violence enacted upon time wasted.

18. Gilles Deleuze, *Cinéma 1: l'image-mouvement* (Paris: Minuit, 1983), 102.

19. A reader wonders if a foreign land is inscribed in the toponym of *Perche*. In his
    edition of the text, Jacques Boulanger remarks that the allusion to apple pickers
    from southern Normandy "was proverbial in order to signify a man in tatters, as if
    his clothing had been torn by the branches of the many apple trees found in
    Perche" (207, n2). Would not Rabelais also be folding an reminiscence of *Persia*
    into *Perche*? Would *Perche* not rhyme with the echoes of Lesbos and Turkey?

20. One thinks of François Rigolot, "The Three Temptations of Panurge: Women's
    Vilification and Christian Humanist Discourse," in Jean-Claude Carron, ed.,
    François Rabelais: Critical Assessments, 83–102.

21. Gilles Deleuze, *"Qu-est-ce qu'un événement?"* in *Le pli: Leibniz et le baroque* (Paris:
    Minuit, 1988), 106.

Bibliography

Berchtold, Jacques. "Le poète-rat." *Bibliothèque d'Humanisme et Renaissance* 50 (1988).

Bon, François. *La folie Rabelais*. Paris: Minuit, 1990.

Brown, Norman O. *Hermes the Thief: The Evolution of a Myth*. New York: Vintage,
1969.

Butler, Judith. *Bodies that Matter*. New York: Routledge, 1993.

Carroll, Michael P. "The Trickster as Selfish-Buffoon and Cultural Hero." *Ethos* 12.2.
(1984), 105–131.

Carron, Jean-Claude, ed. *François Rabelais: Critical Assessments*. Baltimore: The Johns
Hopkins University Press, 1995.

Certeau, Michel de. *L'invention du quotidien*. Paris: Gallimard, 1990.

Conley, Tom. *The Self-Made Map: Cartographic Writing in Early Modern France*. Minneapolis: University of Minnesota Press, 1996.

Cotgrave, Randle. *Dictionarie of French and English Tongues*. 1611.

Deleuze, Gilles. *Cinéma 1: l'image-mouvement*. Paris: Minuit, 1983.

———. *Le pli: Leibniz et le baroque*. Paris: Minuit, 1988.

———, and Guattari, Félix. *1000 plateaux*. Paris: Minuit, 1980.

Duval, Edwin. *The Design of Rabelais's "Pantagruel."* New Haven: Yale University Press, 1991.

Hampton, Timothy. "'Turkish Dogs': Rabelais, Erasmus, and the Rhetoric of Alterity." *Representations* 41 (1993), 58–82.

Jeanneret, Michel. "Du mystère à la mystification: Le sens caché à la Renaissance et dans Rabelais." *Versants* 2 (1982), 31–49.

Lestringant, Frank. *Ecrire le monde à la Renaissance: Quinze études sur Rabelais, Postel, Bodin, et la littérature géographique*. Caen: Editions Paradigme, 1993.

Ohnuki-Tierney, Emiko. *The Monkey as Mirror: Symbolic Transformations in Japanese History and Ritual*. Princeton: Princeton University Press, 1987.

Rabelais, François. *Oeuvres complètes*, ed. Jacques Boulanger. Paris: Gallimard, 1955.

Radin, Paul. *The Trickster: A Study in American Indian Mythology*. London: Routledge & Kegan Paul, 1955

Rigolot, François. *Poésie et onomastie: L'exemple de la Renaissance*. Genève: Droz, 1978.

Roper, Lyndal. *Oedipus and the Devil*. London: Routledge, 1992.

Rosolato, Guy. *La Relation d'inconnu*. Paris: Gallimard, 1978.

Schwartz, Jerome. *Irony and Ideology in Rabelais: Structures of Subversion*. Cambridge: Cambridge University Press, 1990.

Screech, M. A. *Rabelais*. London: Duckworth, 1979.

Soja, Edward. *Postmodern Geographies: The Reassertion of Space in Critical Social Theory*. London: Verso, 1995.

Turner, Victor. *The Ritual Process: Structure and Anti-Structure*. Chicago: Aldine, 1967.

4 🐂

"When the Beasts Spoke"
Animal Speech and Classical Reason in Descartes and La Fontaine

Matthew Senior

> All kinds of animals, birds, reptiles and creatures of the sea are being tamed by man, but no man can tame the tongue. It is a restless evil, full of deadly poison.
>
> —James 3:7–9

> What is speech?
>
> —Montaigne, *Apology of Raymond Sebond*

"One must not confuse words with natural signs that express the passions, and can be imitated by machines and animals, nor think, like some of the Ancients, that the beasts speak, even though we don't understand their language."[1] In this passage from the *Discourse on Method*, Descartes denies language to animals and equates them with machines. The sounds of animals are like the movements of their bodies—reflex mechanical actions explainable by the laws of physics. Animal speech is devoid of *reason*, the uniquely human trait which expresses itself in *words*, discrete, conventional units of meaning.

Descartes was responding specifically to Montaigne's speculations, in the *Apology of Raymond Sebond*, that animals might speak a language that we do not understand, an idea much debated in the ancient world and still compatible with Montaigne's humanism. But with Descartes, language becomes the exclusive vehicle of conscious thought. Human identity is wagered entirely on the use of "words," while the animal body, with all of its inarticulate sounds, is relegated to a mechanical universe of automatons and chiming clocks. This new definition of language would remake the world. Animals would play a crucial role in this mastery of the material world and mastery of language. The nascent discourse of science was an attempt, in the words of the Bible, to tame the animals and to tame the tongue. In the Classical Age, animals would be dissected, studied, and named, while their extradition from human consciousness and speech would allow language to become the transparent instrument of the rational mind.

The technological world was born when animals were silenced and only poets still imagined a time "when the beasts spoke." Animal language had been an open question to Montaigne, much as it is becoming today.[2] He could not say with certainty where animal language ended and human speech began. The Age of Reason dawned when this uncertainty was divided into science and fiction. Real animals vanished. They became the machines of the scientist and the fantasy of the poet. Descartes' contemporary, Blaise Pascal, called this excessive rationalism "another kind of madness," an idea echoed by Jacques Derrida, who has argued that Cartesian rationalism is founded on the "mad audacity of the *cogito.*"[3]

Beast Machines

Although the popular image of Descartes is that of an isolated thinker dreaming of a universal mathematics, the Cartesian redefinition of thought and language had its roots in the material world, in the history of mechanical engineering and biology. Crucial scenes in the elaboration of classical reason take place in the engineer's workshop and the anatomist's dissecting room. Descartes's conception of the animal and its lack of language emerged out of his experiences of dissecting animals and his knowledge of artificial animals. The dead and simulated animals he encountered in the laboratory and the baroque garden are wider evidence of a general de-animation of nature, of which his philosophy is only one example.

The "diverse automatons and moving machines that human industry can make out of a few simple pieces,"[4] mentioned in the *Discourse,* were the work of the French engineer Salomon de Caus, who built animated grottoes and fountains for rich estates in France and Germany. Descartes used these machines to demonstrate how all of animal life, and a good deal of human life, are strictly a matter of engineering and, potentially, *trompe l'oeil.*

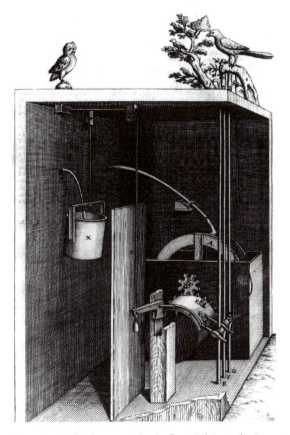

Figure 1. Hydraulic singing birds, from Salomon de Caus, *Les Raisons des forces mouvantes*, 1615. Reprinted with permission of the Department of Printing and Graphic Arts, The Houghton Library, Harvard University.

Figure 2. Detail of hydraulic singing birds.

In the *Treatise on Man*, the philosopher describes at length a fountain designed by de Caus for the royal gardens at Saint-Germain en Laye which contained an animated statue of Diana bathing. Visitors who entered the garden stepped on a hidden lever which caused the robotic Diana to retreat behind a rock. If they continued forward, they were surprised by a trident-waving Neptune or "a marine monster who vomited water in their face."[5]

For Descartes, these automatons were exactly analogous to the human or animal body. The compressed water that made the statues move, talk, or play musical instruments functioned exactly like the *esprit animaux* which rise in the blood, arrive at the brain, and are distributed to different parts of the body, where they produce motion and the mechanical signs of the passions. The spectator who steps on the hidden lever is like a stimulus which strikes the senses, and the automatic, purely mechanical flight of Diana is like the unconscious, reflex action of the body:

> External objects, which by their presence alone act on the senses . . . are like visitors who, entering into the grottoes and fountains cause, without thinking about it, the movements that take place in their presence.[6]

Thus the real meaning of the animated grotto for Descartes is that the spectator sees the animal and human somatic machine in action and appreciates how the body continually responds without conscious thought (*sans y penser*).

The rational human soul is figured in this model by the fountain-master who, hidden in his control booth, like the immaterial soul lodged in the pineal gland of the brain, can adjust or alter the functioning of the machines. Thus animal movement and speech are purely mechanical, while human behavior is either mechanical or the result of the conscious manipulations of the fountain-master.

To prove that animals are indistinguishable from such machines, Descartes challenged his readers to distinguish between a real animal and a clever automaton "which had the figure of a monkey or some other animal without reason."[7] The same would hold true for a human automaton, were it not for the criterion of speech:

> It [the human automaton] could never use words or other signs for the purpose of communicating its thoughts to others as we do. It indeed is conceivable that a machine could be made so that it would utter words, and even words appropriate to physical acts which cause some change in its organs; as, for example, if it were touched in some spot that it would ask what you wanted to say to it; if in another, that it would cry that it was hurt,

and so on for similar things. But it could never modify its phrases to reply to
the sense of whatever was said in its presence, as even the most stupid men
can do.[8]

Words, for Descartes, are the transparent signs of thought. Their sole purpose
is to communicate ideas to other minds. It is clear from this passage that words
which express pain or pleasure are outside the realm of human signification.

A troubling and unintentionally poetic aspect of Descartes's encounter with
the automaton, however, is that humans are easily fooled and quickly attribute
subjectivity to creatures which move or use language. Daniel Dennett has
observed such effects in modern robotics laboratories: "It is, in fact, ridiculously easy to induce powerful intuitions of not just sentience but full-blown
consciousness . . . by exposing people to quite simple robots made to move in
familiar mammalian ways at mammalian speeds."[9]

Descartes meant to prove that only rational language distinguished the
human from the animal and the machine, but what his example uncannily
suggests is that language, the mirror of man, is at once mechanical, animalistic,
and cognitive. The first identifications and the deepest emotions are stirred by
fragments of language and meaningless echo effects. Animal calls are repeti-
tive. They are also different each time. Their monotony has about it a poetic
aptness. All of an animal's being is expressed in its mysterious calls which we
do not understand. When the animal speaks, we hover between an undeci-
pherable fullness of meaning and the extinction of meaning in the mechanical
noise of the machine.[10]

Mechanical Orpheus

One of de Caus's creations, the "Grotto of Orpheus" (Figure 3), is particularly
suggestive of what happened to animals during the seventeenth century. A
mechanical Orpheus plays artificial music on his lyre (updated as a cello) as
statues of animals move back and forth in unison. A system of compressed air,
levers, and pulleys synchronizes his notes with the movement of the animals.
Throughout history Orpheus had symbolized the desire for communication
with animals; his poetic word had been a model for an efficacious sign directly
linked to nature.[11] These aspirations are translated into the language of engineering by de Caus's grotto. Orpheus speaks to the animals in the mechanical
Cartesian language of the passions.

De Caus's grotto of automatons brings us back to Descartes's denial of
speech in animals: "One must not maintain, like some of the Ancients, that

Figure 3. "Grotto of Orpheus," from Salomon de Caus, *Les Raisons des forces mouvantes*, 1615. Reprinted with permission of The Houghton Library, Harvard University.

animals speak even though we don't understand their language." In that passage, Descartes was replying to Montaigne, who had claimed that animals did have a language which was once understood by humans. "Plato in his depiction of the Golden Age of Saturn counts, among the principle advantages of the men of that age, their ability to communicate with animals."[12] By discoursing with animals, men and women had gained perfect knowledge about them firsthand and learned valuable moral lessons from them that were applicable to their own lives.

Adam's naming of the animals in Genesis 2:19 constituted a similar myth of absolute zoological knowledge and linguistic perfection. According to Renaissance speculation on this passage, God revealed the essences of animals to Adam, who gave them names perfectly expressive of their natures. Renaissance linguists and natural historians assumed that this ideal zoological language was Hebrew and that the study of Hebrew etymology could revive Adam's luminous knowledge of animals.[13] Other biblical passages that gave theological weight to the belief in talking animals were Genesis 3:1–5 (Eve's conversation with the serpent) and Numbers 22:22–35 (the story of Balaam's ass). "Eve knew the language of the animals," a seventeenth-century theologian wrote.[14] With this biblical corroboration of talking animals, Renaissance scientists took seriously the claims of ancient philosophers and natural historians that animals could talk. As to the present state of affairs, some thought that animals still spoke a prelapsarian language which men could no longer understand, while another tradition referred to a passage from the apocryphal Book of Jubilees which explained what happened when Adam and Eve were banished from paradise: "On that day was closed the mouth of all beasts, and of cattle, and of birds, and of whatever walks and of whatever moves, so that they could no longer speak: for they had all spoken one with another with one lip and with one tongue" (3:28).[15]

Montaigne was willing to entertain the former possibility and cites a long list of Ancients who understood animal language. According to Montaigne, animals still communicate with humans by their calls and gestures. They use sign language, like certain tribes described by Pliny. Their behavior displays complex reasoning; they weep, like humans. The most important emotions and feelings in humans and animals cannot be adequately expressed in words. Love, for example, speaks through the eyes. Montaigne's phenomenology of speech includes all of these kinds of signifying. It is an activity shared by humans and animals. He concludes his discussion by demanding what speech is: "Qu'est-ce parler?" The polyvalence, timelessness, and hiddenness of animal language, and human participation in this kind of signification, has made it impossible to define speech.

All of this speculation and the world outlook that sustained it were radically reinterpreted with Descartes and Solomon de Caus's mechanical Orpheus. In denying animals any linguist capacities at all and defining language strictly as the reflection of the conscious mind, Descartes participated in the great de-animation and designification of nature that took place during the Scientific Revolution. Before proceeding further with an analysis of the consequences of this change, it is worth reviewing the myth of the great nature poet whom de Caus chose to mechanize.

Living Language

According to myth, Orpheus received from Apollo the gift of the seven-stringed golden lyre, corresponding to the seven vowels of the Greek alphabet. His poetic song "enchanted the wild beasts and made the trees and rocks move."[16] In his work on Greek myth, Robert Graves maintains that the name Orpheus may be derived from *ophruoeis*, meaning "on the banks," and may refer to sacred alder trees that grew there (1:114). His ability to charm animals and trees may be based on a correspondence between his language and the trees since, in the ancient thirteen-consonant alphabet, each character stood for the name of a tree, and the year was divided into thirteen months, each named after a tree.

According to another Greek myth, writing was a gift of the God Hermes, who transcribed speech into wedge-shaped writing because his sacred birds, the cranes, fly in wedge formations across the sky (Graves, 1:182). In Egyptian mythology, writing was a gift of the god Thoth, who is represented in hieroglyphics with the head of an ibis and the body of a man. Plutarch says that is why the first letter of the Egyptian alphabet is shaped like an ibis.[17]

From these "animistic" points of view, animals and humans are linked together in the origin of language. Language is created by hybrid human-animal, human-god, and human-plant creatures. Spoken and written language is alive; it is botanical and biological. Phonemes are living trees and graphemes are flocks of birds flying across the sky in Orpheus's living language.

In the *Metamorphoses*, Ovid describes Orpheus and his enchanted animal audience: "Encircled by wild beasts and fluttering birds, / He tuned his lyre with a delicate hand."[18] Orpheus is the mythical poet-naturalist. His song is a gathering and naming of beasts, plants, and rocks. His poetry reveals the meaning of a natural world where races of men spring from stones, dragon's teeth, or ants, and the speckled breasts of swallows tell human stories of bloodshed and betrayal. The Orphic names are both proper and generic; they are metamorphic names which intertwine the names of people with the names of species: the cypress tree is named after Cyparissus and the hyacinth after Hyacinthus. They designate something common to individual humans and whole species of animals and plants. They violate the modern boundary between humans and other life forms, and they confuse the distinction between the individual and the group.

The paradigm case of Orphic naming in the *Metamorphoses* is the story of Hyacinthus. Apollo tells the dying Hyacinthus that "certain accents of your name shall echo / 'Ai, Ai' within the music of my lyre / And shall be printed letters on frail flowers" (10.206–208). The first syllable of Hyacinthus's name is inscribed in the flower that bears his name: Apollo "wrote the words 'Ai, Ai' across its petals, / The sign of his own grief, his signature" (10.216–220). Human pathos, writing, and biological structure are fused together in the Orphic name.

This kind of naming remained scientifically respectable until the end of the Renaissance. Examples of "signatures" abound in Ulisse Aldrovandi, Edward Topsell, and Conrad Gesner. For example, Topsell says, "Every living beast being a word, every kind being a sentence, and all of them together a large history, contain admirable knowledge and learning, which was, which is, which shall continue."[19]

Dead Language

The sense of the book of nature changed, however, with the Scientific Revolution. As Galileo put it:

> Philosophy is written in this grand book, the universe, which stands continually open to our gaze. But the book cannot be understood unless one first learns to comprehend the language and read the letters in which it is composed. It is written in the language of mathematics, and its characters are triangles, circles, and other geometric figures without which it is humanly impossible to understand a single word of it.[20]

And Galileo closed the book on the old poetic outlook by saying, "Nature takes no delight in poetry" (238).

Galileo means that living creatures are not composed like a poetic language. If there is a divine message to be studied in nature, it is *not* to be read like a literary text. There is no language immanent to the structure of things waiting to be put to music by Orpheus.

The only language of nature is the language of mathematics, and the true Orpheus of that language would "take no delight in poetry." Language was no longer *in* nature; it had retreated, as Michel Foucault says in *Les Mots et les choses:* "Language withdraws from the midst of beings and enters its age of transparence and neutrality."[21]

The retreat of language and the mechanization of nature are part of the same process. Animals become machines and language loses its living link to things. The only animals that Descartes alludes to in the *Discourse* are de Caus's automatons and the dead animals which he invites his readers to dissect: "I would like those who are not versed in anatomy to take the trouble, before they read what follows, to cut up before themselves the heart of a large animal."[22]

The frontispiece of Claude Perrault's *Mémoires pour servir à l'histoire naturelle des animaux* represents a scene of dissection, and it makes explicit the link between reading, writing, and dead animals. A group of naturalists, plus a few curious dilettantes, observe the dissection of an animal while one of their number takes careful notes. Seated in the right foreground, Claude Perrault (1613–88), founder of the Royal Academy of Sciences and brother of the fairy

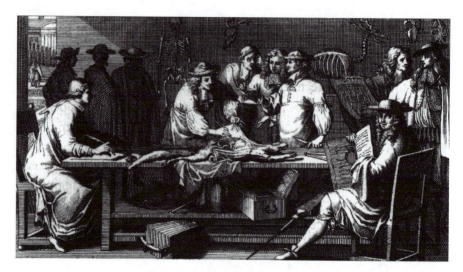

Figure 4. Frontispiece, from Claude Perrault, *Mémoires pour servir à l'histoire naturelle des animaux*, first published in 1669. Engraving from 1731 edition, La Haye, P. Gosse. Reprinted with permission of the Department of Special Collections, Memorial Library, The University of Wisconsin–Madison.

tale writer Charles Perrault, makes eye contact with the reader and points to the text to underscore the link between vision and representation and to suggest that the *Mémoires* were written, literally, on a dissecting board. The other figure in this tableau who meets our gaze is the human skeleton on the wall. The skull, as *memento mori*, adds a note of moral gravity and a seriousness to the scene. Its dominant position on the wall above the animal skeletons is in keeping with what Perrault says of man in the *Mémoires*, that he is "the most perfect animal."[23]

Judging from its tail, the animal the naturalists are dissecting appears to be a fox. One of the more interesting cases related by Perrault involved the otter and its close relative the beaver. Careful dissection of the two animals lead to a clear distinction between the two species and the debunking of an old myth. Ancient naturalists believed that the beaver's testicles contained the valuable drug *castoreum*. According to tradition, the beaver, "knowing that men are pursuing him just to get that liqueur which is so useful in medicine, will tear off his testicles when he sees himself pursued by hunters and abandon them as a ransom" (137). The account of the academy's dissection and the accompanying anatomical drawing proved that *castoreum* is stored in the beaver's scent glands, not its testicles. So, in a sense, as the dissectors strip away flesh from bone, they are also cutting away myth and legend.

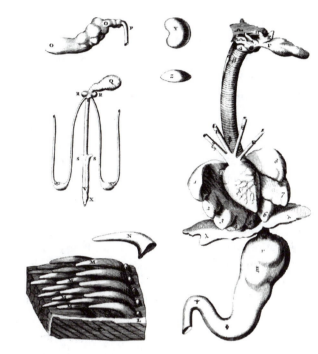

Explication des parties que la diffection du Lion peut faire connoistre.

A. Est la creste du Crane.
BB. Le Zygoma.
CC. La grande & la petite Canine.
D. Les Dents Incisives.
E. L'apophyse Coronoide de la machoire inférieure.
FFF. Les Dents Molaires.
G. L'extrémité du Rayons.
H. L'extrémité du Coude.
IIII. Les os du Carpe.
..... Les quatre os du Métacarpe.
2222. Les quatre os de la premiére Phalange des doits.
3333. Les quatre os de la seconde Phalange.
.... Les derniers os des doits. On en a représenté un separé, & hors de son articulation, lequel avec deux autres marquez 2. 3. qui sont aussi separez du reste de la patte, doit composer un des doits. Il faut rémarquer la bure que l'os marqué 3. a en son extrémité, qui fait un Condyle ou saillie , pour donner lieu au dernier os qui luy est articulé , de se flechir en haut.
KKK. Une portion de la peau de la langue vûë avec le microscope.
LLL. De petites éminences qui sont proche de la racine de chacune des pointes qui sont sur la langue.
MMM. Les pointes dont la langue est hérissée.
N. Une des pointes séparée de la peau,
afin de faire voir sa cavité.
OO. La Vésicule du Fiel.
P. Le conduit de la Bile.
Q. La Vessie.
RR. Les Prostates.
SS. Les ligamens , qui joints avec l'Uréthre composent le corps de la Verge.
T. Le commencement de l'Urethre.
X. Le Balanus.
Y. Le Crystalin qui estoit gasté.
Z. L'autre Crystalin qui estoit sain.
Γ. La Langue.
Δ. Le cartilage Toyroïae du Larynx.
Θ. Le cartilage Cricoïde.
Λ. Le cartilage Arytenoïde.
H. La Glotte.
Σ. L'Epiglotte.
Φ. La partie la plus basse du Ventricule.
Ψ. L'orifice inférieur du Ventricule.
Ω. L'Oesophage.
ββ. L'aspéra Artere.
γ. L'oreille gauche du Cœur.
Δ. Le Cœur.
ζ. L'artére Sousclaviére droite.
ι. La Carotide droite.
θ. La Carotide gauche.
κ. L'artére Sousclaviére gauche.
λλ. Une portion du Diaphragme.
μ. L'orifice supérieur du Ventricule.
νξ. Deux bosses qui estoient au devant du Ventricule.
12345678. Les huit Lobes du Poumon.

Figure 5. Plates representing a dissected lion from *Mémoires pour servir à l'histoire naturelle des animaux*. *Reprinted with permission of Memorial Library, The University of Wisconsin–Madison.*

Descartes's contemporary, Francis Bacon, forcefully proclaimed the need to excise myth by dissecting nature: "Those who aspire not to guess and divine, but to discover and know; who propose not to devise mimic and fabulous worlds of their own; but to examine and dissect the nature of this very world itself; must go to facts themselves for everything."[24] Bacon described his own enterprise as: "a history not only of nature free and at large . . . but much more of nature under constraint and vexed; that is to say, when by art and the hand of man she is forced out of her natural state, and squeezed and moulded."[25] The actors in Perrault's scene of dissection are engaged in such a constraint of nature. By their art and hands they are writing the discourse of comparative anatomy.

The first animals to be dissected by the academy were two lions that had died in captivity at the Vincennes zoo. Careful dissection revealed errors of observation made by Albert the Great, Pliny, and Cardan. The new zoologists were still under the spell of the humoral theory, however, since they believed that one lion died of a excess of bile and the other of an excess of blood, the first brought on—and they are willing to follow Pliny here—by a disease specific to captive lions, *aegritudinem fastidii*.

The plates of the *Mémoires* (Figure 5) represent the final results of the dissection of the lion. The King of the Beasts is disassembled visually and nominally for careful study. His dead body parts are separated and alphabetized by the new scientific discourse. Instead of the living Orphic alphabet, we read the academy's dead letters of dissection. The letters have no sympathetic link with a living animal, just a conventional relation to themselves. Every animal is subject to their arbitrary sequence from A to Z, and every animal would be summoned, named, and dissected; not in Orphic rapture or Dionysian frenzy, but in the dispassionate discourse of modern science.

In *Les Mots et les choses*, Michel Foucault relates the new methodology in botany and zoology to an epistemological break between the Renaissance and the Classical Age and describes the role these sciences would play in a new kind of historical writing:

> The Classical Age gives an entirely different meaning to history: for the first time, things themselves become the object of an exacting gaze which is transcribed into smooth, neutral, faithful words. That is why, in this "purification," the first form of history to be constituted was natural history. Because to construct itself it can simply apply words, without intermediary, to things themselves. The documents of this new kind of history are not other words, texts, or archives, but rather the clear spaces where things are juxtaposed— herbariums, collections, gardens. The locus of this history is an atemporal

rectangle, where, stripped of all commentary, of all accompanying language, beings present themselves side by side with their visible surfaces contrasted according to common traits, and, as a result, already virtually analyzed, and bearing only their names ("*porteurs de leur seul nom*").[26]

In the dissecting room, words are the transparent representatives of rational thought, as Descartes had wished. They record the activity of a conscious human subject who gains mastery over nature by dissection and scientific naming.

"Everything Talks in My Work, Even the Fish"

The poet Jean de La Fontaine's oeuvre was written across the epistemological fault line Foucault describes. The first six books of *Les Fables* were published in 1668, shortly after the date Foucault used to herald the change, the 1657 publication of Joannes Johnston's *Natural History of Quadrupeds*. The remaining twelve books appeared in 1678, after Perrault's first *Mémoire* of 1669. The *Fables* provide a literary reflection of the changing paradigms of animality in the seventeenth century, and they can be used to test the idea of the episteme itself: Is it a useful tool for comparing two figures such as La Fontaine and Descartes, one a poet and the other a philosopher, who had such differing views of animals?[27] Are La Fontaine's talking animals caught in the same web of knowledge and power as Descartes's, De Caus's, and Perrault's animals?[28]

France's great *peintre animalier* inherited a long tradition of fables which united men and animals in the same organic field of language. He was strongly influenced by Plato and Renaissance neoplatonism. In the *Epistle to Horace*, he asks whether his century, with all of its *savants* and *sages*, could find "a single one who approaches Plato."[29] The *Fables*[30] are interspersed with Orphic and Platonic language: "Plants breath . . ." (DS); "Nature has placed in each creature / A few grains of the sphere where souls are formed" (10.14); "We are all . . . hosts of the universe under the names of animals" (DS); "Everything speaks in my work, even the fish" (MD). But he was also informed of the scientific discoveries and controversies of his age. In the salon of one of his patrons, Mme de la Sablière, he came into contact with leading scientists of his day. He read François Bernier's *Abrégé de la philosophie de Gassendi* and adopted its atomism and anti-Cartesian view of animals. In his *Discours à Mme de la Sablière*, La Fontaine cites Descartes by name and attacks the thesis of the *bête machine*. The poet's sympathy for animals and his sense that they fared poorly at the hands of man in the Age of Reason is expressed in his fable, "The Lion in

Love." The tale recounts in poetic fashion the loss of animal speech and a violent end to discourse between humans and animals.

The Lion in Love

In the days when the beasts could speak,
The Lions set about to seek
Communion with humankind.
Why not? They were our equals then;
For both in courage and in mind
They claimed comparison with Men.
. . . .
A Lion of the noblest breed
Met walking in a flowery mead
A Shepherdess of pleasing carriage,
And straightway sought her hand in marriage.
Her father would have wished to find
A less alarming son-in-law.
. . . .
Yet thinking it not wise
To answer "No" without disguise,
"My daughter is delicate," he said,
And when Your Majesty caressed her,
Your claws, I fancy, would molest her.
I'd have them pared, if I were you;
And those sharp teeth need filing too:
Your kisses then would be less rough.
. . . .
Blinded by love, the suitor bold
Went off to do as he was told:
Toothless and clawless he hurried back,
As weak as a dismantled fort.
The father called out his pack of dogs
And the lion was easy prey.

Love, when you seize our hearts,
That moment all common sense departs (4.1)[31]

The first line of the fable evokes the Golden Age, the Adamic time, the *Fabelzeit* when animals talked with humans. It is definitively lost with the arrival of the new episteme. "The Lion in Love" tells the tale of that loss. The poem begins "when the beasts could speak," when humans could communicate their love to animals. By the end of the fable, the wily "classical" father

Figure 6. "The Lion in Love." Engraving by François Chauveau from *Fables choisies mises en vers* by Jean de La Fontaine. Paris: Claude Barbin, 1668. Reprinted with permission of The Houghton Library, Harvard University.

has imposed his order of discourse and knowledge. The wild lion is torn to pieces and silenced forever by the father's domestic dog pack.

François Chaveau's engraving for the fable, which appeared with the first edition of the *Fables* in 1668, captures the drama of the scene. The moment of representation corresponds with the loss of animal language and power. The lion is deprived of its teeth and claws in an enclosed human space which walls out nature and confines animals. The treacherous father is depicted from the side, from an almost anamorphic point of view, which distorts his face, just as his language is oblique and false. The daughter looks on with great concern, displaying emotions that any compassionate human being would feel while watching a beloved animal being operated on. The drawing captures both the rational gaze of the father and the enchanted gaze of the daughter.

On the attractiveness of animals, Montaigne had written: *"Il n'est rien d'eux que nous n'aimons et qui ne plaise à nos sens"* ["There is nothing about them that we don't like and which doesn't please our senses"].[32] Jean Baudrillard characterizes human affection for animals in terms that go well with this fable:

"with animals, seduction achieves its purest form." Human fascination with animals is, for the postmodern French sociologist, the result of "a feline, theatrical nostalgia for finery," an attractive "dizziness, a loss of meaning."[33]

As part of his critique of modern rationalism, Baudrillard has also deconstructed the notion of "animism" which informs most anthropological treatments of talking animals. Bruno Bettelheim defines animism eloquently in *The Uses of Enchantment*:

> To the child there is no clear line separating objects from living things; whatever has life has life very much like his own. . . . The child expects animals to talk about the things which are really significant to him, as animals do in fairy tales. . . . In animistic thinking, not only animals feel and think as we do, but even stones are alive. . . . Everything is inhabited by a spirit similar to all other spirits. Because of this inherent sameness, it is believable that man can change into an animal or the other way around.[34]

La Fontaine introduces his *Fables* with just such a declaration of animism: "Everything talks in my work, even the fish." As a nature poet, he establishes his Orphic and Platonic ancestry at a moment in history when such language was being cut off from rational discourse and confined to childhood and fantasy.

The primitive notion of animism has returned, however, as part of the postmodernist critique of Enlightenment rationality. In *Symbolic Exchange and Death*, Baudrillard argues that: "Primitive people are not under the spell of, as we like to say, 'animism', in other words, of the idealism of the living, of the irrational magic of forces; they do not give priority to either term, 'living' or 'non-living' for the simple reason that they don't even make this distinction."[35]

For Baudrillard, prerational man lives in a symbolic order which understands life and death as exchangeable, not opposed, terms. One lives a life/death which precedes birth and follows death. Whatever the "primitive" attributes to the natural world, it is not the Western concept of "life." In this passage, Baudrillard calls the Western attitude towards life (as defined over and against biological death) an "idealism." The rationalist has an imaginary, "idealist" view of life akin to a religious belief in the soul or the existence of God. For Baudrillard, the modern medical definitions of life and death function as a sort of secular religion.

In the Orphic, poetic worldview, there is a force worth talking about, there is a soul, an organizing principle in things which goes beyond a biological definition of life. There is a life in nature, a life of the planet, which is indifferent to the life and death of individual organisms. Orphic or animistic language does not merely reflect the point of view of a breathing, thinking human being, but rather the life of birds, fish, mammals, and even the geological life of rocks and minerals, a kind of life which, after all, has us in its embrace. We are not just Cartesian minds or breathing bodies pronounced dead or alive on operating tables. We are, in some sense, as Baudrillard says, indistinguishably dead and alive. Animate and inanimate things are happening to us all of the time, as part of our lives, as part of a larger ecological life which is occurring in us all of the time, which, now, is available to us only in the language of poetry and childhood.

The Age of Iron

The lion in love is not the last animal to speak in the *Fables*. Animals continue to speak among themselves and to humans in the Age of Iron. The fate of the lion, however, is prophetic of most dialogues between humans and animals in La Fontaine. Humans are usually rational enough to analyze any situation as a brutal rapport of force and press their tactical advantage. Their language is a means of conquest, an instrument of domination. The irony is that animals also play this linguistic game of exploitation. Throughout his work, La Fontaine continues to demonstrate the continuity between animal and human speech and reason. It is a sometimes bitter version of the old enchanted view. Animals and humans continue to talk, but both now employ the instrumental discourse of science and the hypocritical language of the court. There are also a few rare examples of compassion and generosity in the natural world. One of the most sentimental love poems in the French language is La Fontaine's "The Two Pigeons" (9.2).

Talking Animals

Chance encounters and lasting relationships among the animals are based on linguistic exchange. Because of the brevity of the fable and the wary nature of the animals, conversations are brief performative encounters. Some exchanges are relatively benign—only a piece of cheese is lost for a lesson in flattery. Most of the time, however, the stakes are higher. Rhetorical sparring is the prelude to being left in the bottom of a well, beaten, eaten, or skinned alive.

La Fontaine refers to his animals collectively as *hôtes des bois* ("guests of the woods"). Etymologically, the word *hôte* is derived from the Latin *hostium*, meaning "enemy" or "other." In La Fontaine's forest, one is never sure which meaning of the word will prevail. Formulas of civility and hospitality barely mask the struggle for survival. The fablist believed, following Lucretius, that all of creation was in a constant state of strife, and his *Fables* present the animal world as a rapacious predatory order, an inexorable food chain with man at the top.

This predatory view of nature is summed up in the fable "Nothing in Excess" (9.11). In this poem, nature is described as being constantly in excess; each species is wasteful and overproductive. Wheat proliferates and must be eaten by sheep: "To correct the wheat, God allowed the sheep / To cut back the surplus of the prodigious harvest." Sheep in turn overgraze and are in danger of "ruining everything" were it not for the wolf: "Heaven allowed the Wolves / To eat a few." The greedy wolf would destroy all of the sheep if man did not "punish" him in turn. At the top of this moralized food chain stands man: "Of all the animals, man has the most penchant / To fall into excess." Only the cultural and legal order can curb humankind: "One must bring to justice / The small and the great." In this scheme, human culture is part of a self-regulating, predatory chain of creation, and the poet is himself a predator, one who will carry out the *procès* of correcting and punishing human excess. As a "glutton of vice," the poet, like the wolf, will devour his prey.

Tactical encounters in the forest are the same as those in society. From the top to the bottom of creation, each species is involved in a continual "*procès*," a rational, planned exploitation of its prey according to the most efficient strategy. The wolf and the sheep, the lawyer and the two plaintiffs, the fox and the chicken are all involved in the same strategic jockeying. Some situations call for what Pascal termed "the spirit of geometry," and others, "the spirit of finesse." Sometimes one must seize the high ground and brutally enforce a natural advantage. The wolf is upstream from the lamb; the rooster refuses to descend from his perch; the cormorant imprisons its prey (the crawfish) in a shallow, transparent pond which it guards. An owl isolates mice in the hollow of a tree whose strategic upper branches it occupies; the mice cannot leave the tree because the owl has bitten off their legs. These supreme predators have perfected techniques for identifying and isolating their prey according to species. They are figures of classical science and statecraft. They employ the same tactics as the human animals we see in La Fontaine. As the wolf observes, the ultimate despoiler of the sheep is the shepherd.

The most telling image of man as the tactician of heights is the figure of the poet himself which occurs in fable 14, book 10. In this tale, La Fontaine sets out to demonstrate that "man behaves in a thousand instances like the animals." To prove his point, the author describes climbing up a tree to shoot rabbits: "A new Jupiter from the top of this Olympus / I strike down at my pleasure / An unsuspecting rabbit." The other rabbits scatter when one of their number is killed, but soon reappear, forgetful of the peril that still threatens them from above. La Fontaine puts himself in the same position of sovereign occularity which he identifies with Apollo in another fable, in which a man tries to trick the god by concealing a bird in his hand and asking Apollo whether it is dead or alive. The god replies, cleverly: "Dead or alive, show me your sparrow." Apollo discerns all and is able to name the bird by species, and he adds menacingly: "I see from afar, I strike the same" (4.19). The power to see all things is the power to destroy them, like the poet-hunter in his tree.

Another story which illustrates the need for a simple geometrical strategy for survival is the fable "The Cat and the Fox" (9.14). The fox has bragged to the cat that he has a hundred ways of escaping his enemies; the cat can claim only one. Suddenly the two animals are set upon by a pack of dogs. The cat mockingly calls upon the fox to find a single "sure strategy," and declares abruptly: "As for me, here is mine. / At these words, he scrambled up a tree." The fox stays on the ground, fleeing in circles, and ends up in the jaws of the pursuing hounds. His predicament is reminiscent of Descartes's discussion of the man lost in the woods needing to walk in a straight line. The cat is a good Cartesian, with a firmer grasp of geometry and the need for universal rules of thought.

The most uneven rhetorical exchanges of all occur between humans and animals—can one find a single instance in La Fontaine of an animal outwitting a human or talking itself out of becoming a meal? The little fish pleads for its life, begging the fisherman to release him so that he can grow up to be a big carp and be caught again, only to receive as his answer: "Fish, my dear friend, who try to play the preacher; / You are headed for the skillet, despite what you say. / This very evening you will be fried (5.3)." The "my good friend" is typical of such situations in La Fontaine, where one is usually called "friend" just as the door slams shut or the terrible verdict is pronounced. This fish story concludes with one of La Fontaine's most famous lines: "*Un tien vaut, ce dit-on, mieux que deux tu l'auras*" ["A bird in the hand is worth two in the bush"].

The plaintive cry of animal to man is heard again in "The Vulture and the Plover" (6.15). A bird of prey pounces on a plover, which is itself caught in a huntsman's net. The hawk gets entangled in the trap and finds himself pleading for his own life. "Huntsman, release me . . . I never did you any wrong." The hunter is unmoved: "And the plover, did she harm you?" In another tale, a deer tries to hide among a herd of cattle, at first escaping detection from the hired hands, only to be found by the penetrating "eye of the Master." There is no reprieve: "His tears could not save him from death / He was carried off, salted, and served up in a good many meals" (4.21).

La Bagatelle, La Science

Against Descartes, who decreed a radical separation between humans and animals, La Fontaine seems intent on violating the boundary by showing the animality of man and the (usually cruel) humanity of the beasts. Man is a predatory animal; his reason and science are simply rapacity pursued by other means. Like Descartes, however, La Fontaine does reserve a unique place for man in the natural order. In the *Discours à Mme de la Sablière*, he argues that man has a two-part soul, a "double treasure," half of which he shares with the animals, but the other half of which is a "daughter of Heaven," an immaterial, dimensionless soul which has a beginning but no end, and which can occupy a point in space, yet not fill it.

This is typical of the later, more scientific La Fontaine; this is his theoretical reply to the debate about the animal soul. But at the beginning of the *Discours*, he states that his method is a mixture of science and poetry: "*La bagatelle, la science, / Les chimères, le rien, tout est bon. Je soutiens*" ["Trifles, science, illusions, nothing—everything is good, I maintain."] Like Kipling's, La Fontaine's animal stories are a curious mélange of science and fantasy, in which, finally, science is put on the same level of plausibility and amusement as poetry. La Fontaine lived in an age when the song of Orpheus was silenced by science. The human was defined as the purely rational, so poetry could only be spoken by animals and children. The great Fablist was keenly interested in science, but he was always ready to drop everything for a good fairy tale, if someone were telling the story of "Donkey Skin." "*Si Peau d'âne m'était conté, / J'y prendrais un plaisir extrême, / Le monde est vieux, dit-on; je le crois, cependant / Il le faut amuser encore comme un enfant*" ["If someone told me the story of 'Donkey Skin,' I would be extremely amused; the world is old, they say; I agree, but it must still be entertained, like a child"] (8.4).

Notes

1. René Descartes, *Discours de la méthode*, ed. Etienne Gilson (Paris: Vrin, 1962), 58.

2. The latest conclusion of scientists who study primate language, for example, is that "apes can come to understand even the syntax of human speech, at a level that compares favorably with that of a 2–1/2 year old child." Duane Rumbaugh, "Primate Language and Cognition: Common Ground," *Social Research* 62 (1995), 722.

3. Jacques Derrida, "Cogito and the History of Madness," *Writing and Difference*, trans. Alan Bass (Chicago: University of Chicago Press, 1978), 61.

4. Descartes, *Discours*, 56.

5. Cited in Etienne Gilson, ed., *Discours de la méthode*, 421.

6. Gilson, ed., *Discours*, 421.

7. Descartes, *Discours*, 56.

8. *Ibid.*

9. Daniel Dennett, "Animal Consciousness: What Matters and Why," *Social Research* 62 (1995), 694.

10. On the subject of machinic language in Paul de Man and bp Nichol, see David L. Clark, "Monstrosity, Illegibility, Denegation: De Man, Nichol, and the Resistance to Postmodernism," *Negation, Critical Theory, and Postmodern Textuality* (Boston: Kluwer, 1994), 259–300.

11. Claude Dubois, *Mythe et langage au seizième siècle* (Lyons: Ducros, 1970), 45.

12. Michel de Montaigne, *Oeuvres complètes*, ed. Maurice Rat (Paris: Gallimard, 1962), 430. The passage from Plato's *Statesman*: "In that era God was supreme governor in charge of the actual rotation of the universe as a whole. . . . Savagery was nowhere to be found nor preying of creature on creature, nor did war rage nor any strife whatsoever. . . . Men had abundance of leisure and were at an advantage in being able to converse with animals as well as with one another. . . . As they associated with one another and with the animals they sought to learn from each tribe of creatures whether its special faculties enabled it to apprehend some distinctive truth not available to the rest which it could bring as its contribution to swell the common treasure store of wisdom." *The Collected Dialogues of Plato*, eds. Edith Hamilton and Huntington Cairns (Princeton: Princeton University Press, 1973), 1037.

13. Claude Duret, *Thresor de l'histoire des langues de cest univers* (1613), (Geneva: Slatkine Reprints, 1972), 39–41. See also the discussion of *"adamisme linguistique"* in Dubois, *Mythe*, 46–65.

14. Dubois, *Mythe*, 59.

15. *The Apocrypha and Pseudepigrapha of the Old Testament in English*, ed. R. H. Charles (Oxford: The Clarendon Press, 1974), 2: 17.

16. Robert Graves, *Greek Myths*, 2 vols. (London: Penguin, 1960), 1:111.

17. Louis Charbonneau-Lassay, *The Bestiary of Christ*, trans. D. M. Dooling (New York: Arkana, 1992), 267.

18. Ovid, *The Metamorphoses*, trans. Horace Gregory (New York: Penguin, 1960), 10.145.

19. Cited in James J. Bono, *The Word of God and the Languages of Man: Interpreting Nature in Early Modern Science and Medicine* (Madison: University of Wisconsin Press, 1995), 183. On Topsell and other natural historians, see William Ashworth, "Natural History and the Emblematic World View," *Reappraisals of the Scientific Revolution*, eds. David Lindberg and Robert Westman (Cambridge: Cambridge University Press, 1990), 303–332.

20. Galileo Galilei, *Discoveries and Opinions of Galileo*, trans. Stillman Drake (Garden City: Doubleday, 1957), 237.

21. Michel Foucault, *Les Mots et les choses* (Paris: Gallimard, 1966), 70.

22. Descartes, *Discours*, 47.

23. Claude Perrault, *Mémoires pour servir à l'histoire naturelle des animaux* (La Haye: P. Gosse, 1731), 70. For a discussion of Perrault, see Patrick Dandrey, *La Fabrique des Fables: Essai sur la poétique de La Fontaine* (Paris: Klincksiek, 1991), 144–151.

24. Sir Francis Bacon, *The Works of Francis Bacon*, ed. James Spedding (London: Longman, 1857), 4: 28.

25. *Ibid.*

26. Foucault, *Les Mots et les choses*, 143.

27. Foucault's episteme has been criticized for being a blanket of uniformity that covers all scientific thought at a given period. In *The Growth of Biological Thought* (Cambridge: Belknap, 1982), Ernst Mayr asks how "two seemingly incompatible paradigms may exist side by side, like preformation and epigenesis, mechanism and vitalism, . . ." (113).

28. On classical reason in La Fontaine, see Michel Serres, "Knowledge in the Classical Age: La Fontaine and Descartes," *Hermes: Literature, Science, Philosophy*, eds. Josué Harari and David Bell (Baltimore: Johns Hopkins University Press, 1982), 15–28.

29. Cited in Pierre Bornecque, *La Fontaine fabuliste* (Paris: SEDES, 1983), 190. On neoplatonic influences in La Fontaine, see Alain Niderst, "'Le plus simple animal nous y tient lieu de maistre'," *L'Animalité: Hommes et animaux dans la littérature française*, ed. Alain Niderst (Tubingen: Gunter Narr Verlag, 1994), 115–122.

30. All citations of La Fontaine are from *Oeuvres complètes*, ed. J.-P Collinet (Paris: Gallimard, 1991). References in the text are indicated parenthetically by book and fable number; DS: *Discours à Mme de la Sablière*; MD: "*A monseigneur le dauphin.*" All translations are mine unless otherwise indicated.

31. Translation, slightly altered, from *La Fontaine's Fables Translated into English Verse*, trans. Edward Marsh (London: Everyman's, 1974).

32. Montaigne, *Oeuvres*, 464.

33. Jean Baudrillard, *Seduction*, trans. Brian Singer (New York: St. Martin's Press, 1990), 88–89.

34. Bruno Bettelheim, *The Uses of Enchantment: The Meaning and Importance of Fairy Tales* (New York: Knopf, 1976), 205.

35. Jean Baudrillard, *L'Echange symbolique et la mort* (Paris: Gallimard, 1976), 205.

Bibliography

Bacon, Sir Francis. *The Works of Francis Bacon*, ed. James Spedding. London: Longman, 1857.

Baudrillard, Jean. *Seduction*. Brian Singer, trans. New York: St. Martins' 1990.

———. *Symbolic Exchange and Death*. Iain Grant, trans. London: Sage, 1993.

Bettelheim, Bruno. *The Uses of Enchantment: The Meaning and Importance of Fairy Tales*. New York: Knopf, 1976.

Boas, George. *The Happy Beast in French Thought of the Seventeenth Century*. Baltimore: Johns Hopkins University Press, 1933.

Bono, James. *The Word of God and the Languages of Man: Interpreting Nature in Early Modern Science and Medicine*. Madison: Wisconsin University Press, 1995.

Bornecque, Pierre. *La Fontaine fabuliste*. Paris: SEDES, 1984.

Charbonneau-Lassay, Louis. *The Bestiary of Christ*, trans. D. M. Dooling. New York: Arkana, 1992.

Charles, R. H., ed. *The Apocrypha and Pseudepigrapha of the Old Testament in English*. Oxford: The Clarendon Press, 1974.

Clark, David L, ed. *Negation, Critical Theory, and Postmodern Textuality*. Boston: Kluwer, 1994.

Dandrey, Patrick. *La Fabrique des Fables: Essai sur la poétique de La Fontaine*. Paris: Klincksieck, 1991.

Derrida, Jacques. *Writing and Difference*, trans. Alan Bass. Chicago: University of Chicago Press, 1978.

Dennet, Daniel. "Animal Consciousness: What Matters and Why." *Social Research* 62 (1995), 691–710.

Descartes, René. *Discours de la méthode*, ed. Etienne Gilson. Paris: Vrin, 1962.

Dubois, Claude. *Mythe et language au seizième siècle*. Lyons: Ducros, 1970.

Duret, Claude. *Thresor de l'histoire des langues de cest univers* (1613). Geneva: Slatkine Reprints, 1972.

Foucault, Michel. *Les Mots et les choses*. Paris: Gallimard, 1966.

Galilei, Galileo. *Discoveries and Opinions of Galileo*, trans. Stillman Drake. Garden City: Doubleday, 1957.

Graves, Robert. The *Greek Myths*. 2 vols. London: Penguin, 1960.

Harrison, Peter. "Descartes on Animals." *Philosophical Quarterly* 30 (1992), 219–227.

La Fontaine, Jean de. *Oeuvres complètes*, ed. Jean-Pierre Collinet. Paris: Gallimard, 1991.

Lindberg, David, ed. *Reappraisals of the Scientific Revolution*. Cambridge: Cambridge University Press, 1990.

Marin, Louis. *Food for Thought*, trans. Mette Hjort. Baltimore: Johns Hopkins University Press, 1989.

Marsh, Edward. *La Fontaine's Fables Translated into English Verse*. London: Everyman's, 1974.

Mayr, Ernst. *The Growth of Biological Thought: Diversity, Evolution, and Inheritance*. Cambridge: Harvard University Press, 1982.

Montaigne, Michel de. *Oeuvres complètes*, ed. Maurice Rat. Paris: Gallimard, 1962.

Niderst, Alain, ed. *L'Animalité: Hommes et animaux dans la littérature française*. Berlin: Gunter Narr, 1994.

Ovid. *Metamorphoses*, trans. F. J. Miller. Cambridge: Harvard University Press, 1984.

Perrault, Claude. *Mémoire pour servir à l'histoire naturelle des animaux*. La Haye: P. Gosse, 1731.

Plato. *The Collected Dialogues of Plato*, eds. Edith Hamilton and Hunington Cairns. Princeton: Princeton University Press, 1973.

Rosenfield, Leonora Cohen. *From Beast-Machine to Man-Machine*. New York: Octagon Books, 1968.

Rumbaugh, Duane. "Primate Language and Cognition: Common Ground." *Social Research* 62 (1995), 711–730.

Serres, Michel. "Knowledge in the Classical Age: La Fontaine and Descartes." *Hermes*, eds. David Bell and Josué Harari. Baltimore: Johns Hopkins University Press, 1982.

5 🦎

Revolutionary Monsters

Marie-Hélène Huet

The fall of Robespierre on 9 Thermidor Year II (July 27, 1794) precipitated a dramatic reversal in the politics of the French Revolution. It also marked the beginning of a deliberate effort to disfigure the dead revolutionaries and prevent any idealization of the architects of the most dramatic and controversial upheaval in French history. As early as 10 Thermidor, false documents started circulating in Paris, purporting to uncover the crimes of Robespierre and his friends. The Thermidorians spared no effort to distance themselves from the Robespierrists, shifting the burden of the terror onto their dead shoulders.[1] In the days and decades that followed Thermidor, writers, polemicists, and historiographers strove to expose the iniquities of the French Revolution by focusing on its greatest and most eloquent figures. By 1885, the revolution's meaning, its infamy, its misled ideals had been fully spelled out; and, in spite of much historical work, archival research, and the more-or-less successful rehabilitation of its leaders, the revolution remained forever tainted with both the violence that marred its progress and the verbal ferocity that followed its undoing.

In particular, the images of Danton and Robespierre, as they were conceived, embellished, or tarnished in the nineteenth century, serve to remind us that, from the onset, historical writing was marked by literary concerns that extended beyond style and narrative process: history made room for fiction and for mythical fiction as well.[2] Because the nineteenth century was also a time when Johann Caspar Lavater's theories offered correspondences between physical features and mental or moral dispositions,[3] the French revolutionaries

85

were portrayed in such a way that any reader would shudder at the thought of their ghastly and repulsive appearance, which accurately foreshadowed their words and dreadful deeds. In spite of the devotion Robespierre inspired in an important school of revolutionary historians, not Ernest Hamel, nor Louis Blanc, nor any of the most fervent Jacobins ever succeeded in fully reversing the monsterization their hero had undergone at the hands of Thermidorian politicians and Romantic writers.

The figures of Robespierre and Danton have been extensively analyzed by critics. Recently, Ann Rigney has studied the hermeneutic interventions that helped create the political and physical image of Robespierre in several nineteenth-century narratives.[4] I will argue here that the literary legend of the revolution aimed to transform two of its leaders, Danton and Robespierre, into monsters of mythical proportions. The reasons for that transformation, as we shall see, go beyond political divisions and partisan history.

In 1802, an Englishman traveling to Paris found in a "valuable and curious cabinet" a bust of Robespierre "which was taken of him, a short period before he fell." John Carr noted:

> History, enraged at the review of the insatiable crimes of Robespierre, has already bestowed upon him a fanciful physiognomy, which she has composed of features which rather correspond with the ferocity of his soul, rather than with his real countenance. From the appearance of this bust, which is an authentic resemblance of him, his face must have been rather handsome. His features were small, and his countenance must have strongly expressed animation, penetration, and subtlety. This bust is a real curiosity. It is very likely that not another is now to be found. Mons. le G. is permitted to preserve it, without reproach on account of his art.[5]

The traveler's naive admiration of the handsome face of Robespierre was as rare as beautiful portraits of the revolutionary leader.[6] In fact, contemporary engravings of Robespierre show a thoughtful and rather attractive face.[7] A century later, contemplating a portrait of Robespierre by A. Lefèvre (1792), Hippolyte Buffenoir exclaimed in turn: "One is struck by the nobility of his carriage. Faced with so much dignity . . . the most biased observer, if he is endowed with sincerity, senses the mountains of calumny and error that still surround the personality of Robespierre."[8] But as early as 1802, as Carr noted, the deliberate disfigurement of Robespierre had already started, and the fanciful physiognomy inspired by the "ferocity of his soul" had supplanted images of "his lively and subtle expression."[9] Indeed, nineteenth-century writers made a point of reminding the reader that, in all cases, the monstrous killers of the king had been monstrous to behold.

Figure 1. "Robespierre," engraving by Préval,
Bibliothèque Nationale, Cabinet des Estampes.

In her 1818 *Considérations sur la Révolution Française*, Madame de Staël
described Robespierre in the following terms:

> I once spoke with Robespierre at my father's house in 1789. He was then
> known as a lawyer from Artois, very exaggerated in his democratic views. His
> features were repulsive, his complexion pale, his veins a shade of green. . . .
> There was something mysterious in his manners, something that suggested an
> unspoken terror in the midst of the visible terror his government advocated.[10]

Robespierre, who was then thirty-one years old, is presented like a ghost: the
paleness of his face and the green color of his veins betray the contemporary
fascination with vampires, and would become integral part of his legend.[11]
These details are reproduced, with variations, in countless works on the revolution. In fact, they may have been inspired not only by Madame de Staël's
unlikely encounter with Robespierre, but also by a Thermidorian engraving,
done by Tassart, showing Robespierre "drinking blood" (Figure 2).[12]

In 1821, the Marquis de Ferrières described Robespierre as follows:

He was somber, mournful, suspicious, irascible, vindictive, considering events only in relation to himself. Sober, laborious, and austere in his habits, he nevertheless dressed and powdered with immaculate elegance. His face had something of the cat and the tiger about it. His movements were uneven and precipitate. He turned furious glances upon those he disliked, but averted his eyes uneasily when someone looked at him. The least danger frightened him, and he would hasten to hide himself.[13]

The feline characteristics of Robespierre's face were taking hold of both the popular and aristocratic imagination. Again, they echoed a Thermidorian expression according to which the last months of Robespierre's political life were a "tigro-cratie."[14] In a footnote to his *History of the French Revolution*, Jules Michelet would later report this anecdote:

A young man (who is today a representative) asked one day of the old Merlin, of Thionville, how he had brought himself to sentence Robespierre. The old man seemed to experience some remorse. But then, rising suddenly with a violent movement, he exclaimed: "Robespierre! Robespierre! . . . Ah! if you had seen *his green eyes*, you would have sentenced him just as I did."[15]

The demonic quality of Robespierre's gaze was meant to express, better than any political argumentation, both Robespierre's remarkable ascendancy over the revolution—a hypnotic, mesmerizing effect—and the necessity of destroying him.

In 1831, Nodier, who had never met him, completed Robespierre's physical portrait in these no less extraordinary terms:

Imagine a fairly small, spindly man, with a slender physiognomy, his forehead compressed on the sides, like a beast of prey, his mouth thin, pale and tight; a voice that was hoarse when low, false when the tone was high, and which in moments of intense excitement or anger turned into a howling similar rather like that of hyenas. Such was Robespierre. . . . What characterized his soul, his gaze, was an indescribable shaft of light that flashed from a wild eye, between two convulsively retractile eyelids, a shaft of light that wounded when it struck. . . . With his dreadful good faith, his naive thirst for blood, his pure and cruel soul, Robespierre was the Revolution incarnate.[16]

Nodier's focus on Robespierre's eyes underlined both their hypnotic and animal-like quality. The retractile eyelids suggest a bird of prey. Robespierre is not quite a human being, nor can he be assimilated to a single animal species, for his voice suggests a wild beast endowed with an abnormal quality of speech.

In his 1847 *Histoire des Girondins*, Lamartine contributed in turn to the construction of Robespierre's monstrosity:

> Robespierre was small of stature; his limbs were puny and angular, his walk jerky, his attitudes affected; his gestures without grace or harmony; his rather sharp voice sought for oratorical effects but found only fatigue and monotony; his forehead was rather fine, but small and bulging above the temples, as if the weight and the slow movement of his thoughts had enlarged it through his own efforts. His eyes, very much veiled by the eyelids, and very piercing, were deeply embedded in their sockets; they had a bluish look, rather soft but vague, like steel gleaming in a bright light. His small and straight nose was dilated by nostrils [that were too wide]; his mouth was big, his lips thin and disagreeably contracted at the corners, his chin short and pointed, his complexion a deadly yellow, like that of a sick man, or one exhausted by night watches and meditations.[17]

We can see in these lines the progression of Robespierre's monstrosity. The eyes in particular have kept their animal quality but a new element has been invoked: they gleam like steel, a direct evocation of the guillotine, one that Michelet will repeat a few years later: "His anxious eyes . . . casting a pale gleam of steel" (*HR*, II, 61).

Moreover, if Lamartine's description sounds vaguely familiar, it may also be because, in its style, it echoes the description of Frankenstein's monster, published a few years before:

> His yellow skin scarcely covered the work of muscles and arteries beneath; his hair was a lustrous black, and flowing; his teeth of a pearly whiteness; but these luxuriances only formed a more horrid contrast with his watery eyes, that seemed almost of the same color as the dun white sockets in which they were set.[18]

In the popular imagination fired by early accounts of the French Revolution, Robespierre, like Frankenstein's creature, was death among the living, an unnatural being betrayed by his green veins and his yellow skin, his deep eye sockets and his mechanical gestures. "His automatic gait was that of a man of stone," Michelet would add, punning on Robespierre's surname (*HR*, II, 61).[19]

But Hippolyte Taine, in his passionate hatred of Robespierre, may have given us the most fantastic vision of the revolutionary thinker. Describing Robespierre's withdrawal from the political scene during the months of the Great Terror, he writes:

> In vain he detaches himself from the action, and raises his preacher's eyes to heaven, he cannot help hearing and seeing all around him, beneath his immaculate feet, a cracking of bones and a flowing of blood, the insatiable gaping mouth of the monster he has trained and he bestrides. This mouth grows more ravenous each day, and needs a more ample feast of human flesh, and it is good, not only to let it eat, but even to supply it with food, often with his own hands. . . . This butchery awakens destructive instincts that civilization had long held in check. His cat's physiognomy, which was at first that of a worried, but fairly gentle house cat, became the ferocious expression of a tiger-cat. . . . When he spoke at the Constituent Assembly, he could only moan; when he spoke at the Convention, he could only foam with rage.[20]

The now familiar feline qualities of the portrait are meant to suggest an untamable creature, a man-eating tiger with a suggestion of rabid disease, "foaming at the mouth when he speaks."

Like Frankenstein's creature and, before him, monsters of antiquity, Robespierre was thus thought of as a composite, mythical beast. For Nodier, he was a predator, a hyena with the tawny eyes of a bird of prey, for Taine, a rabid tiger; but for all, indeed (and Michelet will use the word freely), a sphinx. A feline body with a human face, Robespierre was a reincarnation of the monster who devoured the young men of Thebes. But Robespierre became a monster whose riddle was never quite resolved. Michelet describes his strategy as "so obscure Robespierrists were constantly misled" (II, 596). Lamartine may have given the most eloquent definition of the sphinxlike Robespierre: "He was the last word of the Revolution, but nobody could read him" (41).

Historians strove to understand the mystery, with more or less success. As Jean-Joseph Goux remarks: "The Sphinx is a 'head-chopper'. This gives us something to reflect upon. She kills by decapitation to take the soul beyond."[21] The Sphinx, of course, was a female monster—*le sphinx* or *la sphinge*—and Robespierre, the man who would soon be represented as the dictator responsible for all the beheading of the Terror, was also endowed by posterity with an ambiguous sexuality. Known for his austere and celibate life, he became feminized by writers and historians alike. Michelet described him as "more delicate and more feminine" than his sister (*HR*, II, 61). Although his clothes were not the topic of much discussion during his life (during the course of the revolution, he apparently owned no more than three coats), the extraordinary emphasis given by all writers to his habit of dress also suggest the feminization of the monster. Madame de Staël notes: "He was not badly dressed; on the contrary, he alone wore a powdered wig and his clothes were neat" (140–141). Ferrières noted his "immaculate elegance"; Nerval, more maliciously and more explicitely, wrote: "Add to this all the trappings of stuffy, prudish, pouting coquetry, and you will almost have him" (191–192). Hilaire Belloc dedicated a long page to Robespierre's clothes and concluded with words that could apply to an Ancien Régime marquise: "A figure slight but erect and sufficiently well filled, a little dainty and always exquisitely fitted, not disdainful of color but contemptuous of ornament."[22]

The "feminization" of Robespierre's voice also deserves consideration. It is ironic that one of the most successful orators of the revolution was alleged to have had such a strange mode of speech, at times hoarse and low, sharp and false, high, monotonous, impossible to listen to, yet impossible to escape. This also echoes the voice of the Sphinx, when she called on the young men she

le Triumvir ROBESPIERRE

Ce maître impérieux n'est plus qu'un vil coupable,
Il invoquoit la force, et la force l'accable;
D'autant plus malheureux, quand son règne est passé,
Que sur son propre sort lui même a prononcé:
Que rien en sa faveur ne peut se faire entendre,
Et qu'à la pitié même il ne peut plus prétendre
La vengeance publique insulte son trépas,
Et mourant dans la fange, on ne le plaindra pas

Figure 2. "Robespierre," engraving by Tassart,
Bibliothèque Nationale, Cabinet des Estampes.

was about to devour: an indescribable sound, comparable to "a rhapsody," "a song difficult to understand," notes Marie Delcourt.[23] In Euripides' words, it is "a song without a lyre, strange to the Muses," sometimes compared to a muffled rumbling of thunder.[24]

But every monster needs an antidote: Robespierre's deadly sphinx was contrasted with a being that, through his appetite for life and his unequivocal human desires, both counteracted and amplified the funereal qualities of his enemy. And thus was born the legend of Danton. It could be said that Danton was invented by nineteenth-century writers to offset and dramatize Robespierre's quiet and deadly stillness. But Danton, a more resolute regicide than Robespierre ever was, and the main architect of the fearful Revolutionary Tribunal, could not be made chiefly into a glorified victim, so he too became monsterized, a monstrous answer to a monstrous enigma.

From the beginning, it seems that Danton's character and thus his physical description were developed chiefly as a response to Robespierre's. While Robespierre was a hypocrite, Madame de Staël argues, "Danton was factious," and where Robespierre wanted power, "Danton wanted only pleasure" (141).

Michelet, who repeatedly described Danton as "a sublime monster," wrote of Danton at the time of the September massacres: "As I have said, there was something of a lion in this man, but also something of a mastiff, and a fox. And this fellow kept the lion's skin at any price" (*HR*, I, 1073). Later, Michelet acknowledged a strange metamorphosis:

> Those who are familiar with portraits of Danton, in particular the sketches David drafted during the Convention's nightly sessions, know how a man can sink from the lion to the bull—indeed fall as low as the boar, a somber and degraded character, with a distressing sensuality. (*HR*, II, 446)

The mixed animal metaphors that were meant to express Danton's ruthless character and instincts would slowly become absorbed into the mythical image of the Minotaur.

Belloc gave the best account of the composite features that metonymically created the revolutionary myth:

> He was tall and stout, with the forward bearing of the orator, full of gesture and of animation. He carried a round French head upon the thick neck of energy. His face was generous, ugly, and determined. With wide eyes and calm brows, he yet had the quick glance which betrays the habit of appealing to an audience. His upper lip was injured, and so was his nose, and he had been further disfigured by the small-pox, with which disease that forerunner of his, Mirabeau, had also been disfigured. His lip had been torn by a bull

when he was a child, and his nose crushed in a second adventure, they say, with the same animal. In this the Romans would have seen a portent; but he, the idol of our Positivists, found only a chance to repeat Mirabeau's expression that his "boar's head frightened me."[25]

It is said that Danton himself once soberly acknowledged his powerful ugliness by saying that nature had endowed him with *"l'âpre physionomie de la liberté"* [the rude physiognomy of liberty]. But legend took over. Carlyle described Danton sitting "erect with a kind of internal convulsion struggling to keep itself motionless; his lips curling in Titanic scorn" (250).

A later essayist commented:

> [Danton] was enormous; his colossal height dominated the Assembly; his wide shoulders; his bull's neck; his pock-marked face; his thick hair brushed straight back; his high forehead; his piercing eyes; his large, flat, snout-like nose; the scar, which he owed to his adventurous youth, and which swept his face in a sneering grin—all helped to impress people, all contributed to his air of insolent audacity, of threatening, passionate tumult. . . . His whole appearance brought an assurance of strength which his contemporaries tried to embody in the most diverse phrases: "Gigantic Revolutionary," "King of the Revolution," "*real* tribune of the people," "Creator of the Republic," "Cyclops," "Atlas of the Party," "Titan," "Stentor," "Hercules"—such were the various epithets applied to Danton.[26]

As we can see from this portrait, Danton is meant to be, in every detail—height, forehead, nose, eyes, voice, gesture—the opposite of Robespierre.

Taine, whose hatred for Robespierre led him unexpectedly to glorify Danton, described him as follows:

> In temperament and character, he is a *barbarian* and a barbarian born to command his fellows. . . . A colossus with the face of a "tartar" scarred by smallpox, tragically and terribly ugly, he had the distorted mask of a growling "bulldog," tiny eyes sunken beneath the enormous furrows of a throbbing forehead, a thundering voice, a brawler's gestures, overflowing and seething with blood, anger, and energy, the outbursts of a force that seems unlimited like those of nature; his declamation was wild *like the roaring of a bull* [emphasis added], whose sound carried through closed windows as far as fifty steps into the street, with immoderate images, sincere bombast, quivers and shouts of indignation, vengeance, and patriotism, capable of awakening the ferocious instincts in the calmest of souls and the generous instincts in the most brutish; with curses and coarse words, and a cynicism—not monotonous and deliberate like that of Hébert, but gushing forth spontaneously

and naturally, frightfully coarse remarks, worthy of Rabelais, a streak of jovial sensuality and cheeky goodheartedness.[27]

Danton's amplified physique counteracted perfectly Robespierre's small size and delicate features, and Lamartine noted with unmistakable aristocratic scorn: "Everything in him was athletic, coarse, and vulgar like the masses" (I, 176).

The effect of Robespierre's and Danton's transformation into mythical beasts corresponded as well to a way of accounting for their lifestyle and sexuality. Robespierre's epithet, "l'Incorruptible," was given to him during his lifetime. His austerity was proverbial, and no one knew him to have any mistresses. By contrast, historians and commentators emphasized Danton's unbridled sexuality. As Taine noted, Danton spoke to the instincts, the powerful voice of nature. In him, Taine wrote: "There are no repugnances. He has no moral or physical distastes. . . . He can fraternize with drunkards" (180). However, as Belloc duly noted:

> Upon the faith of some who did not know him he acquired the character of a debauchee. For the support of this view there is not a tittle of direct evidence. He certainly loved those pleasures of the senses which Robespierre refused, and which Roland was unable to enjoy; but that his good dinners were orgies or of any illegitimate loves (once he had married the woman to whom he was so devotedly attached) there is not a shadow of proof. (56)[28]

The physical descriptions linking the revolutionaries' monstrous features to their monstrous deeds was spelled out by the nineteenth century, and—surprisingly—transmitted, largely unchallenged, to this day. In a 1937 essay, entitled *Robespierre, the First Modern Dictator*, Ralph Korngold reproduced in great detail the legendary features and habits of dress attributed to Robespierre, from "his green-gray eyes" with a "steely" gleam, to his clothing "immaculate, almost to the point of elegance."[29] In his 1987 film, *Danton*, Andrzej Wajda added yet another element to the enigmatic figure of Robespierre.[30] In contrast to Danton's exuberant heterosexuality, his larger-than-life physique (Danton is played by a robust Depardieu), Robespierre's features are cold, inexpressive, except for a permanent resentment.

In our first encounter with Robespierre, we see him sick, rising painfully from bed to meet his hairdresser. His face is carefully hidden behind a mask and a wig, and he lives in a curious household, under the adoring eyes of the "maid Duplay," whose shy advances he systematically rejects with undisguised repulsion. She, in turn, is first seen coldly beating a naked child who cannot memorize his revolutionary lesson, an unnatural and harsh mother image. (In the end we learn that the abused child is in fact her little brother.) In Wajda's tale (which was also a commentary on contemporary Poland) Danton is fully exonerated: a force of nature, vigorously heterosexual, he prefers a night with a woman to an urgent meeting with his friends. He invites Robespierre to a sumptuous dinner, only to throw away fine dishes, glasses, and carefully prepared food when Robespierre declines to eat. Danton represents life, waste, and excess. He lives luxuriously while the people beg for bread, and he is rich and wasteful, but also devastatingly sincere. In Wajda's interpretation, two momentous scenes seal Danton's and Camille Desmoulins' fate. The first one when Danton, angry at Robespierre, screams: "What do you know of the people? Nothing! Look at yourself! You don't drink wine! You faint at the sight of a naked sword! And they say you've never screwed a woman! So? . . . You want the happiness of men, and you are not even a man." Danton's judgment crudely emphasizes what remains, in Wajda's eyes, Robespierre's most revealing sin: his effeminacy. His unnatural tastes make him unfit to lead the nation. In a second scene, both more cruel and pathetic, Robespierre, who has come to plead with Camille Desmoulins to abandon Danton, is rejected in the midst of laughter and derision. Robespierre, alone in the corridor, hears the mockery and leaves, more than ever determined to have them all executed. Wajda's argument, that Robespierre was in love with Camille Desmoulins—made explicit in a previous scene where Robespierre tenderly puts his arms around Desmoulins's shoulders, but does not succeed in moving the journalist—also serves to show two irreconcilable visions of the revolution: Danton and his friends are resolute heterosexuals, both domestic and decadent, tender with their offspring. They are undisguised (Danton keeps throwing away his disheveled wig). By contrast, in Wajda's eyes, Robespierre's homosexuality comes to symbolize how far the revolution had strayed from its natural course. Everything that comes in contact with him is "abnormal," from the strange domestic arrangement at the Duplay house to the repeated visits of a caricatural Saint-Just, sporting a single earring, heavy makeup, and flowers, and speaking with obscene violence. In the concluding scene, after Danton and Desmoulins have been executed, Robespierre, still sick and in bed, covers his face with a white, shroudlike sheet.

Lest we believe that modern historiography has successfully discarded the monstrous legend created after the revolution, in the *Critical Dictionary of the French Revolution*, Mona Ozouf in turn acknowledges the powerful couple formed by Danton and Robespierre. Far from dismissing the fable so coarsely crafted by decades of conservative and liberal thinking alike, she writes:

> Robespierre has been compared to Danton as virtue to vice, incorruptibility to venality, industriousness to indolence, faith to cynicism. . . . But, one

might equally well contrast the two men as sickly to strong, suspicious to
generous, feminine to masculine (or more accurately, female to male),
abstract to concrete, written to oral, deadly systematizer to lively improviser—such is the Dantonist version.[31]

This astounding series of characterizations, "sickly, suspicious, feminine,
abstract, written," and the punch line "deadly systematizer," undermine the
positive qualities previously listed. "Virtue and incorruptibility," "industrious-
ness and faith," all point to the debilitating sterility of a man who had no
known mistresses, a surprising indictment of his capacity to lead the nation. If
we add up the characteristics of Danton, "strong, generous, masculine, concrete, oral, lively improviser," we find no less than a forceful rehabilitation of
the monstrous Minotaur, saved by his coarse but appealing sensuality, his natural appetites guaranteeing that, had he been given a chance, this bull would
have yielded much profit to the beleaguered revolution.

In economic terms—and we should remember that the legends were forged
in the early days of liberal capitalism—Danton is saved as a figure of intense
economic activity. He takes bribes, buys, borrows, spends, wastes, but gets
rich, immensely rich. The Minotaur rides a bull market, he is a figure of high
investment and profit. Robespierre is further castigated as a figure of sterility,
withdrawal, austerity, and fruitless hoarding.

But such mythical and fanciful images could not have succeeded had they
not responded to a deep anxiety regarding both the inevitability of the revolution and its dramatic unfolding. And this is why the figure of the Sphinx takes
on a special meaning. As Stephen Heath remarks: "For Hegel, the Sphinx stands
at the beginning of the history of consciousness. Or rather, that beginning
comes with a defeat: Oedipus solves the riddle, flings the Sphinx over the rock,
gets rid of the monstrous."[32] Mitchell Greenberg comments: "The politics that
the Oedipus myth represents, the politics that is condensed in and on the figure
of the riddle-solving perpetrator of parricide and incest, is also the originary
moment of Western masculine hegemony."[33] There rests the enduring power of
the revolutionary legend as modern version of the Oedipus myth: it combines
the haunting memories of the parricide/regicide with the plague and the chaos
that preceeded the Sphinx's encounter with Oedipus. From this perspective,
the transformation of Robespierre the statesman, the regicide, the theoretical
founder of the Republic, into the man-eating Sphinx, the feminine figure of
archaic chaos and disorder, forcefully expresses, on the part of the royalist man-
ufacturers of the revolutionary legend, a repudiation of the modern state.

For Michelet, who had different political convictions but was equally in
mourning, the legend of the Sphinx pervaded the history of the revolution in

Figure 3. "Danton," Bibliothèque Nationale, Cabinet des Estampes.

an unexpected manner. Describing Danton's emergence on the political stage, he exclaimed: "What is most terrifying about [Danton] is that he has no eyes; at least one hardly sees them. What! this terrible blindman will be the guide of nations?" (*HR*, I, 505). A few lines later, he commented: "He is a devoted Oedipus, who, possessed by his riddle, carries the terrible sphinx within himself, so as to be devoured by it" (*HR*, I, 505).[34] For this is the failure of the revolution, that Danton, both its Minotaur and its Oedipus, internalized his hidden enemy, the sphinxlike Robespierre, and was blinded *before* he had an opportunity to rid the city of its plague. He would die for it, but still, Michelet repeatedly argued, he would be ultimately responsible for the death of the winged monster. Robespierre, who "swooped down on his prey like a hawk" (*HR*, II, 667), was doomed from the moment he sentenced Danton/Oedipus. The devouring sphinx would perish for it: "Billaud threw Danton to him, a piece fit for a king, but that was difficult to digest, and became deadly for Robespierre" (*HR*, II, 1014).

The Sphinx, of course, was sent to Thebes as punishment for a parricide. Similarly, Robespierre was seen as both agency and punishment for the king's death. Still, nineteenth-century writings made him primarily the devourer of young lives. It is significant, as well, that no one among the Thermidorians could rise as the riddle-solver, the parricide hero, founder of a new order, because the legend of Robespierre as Sphinx also posited that the chaotic unfolding of the revolution could not lead to a new order but, on the contrary, precipitated France into another twenty years of bloody tyranny and war. Varying accounts suggest that the Sphinx threw herself to her death, or else was killed by Oedipus after he solved her riddle. Similarly, there remain varying theories suggesting that Robespierre tried to kill himself just before he was arrested, or that the gendarme Merda, a most unlikely hero, shot him. The Sphinx was dead, but, because no riddle-solver emerged, the chaos remained, and, somehow, Robespierre had to be killed again, explained, "anatomized," to use Michelet's expression, resolved in the endless representations of his revolutionary legend.

The pervasive presence of the legend in nineteenth-century accounts of the revolution also reminds us that the discipline of history in France was developed as an attempt to solve the riddle of the revolution. History took on the task of founding a new science whose dual goal was to account for the past and, at the same time, to indefinitely ponder on the moment when the Sphinx plunged to her death unvanquished, her enigma unsolved, and the illuminating encounter with Oedipus, as well as the birth of the modern state, indefinitely postponed.

Notes

1. In spite of the Thermidorians' personal records as terrorists, their own mediocrity seems to have saved them from posthumous opprobrium. Very little has been written, for example, on Billaud-Varenne, the man Michelet called "pure terror."

2. Many of the influential historical texts published in the nineteenth century were not, of course, written by historians, that is, by writers who were primarily concerned with giving an account of the past. Writers such as Alphonse de Lamartine, Honoré de Balzac, and Charles Nodier—more famous, of course, for his fantastic tales—freely and effectively contributed to the extraordinary legend of the revolution. Madame de Staël, Lamartine, and Nodier were not only giving a highly personalized account of the great upheaval, they were also mourning the Ancien Régime.

3. Johann Caspar Lavater (1741–1801) wrote the extremely popular *Essays on Physiognomy*, which were translated into French under the title *Traité de physiognomonie* (10 vol.) in 1820.

4. See Ann Rigney, "Icon and Symbol: The Historical Figure Called Maximilien Robespierre," in *Representing the French Revolution, Literature, Historiography, and Art*, ed. James A. W. Heffernan (Hanover: University Press of New England, 1992), 106–122.

5. John Carr, *The Stranger in France: Or a Tour from Devonshire to Paris* (Brattleboro: Isaiah Thomas, 1806), 244–245. The book was first published in London in 1803.

6. There were numerous engravings of Robespierre done between 1792 and 1794, now disseminated in the various collections of the Cabinet des Estampes. They show him to have been a rather handsome man. See Hippolyte Buffenoir, *Les Portraits de Robespierre, étude iconographique et historique* (Paris: E. Leroux, 1909).

7. Many of the images printed during the Thermidorian reaction reproduced the existing engravings, substituting an inflammatory text for the former legends.

8. Hippolyte Buffenoir, *op. cit.*, 17. Unless otherwise indicated, all translations are by Henri Dutour.

9. In 1803, the Abbé Proyard, in a book dedicated to Louis XVI, already speaks of Robespierre as a monster: "From this school, [Louis le Grand] will emerge a monster with a human face, a monster of a ferocity unknown to barbarian antiquity; a monster who, after having brought out his king's murder more than anyone else, will himself reign over you and your families . . . will drink the blood of a million men . . . the name of this monster, his execrable name, is Robespierre." Quoted by Gérard Walter in *Robespierre* (Paris: Gallimard, 1961), vol. 1, 20. As Walter notes, Proyard's "allegations are always more or less inexact, his way of presenting facts reflects an obvious bias" (21).

10. Madame de Staël, *Considérations sur les principaux événements de la révolution française* (Paris: Delaunay, Bossange et Masson, 1818), 2: 140–141.

11. Ann Rigney discusses the pallor of Robespierre's face in Louis Blanc's account of the revolution and shows how it is interpreted as a sign of his willingness to sacrifice himself. For Michelet, she suggests, it supports his view of Robespierre as a man of "colorless talent," *op. cit.*, 114–115.

12. Engraving by Tassart, Collection De Vinck, Bibliothèque Nationale, Cabinet des Estampes.

13. Charles-Elie de Ferrières, *Mémoires*, 3 vols. (Paris, 1821–1822), I: 343–344. Quoted in E. L. Higgins, *The French Revolution as Told by Contemporaries* (Cambridge: The Riverside Press, 1938), 135.

14. See the engraving in the Collection De Vinck: "Miroir du passé pour sauvegarder l'avenir/ Tableau parlant du Gouvernement cadavero-faminocratique de 93, sous la *Tigro-cratie* de Robespierre et Compagnie." Paris, Germinal, Year V. Bibliothèque Nationale, Cabinet des Estampes.

15. Jules Michelet, *Histoire de la révolution française* (Paris: Gallimard, 1952), II, 61 (author's emphasis). Later referred to in the text as *HR*. This extraordinary reply was widely circulated in the nineteenth century and is reported, with minor variations, by different writers.

16. Charles Nodier, *Portraits de la révolution et de l'empire* presented by Jean-Luc Steinmetz (Paris: Tallandier, 1988), 191.

17. Alphonse de Lamartine, *Histoire des Girondins* (Paris: Hachette, 1870), I: 41–42. I quote the translation published by Henri Béraud, *Twelve Portraits of the French Revolution*, trans. Madeleine Boyd (Boston: Little, Brown, and Co. 1928), 66.

18. Mary Wollstonecraft Shelley, *Frankenstein or the Modern Prometheus, The 1818 Text*, ed. James Rieger (Chicago: The University of Chicago Press, 1982), 52.

19. Thomas Carlyle himself would be influenced by the now familiar monstrous legend: commenting on the terrible days that preceded Thermidor, he describes "a seagreen Robespierre converted into vinegar and gall." *The French Revolution, A History* (London: J. M. Dent, 1906), 2 vols. II: 329.

20. Hippolyte Taine, *Les Origines de la France contemporaine, la révolution* (Paris: Hachette, 1885), 3 vols. III: 209–210.

21. Jean-Joseph Goux, *Oedipe philosophe* (Paris: Aubier, 1990), 63.

22. Hilaire Belloc, *Robespierre* (New York: Charles Scribners and Sons, 1902), 11.

23. Marie Delcourt, *Oedipe ou la légende du conquérant* (Paris: Droz, 1944), 133.

24. Jean-Joseph Goux gives an illuminating analysis of the Sphinx's voice in *Oedipe philosophe*, 53–55.

25. Hilaire Belloc, *Danton, A Study* (New York: Charles Scribner's Sons, 1902), 53.

26. Henri Béraud, *op. cit.*, 38–39, author's emphasis.

27. Hippolyte Taine, *op. cit.*, 179, emphasis added.

28. Michelet described how Danton, shattered by the death of his wife, had the coffin reopened a week after her death, so as to have a last look at her. Six months later he remarried. His fifteen-year-old bride, Michelet noted, had been chosen by his dying wife (*HR*, II, 444).

29. Ralph Korngold, *Robespierre, First Modern Dictator* (London: MacMillan and Co, 1937), 20–21.

30. Andrzej Wajda, *Danton*, a 1987 Gaumont production, based on the play *L'Affaire Danton*, by Stanislawa Przybyszewska.

31. *A Critical Dictionary of the French Revolution*, eds. François Furet and Mona Ozouf, trans. Arthur Goldhammer (Cambridge: The Belknap Press of Harvard University, 1989), 213–214.

32. Stephen Heath, "The Ethics of Sexual Difference," *Discourse* (Spring–Summer 1990), 128, quoted by Mitchell Greenberg in *Canonical States, Canonical Stages, Oedipus, Othering and Seventeenth-Century Drama* (Minneapolis: University of Minnesota Press, 1994), xxxiii.

33. Mitchell Greenberg, *op. cit.*, xxxiii.

34. In a remarkable essay on Michelet's fascination for monsters, Gilles Marcotte argues that *L'Histoire de la révolution française* contrasts Danton, as sublime monster, to Robespierre, "a man, only a man." It is true that Michelet often underlines the "smallness" of Robespierre's vision; nevertheless, the sphinx image is powerfully at work in his interpretation of the mythical battle between the two men. See "L'Amour du monstre, Michelet, la sirène, Danton." *Etudes françaises*, 30:1 (1994), 122–131.

Bibliography

Belloc, Hilaire. *Danton, A Study*. New York: Scribner's, 1902.

———. *Robespierre*. New York: Scribner's, 1902.

Buffenoir, Hippolyte. *Les Portraits de Robespierre, étude iconographique et historique.* Paris: E. Leroux, 1909.

Carlyle, Thomas. *The French Revolution, A History.* London: J. M. Dent, 1906.

Carr, John. *The Stranger in France: Or a Tour from Devonshire to Paris.* Brattleboro: Isaiah Thomas, 1806.

Delcourt, Marie. *Oedipe ou la légende du conquérant.* Paris: Droz, 1944.

Ferrières, Charles-Elie de. *Mémoires.* Paris, 1821.

Furet, François, and Ozouf, Mona. *A Critical Dictionary of the French Revolution,* trans. Arthur Goldhammer. Cambridge: Belknap, 1989.

Goux, Jean-Joseph. *Oedipe philosophe.* Paris: Aubier, 1990.

Greenberg, Mitchell. *Canonical States, Canonical Stages, Oedipus, Othering and Seventeenth-Century Drama.* Minneapolis: University of Minnesota Press, 1994.

Heath, Stephen. "The Ethics of Sexual Difference." *Discourse* (Spring–Summer 1990).

Higgins, E. L. *The French Revolution as Told by Contemporaries.* Cambridge: Riverside, 1938.

Korngold, Ralph. *Robespierre, First Modern Dictator.* London: MacMillan, 1937.

Lamartine, Alphonse de. *Histoire des Girondins.* Paris: Hachette, 1870.

———. *Twelve Portraits of the French Revolution,* trans. Madeleine Boyd. Boston: Little, Brown & Co., 1928.

Lavater, Johann Caspar. *Essays on Physiognomy,* trans. Henry Hunter. London: J. P. Murray, 1789.

Marcotte, Gilles. "L'Amour du monstre, Michelet, la sirène, Danton." *Etudes françaises,* 30:1, 1994, 122–131.

Michelet, Jules. *Histoire de la révolution française.* Paris: Gallimard, 1952.

Nodier, Charles. *Portraits de la révolution et de l'empire,* ed Jean-Luc Steinmetz. Paris: Tallandier, 1988.

Przybyszewska, Stanislawa. *L'Affaire Danton.*

Rigney, Ann. "Icon and Symbol: The Historical Figure Called Maximilien Robespierre." In *Representing the French Revolution, Literature, Historiography, and Art,* ed. James A. W. Heffernan. Hanover: University Press of New England, 1992, 106–122.

Shelley, Mary Wollstonecraft. *Frankenstein or the Modern Prometheus, The 1818 Text,* ed. James Rieger. Chicago: The University of Chicago Press, 1982.

Staël, Madame de. *Considérations sur les principaux événements de la révolution française.* Paris: Delaunay, Bossange et Masson, 1818.

Taine, Hippolyte. *Les Origines de la France contemporaine, la révolution.* Paris: Hachette, 1885.

Wajda, Adrzej. *Danton.* Gaumont, 1987.

Walter, Gérard. *Robespierre.* Paris: Gallimard, 1961.

6 ✢

Audubon's *Ornithological Biography* and the Question of "Other Minds"

James W. Armstrong

A viewer attending the 1993 traveling exhibition of John James Audubon's watercolors was able to observe firsthand a peculiar change the artist made in his illustration of the golden eagle. In the bottom left corner of the original watercolor sketch (Figure 1), Audubon included a tiny figure carefully inching its way along a fallen tree. This figure, clad in buckskins and carrying a slain eagle over his shoulder, has traditionally been identified as Audubon himself, for it bears a physical resemblance to the artist, and it seems to be engaged in a task typical for him—obtaining specimens for his studies.[1] Yet in the final Havell engraving (Plate No. CLXXXI), Audubon has erased all trace of this autobiographical figure—the log is still there, but the man has vanished (Figure 2). One might ask, what is behind this sudden urge of self-erasure in an artist whose skill at self-promotion was as well developed as his skill at sketching birds? Why does Audubon deny himself this little autobiographical gesture?

One answer would be that it is essential to Audubon's purpose that the viewer should be given no intrusive reference to the artist, the one who in fact orchestrates every aspect of the scene. Audubon aspired to be a master of the realist mode, and realism attempts to fool the eye into believing that what it sees is not a representation, but the thing itself. Therefore, realist painters avoid those traces which draw attention to the technique of the artist (brush strokes, sketch lines, or pentimento) or to the artist's subjective point of view

Figure 1. Detail from Audubon's watercolor painting, "Golden Eagle." Collection of the New York Historical Society.

(unusual perspectives, blurred or expressionistically rendered forms). The focus of a realist work is universally sharp, the perspective and the coloration flawless, so that the viewer does not think "this is a drawing of life made by a human artist," but "this is life." Certainly any visual reference to the artist works against this aim.

Audubon's obsession with objective mimesis is evident in his most enduring accomplishment, *The Birds of America*. Audubon boasted that the two-volume elephant folio edition represented all the native species of American birds, life-sized and in true color—and his claim was for the most part justified. The fidelity of Audubon's images to their original objects was something Audubon took great pride in, as he admits:

> Merely to say, that each object of my *Illustrations* is of the size of nature,
> were too vague—for to many it might only convey the idea that they are so,

Figure 2. Final version of the "Golden Eagle," as printed in Audubon's *Birds of America* (Havell Plate CLXXXI). From the collection of the Mary W. Runnells Rare Book Room of the Field Museum of Natural History, Chicago. Photo by Vision Tree.

more or less, according as the eye of the delineator may have been more or less correct in measurement simply obtained through that medium; and of avoiding error in this respect I am particularly desirous. Not only is every object, as a whole, of the natural size, but also every portion of each object. The compass aided me in its delineation, regulated and corrected each part, even to the very foreshortening which now and then may be seen in the figures. The bill, the feet, the legs, the claws, the very feathers as they project one beyond another, have been accurately measured.[2]

Audubon's concern here is to avoid a representation which is merely "more or less correct," a view according to "the eye of the delineator"—filtered, that is, through a subjective lens. He has resorted to the use of instruments to ensure the consistency and above all the *objectivity* of his results. This insistence on mensuration allies him with Baconian empiricism, and guarantees the scientific usefulness of his images, which he intended to be works of natural history.

But Audubon's concern for accuracy did not stop here. An examination of the original watercolors shows his willingness to be technically innovative in the interest of a precise recording of the various textures and hues of his subjects. As Reba Fishman Snyder has documented, Audubon "used whatever means and techniques were at his disposal to draw the birds as true to life as possible," including novel uses of mixed media and collage techniques.[3] As far as Audubon was concerned, technique was subservient to his "overall intent" of producing as convincing and accurate an image as possible—a pragmatic attitude which was reinforced by the fact that Audubon's paintings were destined to be transcribed onto R. Havell's plates. This transference would assure that Audubon's mixed-media originals would be superseded by engravings whose uniformity of line and standardization of production made them perhaps the closest thing to an "impersonal" medium available to an artist.

The final result of Audubon's labor was to be a vision of pure presence, each plate with its life-sized bird or birds and its detailed background evincing nowhere *within the frame* any trace of the fact that "art" was involved in generating the image. The artist's presence is limited to the guarantee (in small print at the bottom of the page, *outside* the frame) that the image has been "Drawn from Nature by J. J. Audubon." Inside the frame, the hard labor of measuring and sketching, of adding color and textural detail (work that was in fact often done by more than one hand, as Audubon employed various assistants), the labor of the engraver (or engravers) who had to meticulously reproduce the watercolor, is invisible.

Yet to view Audubon as the consummate realist, carefully expunging all trace of himself in his works, would be to present a very one-sided view of the situation. Such a characterization would ignore Audubon's equally great, though much-neglected masterpiece, the *Ornithological Biography*, published in five volumes between 1831 and 1839. This work, always intended as a companion piece to the *Birds of America*, reinserts the author within the frame of each of his bird portraits in a very dramatic and insistent fashion, almost as though it were calculated to undermine the very realism Audubon so carefully cultivated in his images.

The full title of Audubon's work is *Onithological Biography, or an Account of the Habits of the Birds of the United States of America; Accompanied by*

Descriptions of the Objects Represented in the Work Entitled The Birds of
America, *and Interspersed with Delineations of American Scenery and Manners.*
We are immediately made aware by this title that the book is meant to accomplish several different, rather disparate tasks. It is to be an "account" of the
"habits" of the birds of America (and here we deduce that "account" must
mean "narrative," for how else may habits be described?). But it is *also* to serve
as a supplement to Audubon's *Birds of America*, a collection of "descriptions of
the objects" there depicted—as if Audubon, upon reflecting that a picture
equals a thousand words, were suddenly unclear about which side of the equation was superior. Finally, the *Ornithological Biography* promises to provide us
with "Delineations of American Scenery and Manners," that is, sketches (in
prose) of both the American landscape and American society. We are left with
a book that is an ethological narrative, a description of a work of art, and a
travel guide—a strange collection of purposes.

But our awareness of the strangeness of this work only deepens as we ponder its title. There is a curious doubleness manifesting itself here: the phrase
"birds of America" is used to indicate both the actual birds of the American
continent and a work of art by the same title—as though art and life were
somehow interchangeable for Audubon. And why, if the book is meant to provide an "account of the habits of the Birds of the United States," does he not
title the book "Ornithological Biographies"? Or might Audubon be hinting
that the book has a fourth purpose: the telling of his *own* biography, which is
(as he admits in the preface) inextricably entwined both with the birds of
America *and* with the *Birds of America?*

In fact, when we begin reading through the *Ornithological Biography*, we discover that it is not only about the habits of the birds mentioned, it is also
about the habits and thoughts and emotions of Audubon himself—the man
whose qualifications take up such a large block of type on the frontispiece
(Audubon is described as a Fellow of the Royal Society, as well as a "Fellow of
the Linnean and Zoological Societies of London; Member of the Lyceum Of
New York, of the Natural History Society of Paris, the Wernerian Natural
History Society Of Edinburgh: Honorary Member Of The Society Of Natural
History Of Manchester," and so on). The *Biography* could in fact be described
as being *as much* a biography of the teller as it is a biography of the subjects
presented in it. Throughout the book, Audubon tells tales of his own prowess
and heroic efforts—interspersed with descriptions of egg clutches and mating
habits, we get stories of Audubon falling into quicksand or being caught out in
storms; Audubon waxing poetic on the beauties of nature; Audubon commenting on the character of American frontier life. Much of the text is
anecdotal in a way that seems incongruous in a "scientific" work—the result is

that the chapters seem strangely hybrid, vacillating between the poles of nat-ural history and romantic confession (*à la* Rousseau).

For example, in his chapter on the golden eagle, Audubon tells us that he did not, in fact, first view this bird on the jagged peaks of a wilderness moun-tain (as his image would have us believe). Instead, he tells us he purchased his specimen in Boston from a Mr. Greenwood, who had gotten it from a New Hampshire trapper. Nor does he proceed to give us some "account" of the eagle's "habits" (as he previously promised us he would); instead he begins with a rather odd tale of his struggle successfully to exterminate this bird in order better to draw its portrait. At first, he confesses, he vacillates between admiration for the eagle and fidelity to his own task as artist:

> At times I was half inclined to restore to him his freedom, that he might return to his native mountains; nay, I several times thought how pleasing it would be to see him spread out his broad wings and sail away towards the rocks of his wild haunts; but then, reader, some one seemed to whisper that I ought to take the portrait of the magnificent bird, and I abandoned the more generous design of setting him at liberty, for the express purpose of showing you his semblance. (*OB* 2:464–465)

This passage explicitly invokes Audubon's completed watercolor (which places the eagle among "the rocks of his wild haunts," where he is indeed allowed to "spread out his broad wings and sail away"), only to inform us that the eagle's *actual* fate was much less positive; Audubon tells us that, after dis-cussing various means of dispatching the bird ("killing him by electricity, &c."), he decided to suffocate the bird by placing him in a sealed room "into which was introduced a pan of lighted charcoal" (*OB* 2:465). The bird did not, how-ever, prove so easy to destroy:

> I waited, expecting every moment to hear him fall down from his perch; but after listening for *hours*, I opened the door, raised the blankets, and peeped under them amidst a mass of suffocating fumes. There stood the Eagle on his perch, with his bright unflinching eye turned towards me, and as lively and vigorous as ever! Instantly reclosing every aperture, I resumed my station at the door, and towards midnight, not having heard the least noise, I again took a peep at my victim. He was still uninjured, although the air of the clos-et was insupportable to my son and myself, and that of the adjoining apartment began to feel unpleasant. I persevered, however, for ten hours in all, when finding that the charcoal fumes would not produce the desired effect, I retired to rest wearied and disappointed.

The next morning Audubon tried again, adding sulphur to the brasier, but, as he recounts, "we were nearly driven from our home in a few hours by the stifling vapours, while the noble bird continued to stand erect, and to look defiance at us whenever we approached his post of martyrdom." Finally Audubon is driven to "a method always used as a last expedient . . . I thrust a long pointed piece of steel through his heart, when my proud prisoner instantly fell dead, without even ruffling a feather." This accomplishes his aim, but at some cost to Audubon's psyche:

> I sat up nearly the whole of another night to outline him, and worked so constantly at the drawing, that it nearly cost me my life. I was suddenly seized with a spasmodic affection, that much alarmed my family, and completely prostrated me for some days. . . . (*OB* 2:465–466)

After this two-and-a-quarter page anecdotal excursus, Audubon finally turns to a scientific discussion of the golden eagle as a species. By this time, however, any pretense of scientific distance has been destroyed. What we will remember about the eagle is not its nesting habits, but the dreadful image of its "bright unflinching eye" staring at us in the midst of that smoke-filled room. Audubon's narrative, with its air of tortured guilt, its lurid drama of suffocation and stabbing, provides a disturbing contrast to the image of triumphant freedom which greets us in the final engraved plate.

The question then becomes: Having created an image of such mimetic faithfulness that it (along with many other images in his book) would earn him the accolades of naturalists around the globe and ensure him a place among the front ranks of the world's bird artists, why then did Audubon give us a textual supplement in which that masterful illusion of presence is deliberately shattered? His text is a constant reminder to the reader that his images are artifacts, carefully constructed, and that behind the *Birds of America* are the real American birds, each one of which was killed and then mounted on an armature so it could be measured and outlined, for the express purpose of "showing you [the reader, the viewer] his semblance."

Indeed, what do we make of the fact that the *Ornithological Biography* is directed very conspicuously *at the reader*? That is, Audubon is constantly addressing the reader as "you," asking you to "picture" this or that scene, to "imagine" a situation or a setting. Throughout the book's many volumes, Audubon's chatty, solicitous voice comments, expostulates, and pleads in a manner curiously reminiscent of the eighteenth-century novel—for example, in his introduction to his essay on the bald eagle, Audubon says: "To give you, kind reader, some idea of the nature of this bird, permit me to place you on

the Mississippi, on which you may float gently along, while approaching winter brings millions of water-fowl on whistling wings, from the countries of the
north . . ." (OB 2:122). When describing the nest of the American avocet, he
interrupts himself to say:

> You, good reader, will not, I am sure, think me prolix; but as some less con-
> siderate persons may allege that I am tediously so, I must tell them here that
> no student of Nature ever was, or ever can be, too particular while thus
> marking the precise situation of a bird's nest. Indeed, I myself have lost many
> nests by being less attentive. After this short but valuable lecture, you and I
> will do our best to approach the sitting bird unseen by it. (OB 4:170)

Why did Audubon choose such an idiosyncratically *subjective* voice, and why
does that voice seem to be so aware of criticism and so anxious to persuade?

In comparing the *Biography* to the *Birds of America*, one might be tempted
to describe Audubon as psychically split between the demands of scientific
objectivity and those of artistic expressionism—as though Audubon felt driven
to confess the limits of the very objectivity which his art constantly evokes, as
though his voice were at war with the work of his hands. But I suspect that
this would be an incorrect reading—in fact, I would claim that the idiosyncrat-
ic and subjective quality of the *Biography* has a great deal to do with
Audubon's driving ambition *more fully* to represent the birds of America—an
ambition which he realized that his images could only partially accomplish.
This was because what defined the birds of America for Audubon was not
only their physical shape, but also their actions in the world. Prior to
Audubon, bird manuals had shown their subjects in stiff poses, often in pro-
file, with minimal background detail. Their emphasis was on the bird as
object, identified by certain exterior marks—for those exterior marks helped
to place them within the rational hierarchy of the Linnean taxonomy.
Audubon's extensive observation of birds in the wild had led him to believe
that their forms were linked to function—birds were not mere placeholders in
a taxonomic Great Chain of Being, but creatures in process, making love,
catching prey, defending their young. He makes this claim in his prospectus
for *The Birds of America:*

> The Author has not contented himself, as others have done, with single pro-
> file views, but in very many instances has grouped his figures, so as to
> represent the originals at their avocations, and has placed them on branches
> of trees, decorated with foliage, blossoms and fruits, or amidst plants of
> numerous species. Some are seen pursuing their prey through the air, search-

ing for food amongst the leaves and herbage, sitting on their nests, or feeding their young; whilst others, of a different nature, swim, wade, or glide in or over their allotted element. (*OB* 1:n.p.)

This was a more radical claim than contemporary readers often realize; in Audubon's era, the notion of species as existing in relationship with specific material environments had yet to be fully formulated. Most early nineteenth-century naturalists were devout adherents to the notion that God had created each species *ex nihilo* and placed it on the earth at the beginning of the world—and insofar as God might or might not have had a particular ecology in mind for His creatures, this belief tended to emphasize form over function. Audubon, however, could never divorce his birds from the work they had to perform. Audubon excuses his lack of interest in systematics by assuring his reader that:

> . . . although you and I, and all the world besides, are well aware that a grand connected chain does exist in the Creator's sublime system, the subjects of it have been left at liberty to disperse in quest of the food best adapted for them, or the comforts that have been so abundantly scattered for each of them over the globe, and are not in the habit of following each other, as if marching in regular procession to a funeral or a merry-making. (*OB* 1:xix)

The systematizing will come later, Audubon promises; until then, he will "simply offer you the results of my own observation with respect to each of the species." It is the depth and detail of such observations that intrigue him (Audubon is a proponent of what would in our own day be termed "thick description":

> I assure you, good reader, that, even at this moment, I should have less plea-sure in presenting to the scientific world a new bird, the knowledge of whose habits I do not possess, than in describing the peculiarities of one long since discovered. (*OB* 1:xviii)

Audubon's obsession with faithful mimesis pushed him beyond the static representation of the bird as object, toward to the concept of animal biography [from *bios* (life) and *graphein* (to inscribe)]. He wished to inscribe not their structure only, but "their avocations"—their work in the world. This new emphasis on birds as active beings required new standards for accuracy—to fidelity to morphology Audubon added the notion of a fidelity to place. Thus, he assures us that the birds depicted in his plates "were regularly drawn on or near the spot where I procured them" and that "The flowers, plants, or portions of trees which are attached to the principal objects, have been chosen from amongst those in the vicinity of which the birds were found," thus guaranteeing the authenticity of not only the subjects but also their backgrounds (OB 1:xii–xiii). But it also meant a fidelity to certain less easily quantified characteristics. For Audubon the most important "peculiarities" of a species are those concerning what we would call its "character." Because Audubon had observed birds in the wild very closely, he was certain that they experienced emotions like fear, anger, joy, and melancholy. Birds were not merely automatons, as Cartesian scientists were wont to assert, but subjects in the fullest sense of the term—beings with consciousness and volition, capable of displaying such qualities as bravery, malice, loyalty, and tenderness. Audubon wanted to include these qualities as *integral* to any description of the birds of America.[4]

We can see this, of course, in *The Birds of America*. In his most powerful images, Audubon presents the viewer with a representative moment in time which is calculated to display both the individual bird's avocation and something of its character as well. The portrait of the golden eagle is a case in point: Audubon has depicted the bird not just as a predator, but as a *fierce* predator— the bird is caught mid-wingbeat, one talon cruelly piercing the eye of the hare it has seized, its beak open in what we imagine must be a loud and exultant cry. This is in keeping with Audubon's description of the bird as pouncing "with the swiftness of a meteor" on its prey and eating "voraciously." The picture's backdrop of mountains and stormy sky contributes to this characterization, for the eagles are, Audubon says in his essay about the species, "muscular, strong, and hardy, capable of bearing extreme cold without injury, and of pursuing their avocations in the most tempestuous weather" (OB 2:466–467). The backdrop does more than simply illustrate the physical stamina of the bird, however; as Stebbins has pointed out, the dramatic composition and the stormy, alpine backdrop add an expressive level of their own—they recall David's 1801 painting, *Bonaparte Crossing the Great St. Bernard*. That is, the golden eagle is depicted by Audubon as a kind of Romantic exemplar of the heroic will.[5] This is in keeping with the aforementioned prose anecdote from the *Ornithological Biography*, in which Audubon says the eagle possesses an almost supernatural stamina, an unconquerable will, and describes the bird's "martyrdom" in language reminiscent of the novels of Scott or of certain scenes in Cooper's *The Last of the Mohicans*. The bird's ability to "look defiance" at its captors even in the midst of its torture becomes yet another illustration of its fierce but noble nature.

This tendency toward a depiction of character is repeated in many of Audubon's images: his portrait of the passenger pigeon emphasizes the birds' conjugal care for one another; blue jays are rogues and thieves; the great crested flycatcher is fiercely territorial.[6] These character sketches often take the form of moral fables, as in his picture of the turtledoves, who represent "the ideal courtship, where the sincerity of the male pursuer is tested by the virtuous female and found to be true."[7] Sometimes the bird depicted is victim rather than victor, as in Audubon's depiction of a covey of northern bobwhites (or Virginia partridge, as Audubon calls them) under attack by a red-shouldered hawk (Havell Plate LXXVI). The latter picture is perhaps the most spectacular example of Audubon's use of dramatic context to evoke the emotional lives of birds. The image has its origin in Audubon's observation that, when threatened, members of a covey will scatter in many different directions, so as to confuse their enemy. Audubon chooses to depict the explosive moment of that scattering—the adults and young leaping outward in panic as the hawk descends upon them, claws outstretched. Audubon himself states, concerning the picture, "I have represented a group of Partridges attacked by a Hawk. The different attitudes exhibited by the former cannot fail to give you a lively idea of the terror and confusion which prevail on such occasions" (*OB* 5:392). Although the birds' "attitudes" are, strictly speaking, alien to us, their gaping mouths, wide open eyes, and outflung wings are close enough to human "startle" responses that we reflexively read their expressions in human terms. This is abetted by our recognition of the circumstances, which are those of surprise attack: in such a situation, we would feel panic and fright; therefore, we tend to assume the presence of similar feelings in the birds. Audubon's goal was to use our own "terror and confusion" to cause us to sympathize with the timid and vulnerable bobwhites, whose lot it is to be vulnerable to such predation.

And yet is it true that Audubon's picture "cannot fail" to give us these feelings? Whereas the truth about a bird's physical identity is easily obtained by comparing the bird to its taxonomic description, the truth about a bird's internal state of mind is never so easily established. We trust Audubon when he says that he has used a compass to get his proportions correct—why would he lie? However, we do not necessarily trust him when he says he has got the interiority of his subjects correct. We want to ask, first: How could he know? And second: How could he be sure? Do turtledoves really court? Do eagles feel triumphant or defiant? Do bobwhites feel terror?

The fact is, we are rather inclined to dismiss such claims as examples of anthropomorphism. Whereas we do not greatly care what conventions Audubon uses to bring us his representation of birds-as-objects, the fact that his evocation of birds-as-subjects relies to some not inconsiderable degree on the conventions of narrative painting—that the portrait of the golden eagle is possibly alluding to David's *Napoleon,* or that the picture of the bobwhites uses many of the same techniques employed by Poussin in his *Rape of the Sabine Women*—does not boost our confidence.[8] Instead, we wonder if we aren't being duped. The fact that some of Audubon's images seem to fit into the category of moral fable, rather than simply anatomical illustration, creates in us the sudden concern that these narratives might be *only* fables—or, more to the point, romances (that is, Audubon is *romanticizing* the lives of these birds).

I would assert that Audubon is very aware of our skepticism regarding this matter, and that it is this awareness which drives Audubon to give us not only the visual representation of *The Birds of America,* but also the verbal supplement of the *Ornithological Biography.* Visual representation alone cannot fully satisfy us. The presence of other minds—in this case, of the birds' minds or feelings—can only be asserted by the testimony of a thinking subject, and such a testimony is not a "representation" of nature: it is rather more like a promise, or an affadavit.

The difference between the recognition of objects and the recognition of other minds is perhaps most articulately established in the essay "Other Minds," by J. L. Austin. This essay seems particularly suited to speak to the difference between Audubon's ornithological images and Audubon's *Ornithological Biography,* because part of the essay centers on a discussion of the differences and similarities between the statement "There is a goldfinch in the garden," and the statement (made about another person) "He is angry." The former assertion is taken as an example of "a statement of particular, current, empirical fact," Austin says; the latter is commonly considered more problematic. The bulk of his essay explores the significance of this difference.

About our ability to say "There is a goldfinch," Austin states we may reply to the question, "How do you know?" by replying, "'From its behaviour', 'By its markings', or in more detail, 'By its red head', 'from its eating thistles'." It is a matter of recognition:

> Our claim, in saying we know (i.e. that we can tell) is to *recognize:* and recognizing, at least in this sort of case, consists in seeing, or otherwise sensing, a feature or features which we are sure are similar to something noted (and usually named) before, on some earlier occasion in our experience.[9]

This statement is interesting, because one of the salient features of the representation in Audubon's book is that one may, after seeing an image of a bird in that book, subsequently recognize a bird in the world. This experience is very common to bird-watchers, who use the illustrations of bird books to guide them in their quest to learn the names of various species in the wild. It works the other way as well, of course: a bird watcher can identify Audubon's images of blue jays without having to read the title; he or she knows the blue jay in the world, and here are several on the page. They are recognizable.

The situation is not so easy surrounding the statement, "He is angry," according to Austin, for recognizing the interior states of other persons is not simply a matter of ticking off certain physiological signs. In fact, Austin states, "In order to know what you're feeling, I must also apparently be able to imagine (guess, understand, appreciate) what you're feeling. It seems that more is demanded than that I shall have learned to discriminate displays of anger in others: I must also have been angry myself" (*PP* 104). That is, the claim to recognize anger in another is a highly complex one, in the sense that it involves a greater degree of identification between the knower and the object of thought: the recognition involves a "whole pattern of events, including occasion, symptoms, feeling and manifestation, and possibly other factors besides" (*PP* 109). That is, it is not merely the "symptoms" of anger that we recognize, but the situation that gives rise to anger, a situation in which we might imagine ourselves being. Moreover, our familiarity with the subjects involved increases the chance that our ability to recognize states of mind in them will be accurate—individuals from other cultures or classes are harder to "read," as are members of different religious or intellectual traditions (*PP* 104).

Austin's view of the situation corresponds nicely with what we previously said concerning Audubon's mimetic strategy. Audubon's need to portray the inner states of birds pushed him towards narrative, for he had to provide the context in which these interior states might arise and be exteriorized—and thus be recognized by us. Yet by moving from "representation" in its purest sense—that is, the simple reproduction of an object's proportions and identifying marks—to the narration of events in time (events which are, moreover, supposed to reveal the presence of subjective states), Audubon increased dramatically the chances that we might resist his claims to knowledge, for whereas the *object* is (barring its complete disintegration) overt and accessible, bearing, as it were, its own witness, *subjective events* are doubly hidden. They are hidden in the past, because they are sequences and not objects, and they are hidden in the interior of the subjects involved. We must always get the news secondhand—we are utterly dependent upon the testimony of a witness—yet the witness might be mistaken, exaggerating, or even lying.

Moreover, because the recognition of subjectivity, of inner states, is always (as Austin says) a matter of interpretation—a matter calling for complex judgment, rather than simple eidetic correspondence—the chances for error are greatly increased. Austin analyzes the many reasons we may doubt our ability to know what someone else is feeling:

> We may worry (1) as to whether someone is *deceiving* us, by suppressing his
> emotions, or by feigning emotions which he does not feel; we may worry (2)
> as to whether we are *misunderstanding* someone (or he us), in wrongly sup-
> posing that he does "feel like us," that he does share emotions like ours; or
> we may worry (3) as to whether some action of another person is really
> deliberate, or perhaps only involuntary or inadvertent in some manner or
> other. (*PP* 112)

If this is true in the case of our experience with other humans (even, Austin
points out, those humans we feel closest to), it is infinitely more so in the case
of our experience with animals, for the obvious reason that the distance
between species is greater than the difference between even the most disparate
human types. So Audubon is left with the problem of our skepticism, a problem which cannot be solved by mere recourse to "objective" modes of proof,
since there is no "objective" (that is, exteriorized) mark or symptom which
might establish unequivocally the existence of feeling or thought in an animal.
What is left to him? How can he overcome our resistance?

When Austin says, of the authority of written accounts, that "this sort of
'knowledge' is liable to be 'wrong', owing to the unreliability of human testimony," he quickly adds:

> Nevertheless, the occurrence of a piece of human testimony radically alters
> the situation. We say, "we shall never know what Caesar's feelings were on
> the field of the battle of Phillippi," because he did not pen an account of
> them: *if* he *had*, then to say "We shall never know" won't do in the same
> way. . . . (*PP* 82)

We doubt that Audubon can know what birds are feeling and thinking—yet
the same cannot be said for Audubon's statements about his own thoughts and
feelings. Audubon's bird biographies are testimonials which recount his claims
to having recognized animal consciousness, but they are also (and inseparably
so) testimonies to Audubon's own emotions, his own subjective state throughout the event—about which he is in a unique position to judge. As Austin
says, "In the complex of occurrences which induces us to say we know another
man is angry, . . . a peculiar place is occupied by the man's own statement as
to what his feelings are" (*PP* 113). This may provide a clue as to why Audubon
is so anxious to include them. They provide the basis for our trust; they establish his authority.

My thesis is that Audubon felt a need to *write* his own experience of birds as
"other minds" precisely because of his awareness of our skepticism about this

possibility—a skepticism which is an extension of our general skepticism toward the feelings of others. He needed to supplement his images with prose testimony because he had become aware that his only authority for saying that a bird felt thus is essentially, "I was there, and I saw and felt thus." By narrating his experience, Audubon wishes to say that there are some things he knows because they have occurred to him—and he is willing to give us his word to that effect. In other words, where the portraits in the *Birds of America* imply, "It is," the *Biography* states, "I know," which, as Austin has shown, is tantamount to saying "I promise." Austin points out that "When I say 'I know,' I *give others my word: I give others my authority for saying that* 'S is P'" (*PP* 99). The authority for saying a bird is angry or frightened can be established only by another conscious mind, one which has experienced such feelings and can claim to recognize them in a particular situation. His only proof of this is in the telling, of course, and his telling is a kind of affadavit—it is not "proof" in the formal or logical sense sense of the term. And our only obligation to such a witness is that we either take his word for it—take his word as a (poor) substitute for the actual event—or we do not. But what happens if we do?

If we do take Audubon's word, we do not get nature "represented" to us, as we do in his bird portraits. Instead, we are involved in an interesting chain of events: Audubon's observation of the actions of a particular bird or birds causes him to testify that he was (in this particular case) in the presence of "other minds." Our experience of Audubon's narration duplicates this recognition in some fashion—reading words purported to be Audubon's, about events he supposedly experienced which stimulated certain alleged emotions and thoughts, we *may* decide to give these words credence; if we do, we are required at least to entertain the possibility that the conclusions Audubon draws concerning his experience are valid. In this case, the greater the subjectivity of his narrative—the more detail he goes into regarding his own state of mind—the more inclined we are to credit his narrative as true.

For an example of how this might work, I shall turn to a particularly "anthropomorphic" portrait, one which depicts a group of brown thrashers fighting off a black snake (Havell Plate CXVI). The plate depicts three male thrashers vigorously attacking the snake, which is attempting to rob the nest of the female (Figure 3). She appears at the bottom of the painting, draped over the coils of the invader like a Victorian heroine fainting in the arms of her abductor. Most viewers feel that Audubon is taking liberties here—there is something too human in the postures of the birds. Despite the exquisite realism of the image, we are suddenly aware of the artist's hand, of his manipulation of the scene to depict something very like melodrama, with the brave young males banding together to defend the honor of a hapless female.

Figure 3. "Brown Thrashers" (Havell Plate CXVI). From the collection of the Mary W. Runnells Rare Book Room of the Field Museum of Natural History, Chicago. Photo by Vision Tree.

If we turn to Audubon's verbal account, in his chapter on the brown thrasher in the *Biography*, he at first confirms our worst suspicions: "Reader, look attentively at the plate before you," he abjures us; isn't this scene "calculated to excite the compassion of any one who is an admirer of woodland melody, or who sympathizes with the courageous spirit which the male bird shews, as he defends his nest, and exerts all his powers to extricate his beloved mate from the coils of the vile snake which has already nearly deprived her of life?" (*OB* 3:102). The trouble is, this picture seems all *too* calculated—we suspect it has been manipulated in the interest of the moral, rather than in the interest of the truth.

Yet to stop here would be an injustice to Audubon, for the next paragraph demonstrates what I take to be the significant difference between the image Audubon presents us with and its narrative counterpart: "The birds in the case represented were greatly the sufferers," Audubon states: "their nest was upset, their eggs lost, and the life of the female in imminent danger. But the snake was finally conquered, and a jubilee held over its carcass . . ." (*OB* 3:102). He then adds, "I was happy in contributing my share to the general joy, for on taking the almost expiring bird into my hand for a few minutes, she recovered in some degree, and I restored her to her anxious mate" (*ibid.*). Whatever our own interpretation might have been of this event, we are less inclined to dismiss Audubon's conclusions outright because, by mentioning his own "share in the general joy," Audubon reminds us that the scene is being mediated through his own consciousness—and that his consciousness is what makes the detection of "joy" possible. For how could joy be recognized as such, except that it was witnessed by one who knew what joy might be? We might still doubt Audubon's claims about the emotions of birds, but not in the same way that we would doubt them if we were exposed only to his painting of the event.

Even where his image is not overtly anthropomorphic, Audubon's prose can provide an interesting qualification to his realism. For example we might compare the engraving of the American avocet (Havell Plate CCCXVIII) with the prose account. In Audubon's portrait, everything is clearly seen. The bird is pictured in the forground, bent in pursuit of an insect; every detail is crisp, the delicate feathers, the folds of skin around the bird's backward-bending knees, the red eye curiously trained on the observer as if acknowledging our gaze and thus certifying its own authenticity. It seems the perfect inscription of nature, insofar as one who has never seen an avocet could feel comfortable with the belief that he could now *recognize* one in the wild.

Yet there is an enormous difference between our experience of this calm scene and our experience of the corresponding essay in the *Ornithological Biography*. Audubon's words return us, as it were, to the primal scene:

> Although a person can only advance slowly when wading through mud and knee-deep water, it does not take much time to cover forty or fifty yards. I was soon on the small island where the Avocet was comfortably seated on her nest. Softly, and on all fours, I crawled towards the spot, panting with heat and anxiety. Soon I was within three feet of the unsuspecting creature, peeping at her through the tall grasses. Lovely bird, how innocent and unaware she was, and yet how near to her enemy, even though he was also an admirer of her race! There she sat on her eggs, her head almost mournfully

Figure 4. "American Avocet" (Havell Plate CCCXVIII). From the collection of the Mary W. Runnells Rare Book Room of the Field Museum of Natural History, Chicago. Photo by Vision Tree.

sunk into her plumage. Her eyes, unresponsive even to the sight of her mate, were half closed as if she were dreaming of the future. Having seen all this, I was content. (*OB* 4:170)

What is interesting here is that the recovery of the "I" of the observer leads to the recovery of the essential symmetry of the encounter. If the bird is humanized with descriptors like "innocent," "mournful," and "unsuspecting," Audubon is animalized—we are left with the naturalist on all fours, "panting with heat and anxiety." Audubon deliberately depicts himself as a predator creeping up on a defenseless female. Far from a disinterested observer, he becomes the bird's "enemy" and "admirer" at once—a decidedly unreasonable stance, one which problematizes his concluding claim that he is "content" (or perhaps we must say, *he* may be content, but *we* are a little disturbed by the passions he has revealed). But it is precisely the ability of Audubon's narrative to preserve the emotional ambiguities and conflicts of his experience which enables him to testify to the veracity of his claim that the bird has consciousness; his emotions and thoughts are integral to the encounter:

Now she observes me, poor thing, and off she scrambles—running, tumbling, and at last rising on wing, emitting her clicking notes of grief and anxiety, which none but an inconsiderate or callous-hearted person could hear without sympathizing with her. (*OB* 4:170)

If we take Audubon's words for what he says they are worth, then we are obliged, or persuaded, to sympathize with the bird. If we doubt Audubon's words, we are in that class Audubon calls "callous-hearted," a class he knows we are free to join (that is why he is working so hard). The whole thing is a matter of trust, and the reader always has the power to grant or to withhold trust—because we know full well that we cannot be "sure" in such cases.

The conclusion one might draw from comparing the *Ornithological Biography* with the *The Birds of America* is that the former is finally a more compelling testimony to the interiority of birds. Yet this is a difficult conclusion for us to credit, living as we do in a climate of extreme skepticism about language, especially language which purports to preserve the author's intentions (and intention is fundamental to the notion of testimony). This skepticism begins with the scientific notion that language must be purified of its social content, so as to allow for a pure, "objective" discourse in the language of things. In the wake of our failure to achieve that goal, philosophy has tended to take a skeptical view of human communication in general. Derrida in particular has pointed out that if the project depends on a definition of communication as the transfer of object-images from one mind to another, a view which Derrida, in his essay "Signature Event Context," ascribes to Enlightenment figures like Condillac, then the project is doomed from the beginning. Condillac felt that what men have to communicate is "their 'thought', their 'ideas', their representation. Thought, as representation, precedes and governs communication, which transports the 'idea', the signified content."[10] The fact that "The concept of *representation* is here indissociable from those of *communication* and of *expression*" means that there is, in this way of talking about language, an innate prejudice toward the *image*, which is seen as the basic building block both of ideas (thought's content) and language (thought's vehicle). Derrida again quotes Condillac:

> *The most natural means* was thus to depict [*dessiner*] images of things. *To express the idea* of a man or of a horse, one represented the form of the one or of the other, and the first attempt at writing was nothing but a simple painting.[11]

This theory that representation is both at the origin of language and its core content exposes language to Derrida's skeptical critique, which can be elegantly summed up in his famous dictum that "Representation regularly *supplants* [*supplée*] presence" (*LI* 5).

I mention this because Derrida's account of the sign as something which is perpetually evoking that which it in fact erases provides an excellent way to understand Audubon's task as a realistic painter: a task which involves the reparation and modification of the image, so as to mask the essential absence of the referent. In Audubon's case, interestingly enough, the "absence of the sender" from the frame is central to the work of extending presence into the midst of absence. Audubon's realism is (as we have seen) a kind of self-abandonment.

In fact, Audubon's artwork may be the best example of Derrida's notion of the sign as hermeneutic orphan:

> The absence of the sender, of the receiver [*destinateur*], from the mark that he abandons, and which cuts itself off from him and continues to produce effects independently of his presence and of the present actuality of his intentions [*vouloir-dire*], indeed even after his death, his absence, which moreover belongs to the structure of all writing—and I shall add further on, of all language in general—this absence is not examined by Condillac. (*LI* 5)

This is indeed what has happened to Audubon's images: orphaned from both author and intention, they float free in the realm of the aesthetic, endlessly iterated in coffee-table editions, decorator prints, posters, even refrigerator magnets and shopping bags. Their ubiquity and easy exploitation as marketing material seem perfect illustrations of what Derrida calls the "essential drift [*dérive*] bearing on writing as an iterative structure, cut off from all absolute responsibility, from *consciousness* as the ultimate authority, orphaned and separated at birth from the assistance of its father" (*LI* 8).

Yet it is curious that the return to Audubon's *writing* has a tendency to reunite the image with its intended use. For Audubon, the point was always the birds themselves, their power and grace, their biographies. He states in the introduction to the *Ornithological Biography* that his own early life was "unprofitable . . . doubtless because my whole mind was ever filled with a passion for rambling and admiring those objects of nature from which alone I received the purest gratification" (*OB* 1:x). Some of this purity of gratification is what he hopes to pass along to us. His book is thus not only (or even primarily) a scientific field guide, but an introduction to, and an invitation to, empirical experience. He tells us he has placed the "technical descriptions and references," which have been "constructed according to the strictest rules of science," at the end of each chapter "so that you may read them or not, just as you please" (*OB* 1:xx). What you should *not* skip, however, are the "descriptions of the habits of each species," for these will accomplish his purpose. Throughout the book Audubon exhorts the reader and, by implication, the viewer of his works not to be satisfied with merely experiencing the birds of America secondhand—it is Audubon's hope that the reader will go beyond representation to the real thing. As he says of the brown thrasher:

> . . . that I could imitate its loudest notes, surpassed only by those of that unrivalled vocalist, the mocking Bird! But alas! it is impossible for me to convey to you the charms of the full song of the Brown Thrush; you must go to its own woods and there listen to it. (*OB* 3: 103)

Audubon's *Birds of America* was intended as an homage to lives he considered superior to art: the birds of America. We cannot garner this exclusively from his images, however. His art does not usually confess its own limitations; in fact, he has created images so fulsome and rich that we might not want any other world but the world they create. It is only by referring to his words that we recover his intention, which is that his art should change, fundamentally, our attitude toward those beings he passionately loved—by causing us to prefer the referents to the sign.

To say this is to take Austin's side against the Enlightenment theory of language as object-description. It is to agree with Austin when he says that: "Even if some language is now purely descriptive, language was not in origin so, and much of it is still not so" (*PP* 103). It is to see language as a social and contingent act, one in which the world of objects is always gestured toward, but never "represented"—it is to admit that Audubon's writings *cannot present* the world in the way his images do.

In other words, if we do not start with Condillac, if we instead say, with Austin, that: "believing in other persons, in authority and testimony, is an essential part of the act of communicating, an act which we all constantly perform," then language is demoted from a carrier of presence (whether real or fallacious) to the site at which a belief (or disbelief) in other minds is occasioned (*PP* 115). Only with such a theory of language can the notion of an "ornithological biography" be entertained.

Notes

1. Theodore Stebbins, in his article "Audubon's Drawings of American Birds, 1805–38," says that "one cannot help reading the figure as a miniature self-por-

trait. It suggests something of Audubon's continuing struggles to keep his project going in the face of constant difficulties in finding enough backers and in tracking down missing birds." See *John James Audubon: The Watercolors for* The Birds of America. (New York: The New York Historical Society, 1993), 20.

2. John James Audubon, *Ornithological Biography, or an Account of the Habits of the Birds of the United States of America; Accompanied by Descriptions of the Objects Represented in the Work Entitled* The Birds of America, *and Interspersed with Delineations of American Scenery and Manners* (Edinburgh: Adam Black, 1831–1839; Facs. ed. New York: Abbeville Press, 1985), 1: xii. Subsequent citations from this work will be indicated in the text by the abbreviation *OB*.

3. Reba Fishman Snyder, "Complexity in Creation: A Detailed Look at the Watercolors for *The Birds of America*," in *The Watercolors for* The Birds of America (1993), 56.

4. Amy R. W. Meyers, "Observations of an American Woodsman: John James Audubon as Field Naturalist," in *The Watercolors for* The Birds of America, (1993) 50.

5. Stebbins, 20.

6. Meyers, 49–50.

7. *Ibid.*, 51.

8. In her catalog notes on the original Audubon watercolor of the bobwhite, art historian Carole Anne Slatkin states that Audubon uses "foreshortened and unusual views" of his subjects in a series of "overlapping images" to create "a sense of visual confusion that emphasizes the confusion of the event" (see *The Watercolors for* The Birds of America, 149). The same words could easily be applied to Poussin's painting.

9. J. L. Austin, *Philosophical Papers*, 2nd ed. (Oxford: Clarendon Press, 1970), 83–84. Subsequent citations from this work will be indicated in the text by the abbreviation *PP*.

10. Jaques Derrida, *Limited Inc.*, trans. Samuel Weber and Jeffrey Mehlman (Evanston: Northwestern University Press, 1988), 4. Subsequent citations from this work will be indicated in the text by the abbreviation *LI*.

11. The emphasis is by Derrida, as he notes in this passage.

Bibliography

Audubon, John James. *Onithological Biography, or an Account of the Habits of the Birds of the United States of America; Accompanied by Descriptions of the Objects Represented in the Work Entitled* The Birds of America, *and Interspersed with Delineations of American Scenery and Manners.* Edinburgh: Adam Black, 1831–1839. Facs. ed. New York: Abbeville Press, 1985.

Austin, J. L. *Philosophical Papers.* 2nd ed. Oxford: Clarendon Press, 1970.

Cavell, Stanley. *In Quest of the Ordinary: Lines of Skepticism and Romanticism.* Chicago: University of Chicago Press, 1988.

———. *Philosophical Passages: Wittgenstein, Emerson, Austin, Derrida.* Oxford: Blackwell, 1995.

Cheney, Dorothy L. and Robert M. Seyfarth. *How Monkeys See the World.* Chicago: University of Chicago Press, 1990.

Cooper, James Fenimore. *The Last of the Mohicans.* New York: Scribners, 1961.

Derrida, Jacques. *Limited Inc.,* trans. Samuel Weber and Jeffrey Mehlman. Evanston: Northwestern University Press, 1988.

Masson, Jeffrey Moussaieff, and Susan McCarthy. *When Elephants Weep.* New York: Delacorte, 1995.

Meyers, Amy R.W. "Observations of an American Woodsman: John James Audubon as Field Naturalist," in *John James Audubon: The Watercolors for* The Birds of America. New York: The New York Historical Society, 1993. 43–54.

Snyder, Reba Fishman. "Complexity in Creation: A Detailed Look at the Watercolors for *The Birds of America,*" in *John James Audubon: The Watercolors for* The Birds of America. New York: The New York Historical Society, 1993. 55–68.

Stebbins, Theodore E. "Audubon's Drawings of American Birds, 1805–38," in *John James Audubon: The Watercolors for* The Birds of America. New York: The New York Historical Society, 1993. 3–26.

7

What Is "Human"?
Metaphysics and Zoontology in Flaubert and Kafka

Marian Scholtmeijer

O n the outer door of a mall in my town is a sign: "No Animals Allowed."
Look inside, however, and one sees dozens of human animals, browsing through clothing racks or standing behind cash registers. On what do people base their certainty that the term "animals" does not apply to them? The question has to do with experience and belief, not law[1] and logic. Our belief that we are different from other animals is ingrained. Indeed—and somewhat tautologically—that belief shapes our being: we define ourselves and experience ourselves as *distinct from animals*. Modern science seems to have had little influence upon the felt sense that "human" designates a different order of being from that of other species. The trouble is that, while we can point to other animals and say we are not like them, the ontological constructs of "humanity" are hardly secure. What if that which prevents us from experiencing ourselves as animals is an illusion?

One by one, the barriers separating humans from animals have collapsed. Other animals besides ourselves demonstrate rationality, language use, self-consciousness, deceptive behavior, peacemaking, aesthetic interest, and altruism.[2] The remaining province for human difference is metaphysics,[3] and not specific metaphysical claims, such as having a soul, possessing free will, or being conscious of the ideal—no: metaphysical thought by itself seems to affirm human distinctiveness. One might argue that metaphysics is simply a projection of our sense of difference from other animals. We can conceive of the otherworldly, the transcendent, and this capacity alone apparently sets us apart from animals, indeed, holds us above them. The metaphysical is incorporated, literally, into our understanding of who and what we are. Simultaneously as we philosophize about, say, the nature of Being, we are convincing ourselves of our own ontological otherness. Humankind is in the condition of the true believer: stuck inside a system and unable to conceive of alternatives.

In modern Western culture, the nonhuman animal has come along to threaten the whole edifice of human identity—if only, for most people, in theory. Since the time at which human beings imagined themselves sandwiched somewhere between animals and angels on the Great Chain of Being, metaphysics and animality have been in conflict. Two interlinked processes have occurred since then: the reality of the metaphysical—of religious belief, in particular—has come into doubt; and animals have gained power and status. Obviously, the progressive retreat from the concrete and specific of the divide between human and animal benefits animals. They are not as insensate as Western culture thought. More importantly, however, that retreat challenges human status. As the grounds for claiming special status for humanity become increasingly uncertain, the possibility that "human" merely designates one species of animal among others becomes increasingly real. All animals remind us that, in some deeply ontological sense, we are apes trying to be human beings.

Both Gustave Flaubert and Franz Kafka knew that we are apes trying to be human beings, and knew this not merely theoretically, but intimately. They experienced themselves as animals.[4] Or perhaps, to acknowledge postmodern doubt, one should say that they believed they experienced themselves as animals. Their estrangement from the human condition found expression in identification with animals. Jean-Paul Sartre has examined Flaubert's identification with animals in some depth,[5] citing the story Flaubert wrote as a teenager, Quidquid volueris, as the upshot of childhood years spent in virtually mute, animal-like boredom. Quidquid volueris is about an ape-man, Djalioh, and his love for and eventual rape and murder of a young married woman. Djalioh experiences both irrational rage and moments of bliss. He cannot communicate these experiences to others. As an expression of teen angst, Djalioh is near perfect. And as Sartre points out, Flaubert would go on exploring the quarrel between materialism and spirituality implicit in the animal in Quidquid volueris throughout the rest of his life.

Kafka, too, has an ape story within his oeuvre: "A Report to an Academy." One sign of difference between Kafka and Flaubert—and, I would argue, of cultural progress on thinking about animals—is that Kafka's ape is not a biological hybrid of ape and human, as Djalioh is, but an ape who has decided to become human. Imprisoned in a tiny cage on a ship, Kafka's ape realizes that his only way out is to change his essential nature: "I had to stop being an ape,"[6] he reports. He learns to drink schnapps; dazed and drunk, he learns to speak; with the help of teachers, he acquires "the cultural level of an average European" (258). With this story, Kafka represents "humanity" as a series of tricks suitable for the vaudevillian stage, a kind of artificial overlay willed onto animal nature. Of course, there is always the possibility that his ape is deluded. One has to imagine a long-armed, hairy creature explaining to a group of scientists how he became human to catch the full irony of the story. Nevertheless, by means of his ape, Kafka has detached human ontology from essentialist belief.

There can be little doubt that Flaubert and Kafka had personal reasons for their interest in animals. Sartre argues that the root cause of Flaubert's identification with Djalioh is paternal abuse. In making this point, Sartre links Flaubert with Kafka: "that other victim of an abusive father" (345). Critics who have examined Kafka's animal stories do tend to cite his troubles with his father as their source. Ronald Hayman notes that Kafka's father condemned him "with animal imagery";[7] and Ramón Mendoza expands upon the point:

> We know that Kafka's father . . . had a predilection for animal similes when expressing his contempt for a human being. We may possibly assume this influence to be an unconscious reason for Kafka's writing animal stories, and for linking animals with the contemptible.[8]

Such psychoanalytic arguments establish the integral quality of the animal to Flaubert's and Kafka's sense of identity. Where they go wrong is in the assumption that the animal is a degraded being for these two writers. Granted, abuse and self-loathing might have been the mechanism for the entry of the animal into their psyches. Once installed, however, the animal has a much more healthy influence over their imaginations than psychoanalysis has suggested. This is not to say that, like all great artists, Flaubert and Kafka turned their torment into art. Rather, they expanded upon a native affiliation for animals to explore the nature of existence. In their stories, the animal does not represent limitation, lumpish materialism, stupidity. The animal stands as a reasonable ontological alternative to the human state. Animals have power in their stories. Specifically, they have the power to challenge metaphysical values and thoughts.

Neither Flaubert nor Kafka, however, works with a straightforward antagonism between animality and metaphysics. Their animal stories are experiments in the fusion of animal ontology with the metaphysical.[9] Because they take animals seriously enough to wonder whether or not metaphysical values survive contact with animal ontology, they call the term "human" into question on two fronts: from the top down, as it were, they detach metaphysics from humanity; and from the bottom up (again, as it were), they raise the animal into direct competition with humankind. On both fronts, they deconstruct human identity. The process is reciprocal and dynamic: the animal serves to deconstruct the image of the human being; and a preexisting mistrust of the human state enhances the power of the animal. None of this could occur if Kafka's and Flaubert's felt connection with animals was one of kinship in degradation or subhuman status.

I shall be examining this process as it appears in two familiar stories: Flaubert's "*Un Coeur simple*" from *Trois Contes*—hereafter, "A Simple Heart"— and Kafka's "*Die Verwandlung*," known in English as "The Metamorphosis." As well-covered as these stories have been, I believe that an animal-centred approach proves illuminating. This approach demonstrates, for one thing, the radical nature of Flaubert's vision and argument in "A Simple Heart." His story is more subversive, on a greater scale, than is usually realized. With "The Metamorphosis," an animal-centred approach helps to explain the disorientation that most readers feel when they read a Kafka story. The foundations of the reader's existence are shaken by Kafka's stories. Indeed, this is a fair description of what is occurring to human identity in modern Western culture as animals gain power. Between Flaubert's time and Kafka's, culture had opened itself even wider to the influence of the animal, as I shall suggest later in the discussion.

"A Simple Heart"

The primary debate initiated by "A Simple Heart" is whether or not its conclusion is ironic. Indeed, this question arose as soon as Flaubert circulated the story idea among his friends, and thus Flaubert himself had the opportunity to respond. At the same time, he provides a summary of the story:

> The "Story of a Simple Heart" is just the account of an obscure life, that of a poor servant girl [Félicité], pious but fervent, discreetly loyal, and tender as new-baked bread. She loves one after the other a man, her mistress's children, a nephew of hers, an old man whom she nurses, and her parrot. When the parrot dies she has it stuffed, and when she herself comes to die she confuses the parrot with the Holy Ghost. This is not at all ironical as you may suppose but on the contrary very serious and sad. I want to move tender hearts to pity and tears, for I am tender-hearted myself.[10]

Of course, irony played out upon the innocent *is* serious and sad—and Félicité is as innocent a being as can exist in human form. In fact, one wonders how the story can be sad at all if Félicité's dying vision were not ironic. In the final moment of her life, a harmless, trusting soul is duped with an image of grace and salvation spawned by her own deluded brain—and a "grotesque"[11] image at that. Furthermore, it would be not only sad but tragic if, in the last moment of her life, this innocent anticipates the great reward which every reader would grant she deserves, when in fact her fate is to be sunk into the greater obscurity of the grave. With Félicité's vision, the problem Flaubert is confronting in this story is heightened and intensified to the point of impasse. No matter how knowing or cynical we might be, we are all victims of the irony centered on Félicité at this culmination of her narrative.

Flaubert subjects metaphysics to the ultimate test: Does the metaphysical have any reality outside of the human mind? He has chosen an interesting mind for this test: Félicité is no philosopher. Her mind is uncorrupted by learning. Measured by conventional qualities determining human identity, she is very close to the animal. Critics analyzing her character most often invoke the term *la bêtise*,[12] rather misleadingly translated as stupidity and better conceived of as "animal-like simplicity."[13] If this mind conflates the Holy Ghost with a long-dead, stuffed, and now worm-eaten parrot, does that certify the purity of the vision? Can we say with greater confidence that the spiritual is real because an untainted mind has found glory in an object that more "human" sensibilities find grotesque? Surely, if one could determine that animals felt the presence of the divine, that determination would vouch for the metaphysical in a way that assertions by encultured, self-invented beings do not. Thus animality is a key factor in "A Simple Heart" in three respects: the principal character is animal-like; the real-life object of her passion is an animal; and the form taken by her religious ecstasy is animal.

It is necessary to turn to the middle term in this tripartite structure, the actual parrot, to capture the stringency of Flaubert's experiment. Félicité's animal innocence—her devotion, her suffering—lends her a kind of saintliness. In and of itself, detached from the actual parrot, the Holy Ghost/parrot is unquestionably sublime. The parrot, Loulou, who sits at the heart of the equation is another matter altogether—a most unromantic bird. Indeed, Flaubert goes out of his way to suppress features that might make Loulou attractive. He does not mention glorious plumage, but lists only the colors of the various parts of the bird in flat, deliberately unimaginative sequence: body green, wing tips pink, head blue, breast golden.[14] He does not detail the parrot's charming quizzical looks or instant responsiveness to his owner's presence.[15] Instead, he touches on raucous noises; feathers and droppings making a mess everywhere; a growth on the parrot's tongue, a growth which Félicité has to remove with her fingernails. He describes the parrot's meaningless reiteration of the same tiresome phrases and the hatred other people besides Félicité feel for the parrot. The portrait of Loulou is not drawn from affection in the usual sense.[16] Even Félicité's attachment to Loulou seems to exist at several stages removed from the parrot himself: the bird invokes the Americas, the place to which, several years before, her beloved nephew had traveled, and where he had died. A reader seeks a way "in" with Loulou, a way to engage humanly or culturally with the creature, and is thwarted. In this way, Flaubert ensures that Loulou remains animal and that whatever meaning is to be derived from the philosophical problem into which the parrot factors is not diverted from animality by some cultural or social construction.

In the hands of a less intelligent writer, all of this would be entirely in keeping with convention: animal ontology entails the primacy of body functions, stupidity, indifference to social niceties. To compose the image of an animal out of such values appears to confirm rather than defy habitual beliefs about animal ontology. Furthermore, if we are compelled to choose between existence at the level of Flaubert's Loulou and existence at the level of the divine, there is almost no contest. Give us the divine any day, over dung and disease and utterance indistinguishable from noise. Notice, however, that Flaubert forces his reader into the position at which choice is necessary. In alienating readers from Loulou, he isolates an ontological category for the parrot. The few actions that Loulou performs are not unfamiliar to readers. The parrot commits the deed even more unmentionable in Flaubert's day than sexual intercourse: he defecates. He is the victim of moulting and skin growths. He pecks mindlessly at his perch: the animal equivalent, perhaps, of playing cards. In this instance, alienation does not mean denial of resemblance but recognition of animality denied. Flaubert's refusal to make the parrot endearing dehumanizes actions we share in common with the bird. That is to say, he removes the human attachment to acts that are ours.

The effect is most striking, of course, when it comes to language. Loulou is, according to Luc Dariosecq, *"un personnage Flaubertian par excellence"* because the parrot *"ne fait que caricaturer la médiocrité des rapports entre les hommes."*[17] We speak words; this makes us human. Yet as Dariosecq points out, Flaubert's characters have a habit of chattering away without meaning much of anything. Ironically, Loulou's utterance imitates human speech in its disconnection from signification.[18] In Flaubert's stories, a good deal of human speech is reduced to the level of mere, automatic parroting.

On this score, too, however, Félicité's "simple heart" has to be taken into account. In middle age, she becomes deaf, deaf to every sound except those Loulou makes. The circle of her contacts with others has shrunk progressively, and in her deafness, her most vital meaningful exchanges occur with her parrot: they "held conversations together, he repeating *ad nauseam* the three phrases in his repertory, she replying with words which were just as disconnected but which came from the heart" (47). What are we to do with this image? Loulou's words do not come from the heart; one can doubt that, in a crucial operative sense, they actually come from the brain: from conscious, intentional cerebration. In turn, Félicité communicates loving words to Loulou; the content of her broken speech is less meaningful than the fact that she is communicating affection. One could argue that Félicité's simple heart has been betrayed again, tricked into the illusion of commensurability. But since Loulou intends no deception, is not locked into the conventions which cause the depreciation of human utterance, he is not implicated in the system of signification that would make a dupe of Félicité in this instance. In view of the discrepancy between the value of human discourse in theory and its value in actuality (in a Flaubert story), Jonathan Culler proposes that, in fact, the point to be derived from Félicité's intercourse with Loulou is this: "Arbitrary signs, which make no pretense of accurately conveying human feelings, seem to be, for that very reason, the forms which contain the greatest depths."[19] At a personal level, when an exchange of noises satisfies the import of the interaction, Félicité's loving response is sufficient to humanize the whole, including Loulou's parroted phrases.

As with language, so with metaphysics? One must wonder whether Félicité's simple heart is great enough to authorize her version of the Holy Ghost and ultimately the "Holy Ghost" *per se*. In view of the ludicrous disparity between the decrepit stuffed parrot and the glorious, sheltering image which comes to usher Félicité into heaven, it is hard to disagree with Bernard Stoltzfus's thesis that the story represents "Flaubert's attack on organized religion and the church."[20] Drawing on Luc Dariosecq's commentary (mentioned above), Stoltzfus argues that those who have faith in the church go beyond psittacism (parroting) to psittacosis: a fever communicated to humans by parrots. They are deranged (24), and poor Félicité is just one more victim of the disease. In Stoltzfus's reading of the story, the metaphysical does not survive contact with the animal. Expanding upon his argument, one could say that religion is the disease of animals who think they are more important than they actually are.

To conceive of the story as an attack on religion, however, does not invalidate Félicité's vision. Her religious responses have been unique throughout the story. The church invokes the Lamb of God without giving a thought to real lambs. Félicité, in contrast, "loved the lambs more tenderly for love of the Lamb of God" (30). Likewise, and working in the opposite direction, she later finds that parrots are a reasonable symbol of the Holy Ghost, and thus the Holy Ghost "acquired new life and meaning in her eyes" (50). One can add, of course, that the Holy Ghost would acquire new life and meaning in general were it possible to cite something specific in the world that *is* the Holy Ghost. It is far more intelligent and useful to find an earthly correlate for metaphysical entities than to indulge in endless debate about the real nature of concocted beings. Instinctively and creatively, Félicité actualizes an image religion has made abstruse and inhuman.

Finally, it is important to take note of the fact that, despite what Flaubert says in his letter explaining the seriousness of "A Simple Heart," he makes no mention of the Holy Ghost in the story's final paragraph. What comes to Félicité at the close of her life is unequivocally "a gigantic parrot." Religious doctrine is irrelevant. The story itself does not indicate that this vision, in this moment, is meant to be the Holy Ghost in the form of a parrot. The image is that of an animal. Unencumbered by investment in the association of human identity with metaphysics, Félicité's mind turns to the animal at the extreme limit of its expression. At most, metaphysically, Félicité's parrot is the Platonic ideal of "Parrot": the essence of Loulou and all his kin in magnificent form. The metaphysical problem hinges on animal ontology. Is animal being amenable to spiritualization on this scale? Within Flaubert's view of the world, very likely not, and that is the point. The religious images most longed for are human-created fantasies. Félicité's parrot opens the question as to whether an animal can qualify for divine status: the same question that confronts post-Darwinian humankind. If it is laughable that a parrot should occupy the position of the Holy Ghost, it is equally laughable that any quasi-human entity should. Félicité's choice is arbitrary: why not a gigantic giraffe, or a gigantic panda bear? Similarly, the choice of a human image to represent the holy is arbitrary. Her choice is personal: it reflects nothing more than the peculiarities of Félicité's own experience. Similarly, one must look to humankind and its needs for explanation of the divine. The irony remains the same: Félicité's fate as an animal is to decay into oblivion. Her own metaphysics imply the conclusion. Her stuffed parrot will "survive" longer than she will. The joke, however, is not on her, but on the reification and vast inflation of humanity's desire for immortality. We should be able to find humanized images of divinity as quaint and comical as Félicité's parrot. The fact that most of us cannot (I, for one, am unable to—except in theory) indicates the depth of our attachment to mistaken beliefs about human ontology.

"The Metamorphosis"

Flaubert employs the animal in an argument about metaphysics. His target is religion, and he succeeds in legitimating animality at religion's expense. He works with three clear and isolable domains of thought: animal, human, and metaphysical. Thirty-six years later, when Kafka wrote "The Metamorphosis," these domains of existence were hardly as separable as they were in the last quarter of the nineteenth century. Granted, Kafka is a singular thinker. He is ahead of his time, and ahead of ours, in fact. Nonetheless, his works signal change in the potentialities of cultural expression. Kafka's stories may be unfathomable to logic. His animal stories are particularly inclined to reach impenetrable ironies and paradoxes. Yet readers sense the truth of his stories— or truths—and thus it is fair to say that something in the culture we share is ready for a strange vision like Kafka's.

I would speculate that two incipient cultural forces had gained ground between Flaubert's period and Kafka's. One is obvious: humankind was becoming more deeply estranged from traditional views of itself. The other is occurring in a less obvious, more underground fashion: animality has a more formidable presence in and influence over thought in Western culture. One sign of this latter development is the fact that the whole idea of animality, of what it consists of and how far it extends, has become less clear. No longer confined to well-defined categories, it has greater power. Kafka himself believed that a story like "The Metamorphosis" came from the spirit of his age. He said as much in a conversation reported by Gustav Janouch about another tale of metamorphosis into an animal, *Lady into Fox* by David Garnett:

> He didn't get that from me. It's a matter of the age. We both copied from that. Animals are closer to us than human beings. That's where our prison bars lie. We find relations with animals easier than with men. . . .
>
> Every man lives behind bars, which he carries within him. That is why people write so much about animals now. It's an expression of longing for a free natural life. But for human beings the natural life is a human life. But men don't always realize that. They refuse to realize it. Human existence is a burden to them, so they dispose of it in fantasies.[21]

Kafka knew and conveyed the strangeness of the animal. In fact, he incorporates that strangeness into all of his stories, not just the animal ones. The world of his stories is weird, dark, tortuous, I would argue, because he adopts an animal point of view.[22] Animality is built into the structure of his narratives.

In his essay, "Human Literacy," George Steiner makes this assertion: "He [or she] who has read Kafka's 'Metamorphosis' and can look into his [or her] mirror unflinching may technically be able to read print, but is illiterate in the only sense that matters."[23] His statement captures the full estrangement from the human image effected by Kafka's story; and this despite the fact that not one of us has ever been transformed overnight into a gigantic insect as Gregor Samsa is. Steiner conveys the invasion of our sense of being that comes from our involvement in the story and Gregor's strange condition. I suspect that most readers identify with Gregor in his new form. For all that it is entirely alien from a realistic perspective, there is something about his insect state that is painfully familiar. "[W]hat is so disorienting about Kafka's 'Metamorphosis,'" says Michael Levine, "is the strange familiarity of it all."[24]

Common sociopsychological experience probably explains some of that sense of familiarity. No doubt we have all, at some moments, felt like strangers and outcasts within our own families: hidden in our rooms, feeling rejected and ashamed. That common experience represents Kafka's way in to larger ontological questions. All the particulars—Gregor's confinement to his room, his compulsive desire to follow the regular morning routine despite what has happened to him, the hostility of his family, his need for understanding, his inability to explain himself—all these humanize Gregor's insect state. As he himself reasons when he imagines his hated chief clerk suffering the same transformation, if it happened to him, it could happen to anyone: "one really could not deny that it was possible" (95).

With the rigid boundary between human and animal thus transgressed, Kafka breaks free of the ontological prison of which he spoke in his conversation with Gustav Janouch.[25] The fact that this marvelous freedom in the ontological field seems to entail extreme stricture[26] for Gregor is typical of Kafka's parabolic thought. Gregor has had freedom forced upon him. A kind of wish fulfillment informs the story: Gregor is no longer obliged to perform as a human being. He does not have to go to work; he does not have to support his family; as time goes by, he realizes that he does not have to be particularly sociable. His efforts to maintain these human routines and human bonds indicate how deeply we are in the grip of the artificial constructs that compose our identities. Humanness is made up out of trivial habits, and because our identities are bound up in these trivial habits, we are not free to abandon them. To do so is to lose ourselves.

There is a striking moment in "The Metamorphosis" which brings home the ontological implications of the great divide Gregor has crossed. After a long and frequently absurd struggle to bring his immense insect body and tiny legs under control, to get out of bed and then open his door, Gregor the insect emerges to confront, not only his family, but a photograph of himself as he was: "in military service, as a lieutenant, hand on sword, a carefree smile on his face, inviting one to respect his uniform and military bearing" (101). Critics who find the animal state a state of degradation in Kafka would have to have a unidirectional response to this *tableau vivant:* how far poor Gregor has fallen! Once free and proud, he is now a monster, a thing of shame. The confrontation works two ways, however: the premetamorphosis Gregor's image is more obviously image and more obviously absurd when held up next to Gregor's new state of being. Gregor had fabricated himself for the photograph, had imitated an image for the moment no less than he had imitated images in his life as a human being: lieutenant, salesman, son, and brother. "The Metamorphosis" destroys the belief that there is some ultimate reality in the images human beings assume as their identities.

It is not really necessary to determine the kind of insect Gregor becomes to explore the ontological questions Kafka initiates. Nonetheless, the term Kafka uses in the opening statement of the story is a useful pivot: Gregor is transformed into an *"ungeheures Ungeziefer,"* an "enormous vermin," or, more specifically, a creature unfit for sacrifice, and a very large one at that. The description possesses a fine irony: what kind of temerity does it take to decide that the huge and frightening being Gregor has become is either fit or unfit for sacrifice? Metaphysical issues turn on the idea of sacrifice. According to the religious traditions in which Kafka was steeped, it is an honor to an animal to be fit for sacrifice. Karl Erich Grözinger describes this as "redemption via the knife."[27] One has to imagine, however, that the actual animal would prefer not to be the object of such an honor. But since, according to the tradition, redemption for the animal comes through sacrifice, one can speculate further that human beings might want to be the kind of creature that is fit for sacrifice without actually ever having to suffer the consequences. As arbitrary as these mystical devices are, the essential nature of the being judged fit or unfit for sacrifice is presumed to be changed by that judgment.

Because human sacrifice is no longer available by the physical route, the Kafkaesque individual (and which of us is not a Kafkaesque individual) tries to effect personal sacrifice by less certain means: by service to others, by feeling guilty or believing him- or herself a burden. Although self-abnegation of this sort is sanctified by Judeo-Christian belief, in the absence of the authoritative mechanism of literal sacrifice, no one can determine whether these self-adopted self-sacrifices qualify the human being for redemption. In "The Metamorphosis," the whole problem is taken out of Gregor's hands. He no longer has to worry whether or not his personal sacrifices qualify him for redemption because he is no longer the kind of being who has to remake his identity to render himself suitable for sacrifice. That route to redemption—and anxiety over the whole issue could itself qualify as such a route—is closed to him.

Excluded by his very nature (and as an unsacrificable animal he is truly a *natural* being) from the metaphysical dilemmas that compose human identity, he is compelled to generate spiritual value out of himself alone—literally. His decision to sacrifice himself for his family by dying and removing the burden of himself from them—if it can be called a decision—begins with his response to music. Moved by his sister's violin playing, he wonders (and Kafka wonders): "Was he an animal, that music had such an effect upon him?" (130). Since Kafka often associates animals and music,[28] the question is wide open. It could be rhetorical: Gregor's responsiveness to music proves he is human.[29] It could be genuine: Gregor's pure and whole-souled response to the music proves he is animal. At the precise moment that his true identity is as open as this, his sister angrily denies him: "'How can it be Gregor? If this were Gregor, he would have realized long ago that human beings can't live with such a creature, and he'd have gone away on his own accord'" (134). This assertion puts Gregor in a terrible ontological bind: to prove himself Gregor he has to disburden the family of his, to them, loathsome presence, yet to do so simultaneously proves that he is not Gregor but an animal (bracketing the difficulty that even as Gregor he was an animal). His decision to die should establish his humanity and, indeed, redeem him. No animal, by traditional belief, kills him or herself. Assuming that he does perform this sacrifice voluntarily, one irony is that he has eliminated the only witness to the redemptive nature of his death; that is, himself. He is known to himself alone. Even his final loving thoughts of his family are wasted, for while anthropocentric belief might expect the human being to experience noble sentiments on the point of death, the animal is given no such credit. What Gregor leaves behind is evidence that wholly contradicts his bid for human status: a large but desiccated animal corpse. In the godless world of Kafka's stories, Gregor's means of asserting his humanness has a completely opposite effect. Perhaps the futility of his effort is the most Kafkaesque proof of all that Gregor is a post-Darwinian human being.

What metaphysical values survive contact with the animal in "The Metamorphosis"? As one would expect, Kafka's discovery is paradoxical: the only remaining value is self-annihilation. The sole method by which a human animal can establish his or her humanity is to cease to be anything. The conclusion is not as pessimistic as it might seem. Kafka is well aware that the idea of "humanity" is contingent. As the metaphysical props to human identity collapse, the modern person is left with the self-defeating alternatives Kafka delineates. The metaphysical spiral has gone into reverse. Metaphysics no longer supplies humanity with an inflated identity; to continue to attach human ontology to the metaphysical means sinking humanity below animal vitality. Allegorically speaking, in modern Western culture, the animal has humanity cornered in the ontological paradoxes Kafka discloses in "The Metamorphosis."

Conclusion

A small aside in a critical article consulted for this paper states most acutely the burden of its argument. In "*Quidquid volueris:* The Scriptural Education," Leyla Peronne-Moisés offers the following, highly pertinent comment on Flaubert's ape story: "*Quidquid volueris* is . . . the story of an ape told by another ape."[30] This observation warrants further thought. In a post-Darwinian world, *all* stories are stories about apes told by other apes—or at least primates. Implicitly, all stories are about the struggle of a particular species of ape to invent and preserve a nonanimal identity for itself. Only a few writers consciously incorporate that struggle into the bodies of their texts. Flaubert and Kafka are foremost among them. They write out of a consciousness that animality has not been defeated by the metaphysical, neither outside nor inside the human being. Unconvinced by the rigid ontological categories given to them by their culture, they move freely between states of being in their stories. They realize, in the fullest sense of the word, that animals threaten the sociocultural constructions designed to erase them. In a culture at last making clumsy efforts to retrieve animals and animality, Flaubert and Kafka exemplify what it means to take the animal seriously. Their stories reveal the extent of the disruptions to the ontological field that occur when animals are truly allowed in.

Notes

1. Legally, of course, each human being is a "person," and thus may pass through doors marked "No Animals Allowed." In this context, it is important to take note of the courageous work of contributors to *The Great Ape Project: Equality beyond Humanity* (eds. Paola Cavalieri and Peter Singer [London: The Fourth Estate, 1993]), who seek the legal designation of "person" for our near primate relatives.

2. The following are just a few sources for these points: Donald R. Griffin, *Animal Minds* (Chicago: University of Chicago Press, 1992); Michael Bright, *Animal Language* (London: British Broadcasting Corporation, 1984); Jeffrey Masson and Susan McCarthy, *When Elephants Weep: The Emotional Lives of Animals* (New York: Delacorte Press, 1995); Robert W. Mitchell and Nicholas S. Thompson, eds., *Deception: Perspectives on Human and Nonhuman Deceit* (New York: State University of New York Press, 1986); Frans de Waal, *Peacemaking among Primates*

(Cambridge: Harvard University Press, 1989); and Desmond Morris, *The Biology of Art: A Study of the Picture-Making Behavior of the Great Apes and Its Relationship to Human Art* (New York: Alfred A. Knopf, 1962).

3. I am asking the term "metaphysical" to do double service in this paper. It is to refer to both the investigation of such nonphysical principles as Truth, Being, and Knowing, and its colloquial usage as a designation of such nonphysical phenomena as religious belief, spirituality, and the ideal. If a reader is inclined to ask, "Just precisely to what does 'the metaphysical' refer?" that is not an inappropriate response. In Western culture, we believe that the metaphysical designates a real and discussable category. Slippery as it might be, the semantic term does identify a powerful domain of human thought and action.

4. The question will naturally arise as to what it means to "experience" oneself as an animal. Unfortunately, the question is unanswerable, especially given that it is difficult to escape the conventions that would have us trying to shut down "human" capacities in order to think ourselves into an animal state. By convention, trying to experience ourselves as animals is a little like trying to experience our own death: our live self, and with animals our human self, keeps popping up to ruin the exercise. This problem does not, however, make nonsense of the assertion. There are beings in the world whom we call animals, and even if we cannot state with certainty that to be an animal means this or that, animals have sufficient Being to disturb human complacency.

5. *The Family Idiot: Gustave Flaubert 1821–1857*, vol. 1, trans. Carol Cosman (Chicago: University of Chicago Press, 1981), particularly 138–139 and 345–346. For further discussion of Flaubert and animals, see Benjamin F. Bart's "Psyche into Myth: Humanity and Animality in Flaubert's *Saint-Julien*," *Kentucky Romance Quarterly* 20 (1973), 317–342; and *Animal Victims in Modern Fiction: From Sanctity to Sacrifice* (Toronto: University of Toronto Press, 1993), 228–244, by the present author.

6. In *Franz Kafka: The Complete Stories*, trans. Willa and Edwin Muir, txt. ed. Nahum N. Glatzer (New York: Schocken Books, 1971), 253. Unless otherwise noted, citations of Kafka's works are from this source.

7. *Kafka: A Biography* (New York: Oxford University Press, 1981), 150. Most Kafka critics mention animals; they are a salient feature of his work. A couple of particularly useful sources are Pietro Citati's *Kafka*, trans. Raymond Rosenthal (New York: Alfred A. Knopf, 1990), 50–73, and Margot Norris's *Beasts of the Modern Imagination: Darwin, Nietzsche, Kafka, Ernst, and Lawrence* (Baltimore: Johns Hopkins University Press, 1985), 118–133 and passim.

8. *Outside Humanity: A Study of Kafka's Fiction* (Lanham, MD: University Press of America, 1986), 90.

9. Haven't human beings always included animals in their metaphysics? Do not animal gods, totem animals, mythic animals, and, more recently, Romantic animals, demonstrate the investiture of animals into the realms of the transcendent? Indeed, they do. Yet they also represent a one-way process in which human beings apply the metaphysical almost by force. Animal ontology does not factor conceptually into these constructs. For all that animal sciences might be overconfident in their assertions about animals, they have introduced animals as a genuine problem within the world that humans construct. I am assuming, as well, that

with the work of natural history, zoology, ethology, and zoosemiotics, we know animals better than we did before, and that our new understanding of them conflicts with earlier conventions.

10. Letter to Mme Roger des Genettes, June 19, 1876. Cited in Robert Baldick's introduction to *Three Tales*, trans. Robert Baldick (Harmondsworth, Middlesex: Penguin Books, 1961), 15.

11. Börge Gedsö Madsen, "Realism, Irony, and Compassion in Flaubert's *Un Coeur simple*," *The French Review* 27 (February 1954), 257.

12. See, for instance, Robert Griffin, *Rape of the Lock: Flaubert's Mythic Realism* (Lexington, Kentucky: French Forum, 1988), 295; and Jonathan Culler, *Flaubert: The Uses of Uncertainty* (London: Paul Elek, 1974), 158–179, on *la bêtise* in general, and 208–210, on Félicité and *la bêtise*.

13. Françoise Gaillard, "A Little Story about the *bras de fer*; or How History Is Made," in *Flaubert and Postmodernism*, eds. Naomi Schor and Henry F. Majewski (Lincoln: University of Nebraska Press, 1984), fn, 99.

14. *Three Tales*, trans. Robert Baldick (Harmondsworth, Middlesex: Penguin Books, 1961), 44. All references are to this edition.

15. Ironically, Loulou is more charming when he is stuffed. He looks "magnificent" standing with his head cocked on one side and biting a gilded nut (49).

16. This is not to say, of course, that Flaubert felt no affection for parrots. In an early letter (1845), he writes "I look on animals and even trees with a tenderness that amounts to a feeling of affinity." *The Letters of Gustave Flaubert, 1830–1857*, ed. and trans. Francis Steegmuller (Cambridge, MA: Belknap Press of Harvard University Press, 1980), 32. That tenderness might never have found its way into his stories in sentimental depictions of animals, but it certainly presupposes a more cheerful attachment to animals and their less than glamorous habits than conventional responses postulate.

17. "*A Propos de Loulou*," *The French Review* 31 (1958), 322.

18. Flaubert has gone in the opposite direction as well. In "The Legend of St. Julian Hospitator," he puts into the mouth of an animal that most meaningful of utterances: the true prophecy (*Three Tales*, 67).

19. *Flaubert: The Uses of Uncertainty* (London: Paul Elek, 1974), 209.

20. "Point of View in 'Un Coeur simple'," *The French Review* 35 (1961), 20.

21. *Conversations with Kafka*, trans. Goronwy Rees (Frankfurt-am-Main: Andre Deutsch, 1971), 22–23. While not exactly expressing tenderness for animals, these remarks do contradict critical assertions to the effect that Kafka was repulsed by animals and by all that he shared with them.

22. Because of legitimate doubts as to what an "animal" point of view might be specifically, I could qualify this statement by phrasing it as "a point of view which could be characterized as 'animal'." Or I could appeal to the idea of "otherness," the outsider's perspective. It is, however, hard to conceive of any *point of view* outside the human point of view other than an animal's—and one does need to imagine a nonhuman point of view to comprehend what Kafka achieves. The animal constitutes a real-life reference point. Moreover, identifying the point of view in Kafka's narratives as specifically animal captures both the strangeness *and* the wholeness of his perspective.

23. *The Critical Moment: Essays on the Nature of Literature* (London: Faber and Faber, 1964), 30.

24. *Writing through Repression: Literature, Censorship, Psychoanalysis* (Baltimore: Johns Hopkins University Press, 1994), 170.

25. Peter Stine makes some excellent comments on Kafka's prison metaphor and the animal in "Franz Kafka and Animals," *Contemporary Literature* 22 (Winter 1981), 58–80. He cites Kafka's bodily sense of entrapment: the human being's "'own frontal bone bars his way'" to true introspection (Stine, 59).

26. I am referring, of course, to the fact that, aside from three dramatic forays into the living room, Gregor's movement over the remainder of his life is restricted to his own room. Unfortunately, the constraints of the argument do not allow coverage of the joyous animal freedoms Gregor discovers: his insect legs (like our own legs) strive "to carry him forward in whatever direction he [chooses]" (102); when food that he likes is presented to Gregor, "Gregor's legs all whizzed toward the food" and he eats with "tears of satisfaction in his eyes" (108). He can crawl up the walls and over the ceiling: "He especially enjoyed hanging suspended from the ceiling; it was much better than lying on the floor; one could breathe more freely; one's body swung and rocked lightly" (115).

27. *Kafka and Kabbalah*, trans. Susan Hecker Ray (New York: Continuum, 1994), 111.

28. See, for example, "Josephine the Singer, or the Mouse Folk" and "Investigations of a Dog."

29. Hanz Politzer makes the case for this interpretation in *Franz Kafka: Parable and Paradox* (Ithaca, New York: Cornell University Press, 1966), 76–77.

30. In *Flaubert and Postmodernism*, eds. Naomi Schor and Henry F. Majewski (Lincoln: University of Nebraska Press, 1984), 144.

Bibliography

Bart, Benjamin F. "Psyche into Myth: Humanity and Animality in Flaubert's *Saint-Julien.*" *Kentucky Romance Quarterly* 20 (1973), 317–342.

Bright, Michael. *Animal Language.* London: British Broadcasting Corporation, 1984.

Cavalieri, Paola, and Peter Singer, eds. *The Great Ape Project: Equality beyond Humanity.* London: The Fourth Estate, 1993.

Citati, Pietro. *Kafka*, trans. Raymond Rosenthal. New York: Alfred A. Knopf, 1990.

Culler, Jonathan. *Flaubert: The Uses of Uncertainty.* London: Paul Elek, 1974.

Dariosecq, Luc. "A Propos de Loulou." *The French Review* 31 (1958), 332–334.

de Waal, Frans. *Peacemaking among Primates.* Cambridge: Harvard University Press, 1989.

Flaubert, Gustave. *The Letters of Gustave Flaubert, 1830–1857*, ed. and trans. Francis Steegmuller. Cambridge, MA: Belknap Press of Harvard University Press, 1980.

———. *Three Tales*, trans. Robert Baldick. Harmondsworth, Middlesex: Penguin Books, 1961.

Gaillard, Françoise. "A Little Story about the *bras de fer;* or How History Is Made." In *Flaubert and Postmodernism*, eds. Naomi Schor and Henry F. Majewski. Lincoln: University of Nebraska Press, 1984. 84–99.

Griffin, Donald R. *Animal Minds.* Chicago: University of Chicago Press, 1992.

Griffin, Robert. *Rape of the Lock: Flaubert's Mythic Realism.* Lexington, Kentucky: French Forum, 1988.

Grözinger, Karl. *Kafka and Kabbalah,* trans. Susan Hecker Ray. New York: Continuum, 1994.

Hayman, Ronald. *Kafka: A Biography.* New York: Oxford University Press, 1981.

Janouch, Gustav. *Conversations with Kafka,* trans. Goronwy Rees. Frankfurt-am-Main: Andre Deutsch, 1971.

Kafka, Franz. *Franz Kafka: The Complete Stories,* ed. Nahum N. Glatzer. New York: Schocken Books, 1971.

Levine, Michael. *Writing through Repression: Literature, Censorship, Psychoanalysis.* Baltimore: Johns Hopkins University Press, 1994.

Madsen, Börge Gedsö. "Realism, Irony, and Compassion in Flaubert's *Un Coeur simple.*" *The French Review* 27 (February 1954), 253–258.

Masson, Jeffrey, and Susan McCarthy. *When Elephants Weep: The Emotional Lives of Animals.* New York: Delacorte Press, 1995.

Mendoza, Ramón. *Outside Humanity: A Study of Kafka's Fiction.* Lanham, MD: University Press of America, 1986.

Mitchell, Robert W., and Nicholas S. Thompson, eds. *Deception: Perspectives on Human and Nonhuman Deceit.* New York: State University of New York Press, 1986.

Morris, Desmond. *The Biology of Art: A Study of the Picture-Making Behavior of the Great Apes and Its Relationship to Human Art.* New York: Alfred A. Knopf, 1962.

Norris, Margot. *Beasts of the Modern Imagination: Darwin, Nietzsche, Kafka, Ernst, and Lawrence.* Baltimore: Johns Hopkins University Press, 1985.

Peronne-Moisés, Leyla. "*Quidquid volueris:* The Scriptural Education." In *Flaubert and Postmodernism*, eds. Naomi Schor and Henry F. Majewski. Lincoln: University of Nebraska Press, 1984. 139–159.

Politzer, Hanz. *Franz Kafka: Parable and Paradox.* Ithaca, New York: Cornell University Press, 1966.

Sartre, Jean-Paul. *The Family Idiot: Gustave Flaubert 1821–1857.* Vol. 1, trans. Carol Cosman. Chicago: University of Chicago Press, 1981.

Scholtmeijer, Marian. *Animal Victims in Modern Fiction: From Sanctity to Sacrifice.* Toronto: University of Toronto Press, 1993.

Steiner, George. "Humane Literacy." In *The Critical Moment: Essays on the Nature of Literature.* London: Faber and Faber, 1964. 21–30.

Stine, Peter. "Franz Kafka and Animals." *Contemporary Literature* 22 (Winter 1981), 58–80.

Stoltzfus, Bernard. "Point of View in '*Un Coeur simple.*'" *The French Review* 35 (1961), 19–25.

8 🦎

Taming the Beast
Animality in Wedekind and Nietzsche

Jennifer Ham

Morality is a menagerie. . . .

—Nietzsche, *Genealogy of Morals*

I lose nothing when I lose my life. I am not much more than a beast that has
been taught to dance by blows and a few meager morsels.

—Nietzsche, *Beyond Good and Evil*

Today I appeared to myself to be an animal tamer, who leaves the lion cage
backwards always keeping the beasts in sight so as not to be devoured from
behind, and this until the cage door is shut.

—Frank Wedekind, *Tagebücher*

Unlike the plow horses and other beasts of burden used in tilling and har-
vesting the land in an earlier, more agrarian age, many animals at the turn
of the century worked within the architecture of Europe's rapidly evolving
modern metropolises—Paris, Berlin, and Munich. As these cities became
increasingly industrialized, as the iron horse replaced the real horse, animals
vacated their roles in production as harnessed laborers and were subjected to
more nuanced and subtler forms of domestication as house pets,[1] zoo attractions, and circus entertainers. In the age of Darwin, when evolutionary theory
relaxed the boundary between humans and animals, the newly declared relative of man—the animal—was, in the experience of most urbanites, more
likely to be an exotic *fauve* from Africa or a dancing circus bear than a com-

mon herd animal. Modern Europeans had to renegotiate a relationship to animality in terms of exoticism, wildness, and clever performance.

As Germany and France colonized distant lands and brought foreign cultures within their national borders, and as cities incorporated an increasing number of parks and zoological gardens within their limits, man sought to domesticate new zones of animal wildness. Taming and training were the practices and allegories of these gestures of inclusion and exclusion, of the simultaneous narrowing and widening "distance within" the civilizing process. As a speechless subproletariat in the urban jungle, animals were unable to defend themselves against the abuses of the modern subjectivization process. Yet like the "downtrodden" of nineteenth-century socialism, the category of the animal also promised the most radical possibility for the political and philosophical re-invention and reinvigoration of the human race, an endeavor to which, as Heidegger notes, humanism itself had only served to obfuscate.[2] Animal savagery, victimhood, innocence, and vitality afforded the most daring *fin de siècle* theorists a space within which to think beyond traditional conceptions of humanism.

Two vitalist thinkers in particular, one a dramatist and the other a philosopher, were intrigued by the profound unknowability of animal experience and the implications that chasm held for the "all too human" human being. Before Artaud, Frank Wedekind invented a theater of animal cruelty and, before Brecht, delved to the depths of society, to the depths of monstrosity (Jack the Ripper), to define the human, while Friedrich Nietzsche spoke his philosophic voice through the mouths of lions, camels, and cows. Before discussing their writings individually, the specific historical practices that shaped the animals they encountered merit a closer look.

Animal Attractions

Popular entertainment, particularly at the zoo and the circus, provided spaces in the city where such continuities and discontinuities between man and animal could be dramatized, where humans could gawk at the great diversity in the animal kingdom and create their own animal acts, with and as animals. Zoos and circuses, however, having different institutional histories, offered these visitors different experiences of animality. As a product of the Classical Age, the zoo insisted on the radical separation and enclosure of species and emphasized their distance from man. The modern circus, on the other hand, harkens back to ancient hippodromes and more recently to the Renaissance, where it celebrated carnivalesque inversions and the exchange of human and animal identities.[3] These two institutions also domesticate the animal in different ways. In both displays animals are confined, in both they are caged; one alone, one together with man; one entrapping the animal in a deterministic discourse of science and instrumentality, the other centered on the release of animal vitality.

Menageries were some of the oldest displays of animals in captivity. Originally private collections at court, where animals were presented as royal decorations and living gifts, menageries later developed into zoological gardens which served primarily as static classification galleries and catalogues of natural history. As zoos began to employ hunters and trappers to expand their animal collections, new animals were added into the classificatory system—into the monkey house, the bear pit, and the raptor cage—according to their visual similarities with other animal forms, a practice Foucault refers to as a "nomination of the visual."[4]

But zoological gardens were undergoing institutional changes in the nineteenth century, changes which affected the public's understanding, attitudes toward, and firsthand knowledge of the category of animal.[5] Zoos lost some of their primary purpose as collections of living portraits and catered increasingly to public demands for sensation. Open animal parks allowed for the study of otherwise "unseen" aspects of animality as revealed by their instinctual and habituized behavior. Animal behavior in captivity fascinated large crowds, as did their trained aping of human behavior. Beyond their performances in private households as trained pets, riding toys, and hunting lures, urban animals were taught to perform strange acts ranging from apes eating with table utensils and sipping from teacups and Bengalese tigers playing hand organs, to kangaroo boxing matches and pigs walking tightrope. On stage, animals performed lead roles, appeared in processions, and were used as scenery. More violent public displays pitted animals against each other, as for example in badger- and bear-baiting meets and dog and cockfights in sporting clubs, variety theaters, and circus arenas. Citydwellers became more interested in animality as a vital and often dangerous organic force, rather than merely as a subject of morphological comparisons and erudite speculation. Staged animal violence, particularly those animal acts which riveted onlookers by their attempt to display animality unbound, seemed to threaten the modern sense of "civilized" society. On the heels of Germany's first *Tierschutzvereine* in Berlin and Munich, animal protection leagues helped to enact legislation in the early 1880s to repress such brutal displays of animal wildness in baitings,[6] and, in order to hide them from public view, to push them into suburbs and outlying areas.[7] However, modern society had not rid itself of the bestial, and popular entertainment continued to produce scenes of animal violence. After Joseph II lifted the ban on displaying ravenous animals to the public, zoos began staging regular attractions such as "feeding times," which featured dramatic attempts to stimulate animal appetite and voracity before the learned and poised public of the *Tiergarten*. Especially popular were the boa constrictors and exotic beasts of prey in the *Raubtierhaus*. Visiting the zoo at the turn of the century increased to the point of becoming a Sunday outing *de rigueur* for the bourgeoisie.

With the massive importation of exotic beasts from Asia, Africa, and India, visits to animal tents and zoological gardens in the 1890s also took on expanded functions, serving viewers not only as holding pens for scientific investigation, but also as crude exhibits of imperialist power. Exotic animals no longer existed merely in distant photographs and drawings from the "Dark Continent," but could be experienced as the colonized in firsthand, eye-to-eye encounters.

Paul Meyerheim's painting "In the Animal Tent" depicts a dramatic sideshow, a mixing of races, classes, and animals, and the conflicting discourses that define them all. In the background are traces of the older classificatory system and its cages, which the animals have somehow managed to escape. The artist has captured the unpredictable moment when humans become temporarily oblivious to their humanity, enthralled with the spectacle of exotic wildness in their

Figure 1. "In the Animal Tent," Paul Meyerheim. Sächsische Landesbibliothek, Dresden. Abteilung Deutsche Fotothek/Hüttel LD 1921 a.

Figure 2. "Der Hagenbeck kommt." Holzstich nach einer Zeichnung von W. A. Wellner für die "Lustigen Blätter," 1911. Bildarchiv Preussischer Kulturbesitz, Berlin.

midst. With a mixture of fascination and squeamishness, the bourgeois are drawn to the exotic animals and the "primitive" outsiders who display them. A strange mimicry prevails in which the colonial other helps the stifled Europeans through staged display to reconnect with their animality.[8]

This interest in the exotic coincided with an architectural shift toward openness which Carl Hagenbeck initiated in his famous animal park in Stellingen, outside Hamburg. His desire to create the illusion of animals' freedom in his expansive exhibits is literalized in the sketch above, where his uncaged imported animals are portrayed reciprocating the Kaiser's 1911 visit to the Stellingen zoo by storming the Brandenburg Gate and overrunning the streets of Berlin.

Although zoos still retained their primary function as catalogued collections, the animals were no longer to be caged by individual species in narrow pens, but rather in groups of multiple species, separated by deep nearly invisible moats, in huge panoramas. These panoramic exhibits served as *tableaux vivants*, as barless animal enclosures, affording total visibility and an increased sense of liberation. A recent photographic advance much popularized by aerial shots on city tourist postcards, panoramas in zoos transported the animals and, by extension, those attracted to them, back to the expanses of the animals' native wilds. An even more marked architectural shift toward openness occurred in the circus arena, where focus was directed from the riding ring up into the lofty heights above it and expanded to include additional outbuildings for the sideshow.

Wedekind's Circus Mundi

A great enthusiast of the circus, Frank Wedekind welcomed this move toward liberation, claiming: "In the circus one has freedom to move, that's something special."[9] In his play, *Fritz Schwigerling*, Katharina asks "Is it true, that one has free reign over one's person in the circus?"[10] Several other dramatists also saw the potential the circus had for revitalizing modern theater. Max Reinhardt was so impressed with the huge expanse of the Schuhmann Circus in Berlin that he refurbished its interior and transformed it into what became his famous *Großes Schauspielhaus* in 1918. The Futurists also believed in the theatrical promise of the open circus arena. Here Marinetti contrasts it to the zoo:

> The conventional theater exalts the inner life, professorial meditation, libraries, museums, zoos, monotonous crises of conscience, stupid analyses of feelings, in other words, psychology, whereas on the other hand the circus and variety theater exalt action, heroism, life in the open air. . . .[11]

Whereas the zoo, like conventional theater, encouraged static analyses, animal acts in the circus and variety theater exalted action and daring, not merely reenacts of the age-old struggle for physical primacy between man and beast, but a new dynamic which pitted a raw vitality of nature against what was increasingly seen as an effete and decadent culture of the 1890s.

Wedekind's experience of animals extended beyond his familiarity with the domesticated herd animals he encountered in Aarau, the rural Swiss village of his youth. His move to Paris in the late 1890s provided him opportunity to witness the public's fascination with animals performing for social amusement. The dramatist spent countless hours watching animals in such urban settings, behind the *Cirque d'Hiver*, at the *Jardin des Plantes*[12] and in the *Berliner Tiergarten* where he encountered them in captivity, as part of collections, but also on stage and in the ring, as dramatic performers. A frequent visitor to the zoological garden, Wedekind experienced the menagerie at feeding time and understood animals as powerful and dangerous creatures with rapacious appetites and survival instincts. He records in his diary the crowds' raucous enthusiasm at these displays of raw animal strength and viciousness and relates his commentary verbatim to audiences' hunger for good entertainment in his 1894 essay "The Middlesex Music Hall," which describes the tumult after the curtain falls on a variety act as "a cry to battle, a howling as in the muzzle of a beast, a roaring, screeching and shrieking like in a menagerie, when meat appears in front of a cage."[13]

Inspired by such scenes of animality, Wedekind not only enlisted live animals to perform alongside humans in some of his shorter dramatic narratives, particularly in the ballets and pantomimes he wrote for the Folies Bergère,[14] but he also relied on his personal experiences with these powerful creatures to demonstrate on stage the rootedness of animality in human behavior. In Act III of the "*Monstretragödie*," *Erdgeist* (Earth Spirit), Alwa depicts the audience reaction to Lulu's performance similarly: "A long boisterous applause and calls of Bravo are heard from outside—It's rocking as in the menagerie, when food appears before the cages."[15] The sensationalism of these descriptions of wild, frenzied audiences was heightened by the fact that, by the 1870s, outbursts of uncivilized public conduct in the theater were restrained. Audiences were brought under control and were no longer permitted to talk or call out in such fashion for repetitions during the performance.[16] Entrepreneurs and artists like Wedekind capitalized on the potential excitement such dangerous creatures could unleash in controlled society, an unfettered instinct, which Wedekind, like many Social Darwinists of his day, equated with the human response to fierce competition in societies based on free enterprise. According to Wedekind, when faced with such struggles for survival, humans consult with animal "wisdom" and adopt a *Raubtiermoral*, a morality of beasts.

Wedekind aims to demystify human morality by revealing its instinctual basis. In an essay entitled "Thoughts about Christmas" (1912), Wedekind contrasts this animal "ethic" to Christian morality and points to its biological origin in predatory instinct. He states:

> A lion captures an antelope after an arduous hunt and an eight-day fast. The act means first his sustenance and secondly the fulfillment of his social duty. Because the lion has the upper hand on the antelope and can therefore prevent the extinction of the Jericho roses, which the antelope devour with such relish. Does this act constitute work, play or pleasure?[17]

The question is meant as a rhetorical one—the lion exists outside such human categories and thwarts man's attempt to understand animal motivation in such anthropomorphic terms. The vigorous release of animal aggression, this instinctual "morality" flowing from some primal will to power, is not calculated and knows no ambition or malice. Its ethic is one of instinctual release, beyond good and evil. Wedekind claims "life itself is a damned clever beast, and it is not easy to subjugate it. Such beasts are pushed out of ethics, ethics leads an unrelenting battle against them, which usually ends with the executioner's axe. Result: Here ethical people, there the cursed and the damned."[18] Whereas animal violence is innocent, it is man who wields the executioner's axe and condemns the beast.

Perhaps nowhere in the urban landscape is the struggle between vitality and morality, between animal violence and cultural violence, staged more dramatically than in the circus ring, where the beast of prey encounters the ringmaster. In the *Prologue* to his play *Erdgeist*, Wedekind himself appears as an animal tamer: "Step right inside to look around the zoo, with burning pleasure, icy shudders too, come see the soulless brutes tamed by human genius. Come in, the show is just beginning!"[19] The tamer evokes the familiar dichotomy of "genius" and "soullessness," a wealth of intelligence facing a lack of conscience or moral subjectivity, and seems to emphasize the distinctness of these spheres; yet the gesture also invites in and implies the possibility of shared experience. Part of the irony of this passage is derived by the fact that "the soulless brutes tamed by human genius" refer to humans as well, that the downtrodden are also "soulless brutes," and that more clever "human geniuses" like Lulu and Dr. Schön manage to "tame" them. Wedekind is reversing the normal animal show—he is showing us his Nietzschean "menagerie" in which humans are animals tamed by other animals, in a show of "cruelty fighting cruelty."

Nietzsche uses the image of the animal tamer to comment on morality. From his *Genealogy of Morals:*

> Morality is a menagerie, its premise is, that iron bars are more useful than freedom, even for the captive, its other premise, that there are animal tamers who do not shrink from frightful means, who know how to handle red-hot iron. This horrific species, which accepts battle with the wild animal, calls itself "priest."[20]

From *Zarathustra:* "Cursed I call all who have only one choice: to become evil beasts or evil tamers of beasts; among such men I would not build my home."[21] For Nietzsche, these enforcers of civility are an even more brutal version of the very beasts they are trying to tame. Because their taming is self-interested, directed, sadistic, such masters of the ring represent for him "the cruelest animals." This process of "civilizing," of taming the wild, is a violent endeavor, one in which acts of cruelty are renamed cultural events. Nietzsche states:

> Virtually everything we call "higher culture" rests on the spiritualization and sublimation of cruelty [*Grausamkeit*]—that is my proposition; the "wild ani-

mal" has not been exterminated at all; it lives, it thrives, it has only become—deified. (III:139)

For Nietzsche, the circus act exposes the real ferocity of society: the drama of innocent human/animal natures subdued by cruel disciplinarians into conformity, efficiency, and productivity within the capitalist enterprise, an act of taming similar to the representation process. To make sense of the world, humans impose reason to domesticate images, to halt them, fix them in abstractions and static conclusions for easier consumption. In both acts, rational man attempts to discipline, to gain "power over," but in the process he loses touch with the source of that power, his animal vigor. Nietzsche posits these acts of animal instinct to be pure and unmediated, while human motivation appears as filtered through consciousness and as interested and potentially deceptive. Like Wedekind, Nietzsche understands animal aggression to be an unadulterated discharge of competing instinctual drives. While harsh and violent, it is not conniving, manipulative, or sadistic. For Nietzsche, since animal acts, particularly violent ones, operate in ignorance of moral constructs, their perpetrators, unlike man, are innocent: "Would that you were as perfect as animals at least! But animals have innocence."[22] Cultural acts, particularly violent ones, are immoral and perverse, and often make an art out of torture and killing. The *Tierbändiger* for Nietzsche is a most cruel monster, training animals to perform meaningless and inconsequential acts not for survival, but for others' amusement.

Wedekind and Nietzsche, while sharing the liberatory aspect of the circus act, held slightly different views of what was actually transpiring with the *Tierbändiger* in the lion cage. In Nietzsche, the animal tamer is an image of the cruelty and oppressiveness of contemporary Western culture forcing animal vitality into submission. Wedekind's view of the act of taming is more nuanced, deduced in part from his more intimate connection to circuses. Wedekind was fascinated by the subject of taming animals. He took a personal interest in animal tamers, played the role of *Tierbändiger* in his own plays, and even fancied himself to be one. "Today I appeared to myself to be an animal tamer, who leaves the lion cage backwards always keeping the beasts in sight so as not to be devoured from behind, and this until the cage door is shut."[23] The playwright informed himself in detail about taming practices through his contacts with some of the most famous animal trainers of Europe, such as Tescho, Herr Valende, and the Russian, Anatol Durow, who handled animals at the Folies Bergères.[24] Wedekind wrote a brief history of equipage and most likely witnessed the common assembly of flea circuses, learned pigs, singing mice, dancing bears, orangutans in pajamas, and bears on skates on the variety hall stages he also frequented.

Most animal tamers performing on European stages, including those Wedekind knew personally, had some familiarity with Carl Hagenbeck and the animal obedience school he founded. The school heralded a new approach to taming, one based not on the *wilde Dressur* of hot irons and revolvers, but rather on what Hagenbeck called the *prügelfreie Erziehungsmethode*, the concept of positive reinforcement. Hagenbeck claimed: "The period when unfortunate animals were driven to jump over a bar from dread of a whip or a red-hot iron—a disgrace to the humanity of man—is gone by. Sympathy with the animal, patience with its deficiencies has brought about a perfection of education which cruelty altogether failed to secure."[25] Von Osten, the trainer of the famous counting horse, Clever Hans, noted the connection between this *kinder, gentler* form of animal training and the one introduced as part of current childhood education reforms. Gustav Wyneken, an opponent of such school reforms, favored instead a "coercion of nature, an overcoming of the beast in humanity." Familiarity with this method of taming without physical violence prompted Wedekind to compare education and domestication in his play *Fritz Schwigerling*. Schwigerling, an animal tamer himself, is employed as a house tutor of languages for Prince Rogoschin's children, where instead of employing the whip he tells his pupils: "For every word you remember you will get a piece of sugar."[26]

Wedekind describes this more subtle approach to the civilizing process as an attempt to awaken the invisible aspects of the organism:

> And what we demand of humans on the highwire, on the trapeze, in the ring, in Roman wrestling matches, that is what we attempt through the most careful invisible means of education to awaken. The spirit, the soul, that lies sleeping in the beautiful organism, must awaken and come to its full rhythmic form.[27]

Wedekind senses right away, like Nietzsche, that the confrontation between wild *fauves* and tamers is a cruel spectacle reminiscent of similar demonstrations of brute strength in power struggles in society. But drawing from his own circus experiences, he suggests that taming is not always a matter of such crude domination, that, given the right pedagogy, humans and animals can collaborate in a learning that is in fact not oppressive but liberatory.

> Tickle ambition! Awaken self-esteem! In the circus one finds new concepts of education (*Bildung*). An animal must acknowledge his pride in order to overcome any conceivable obstacle with dignity, with assurance. I relax the limbs, so that the spirit pulses through, so that freedom and joy quiver in

every vein, until the wonder of it explodes in bright sparks from both eyes. The animal must swell his muscles and feel his breast heave whenever he confronts the world.[28]

Adorno echoes this notion in his *Dialectic of Enlightenment*, where he states: "Every partial stupidity of a man denotes a spot where the play of stirring muscles was thwarted instead of encouraged."[29]

Wedekind's animal tamers' ambition is to teach their subjects to overcome obstacles. He comments on this process of *overcoming* when describing Emerald the Jumping Horse performing in the circus ring:

> Many do not make it over the barriers their whole lives, others succeed at the first jump, others, it is only on the hundredth attempt. Emerald succeeded without difficulty, that is, he glided as if carried by an invisible hand, this after he failed two times, but with a new approach he lifts himself up and over the superhuman barrier.[30]

This is positive training, one that does not punish and censor through violent mimicry, one that attempts instead to release the natural power of animal vigor and assist creatures in overcoming their limitations. This is the drama of resistance, dependent on the strategy Wedekind found so attractive in the circus—its liberatory aesthetic. Unlike Nietzsche, Wedekind also admired the tamer. At least he, among cultural masters, risks his own life in the confrontation and has priviledged access to what both Wedekind and Nietzsche were after: the primal vital force of the lion—and the man. To free the animal, the unconscious, the body, and to harness it to perform astounding and creative acts of "becoming" rather than subjugate it in slavish attempts at imitation—that was the inspired role of tamers and handlers of beasts.

Nietzsche and Animals

Animals are central to Nietzsche's thinking. For Nietzsche, man is "the not-yet-fixed animal," the "cruellest animal," the "bravest animal," the "most interesting animal," indeed the "superanimal," but also the "sick animal." No other thinker in the Western tradition, except perhaps Aesop, has donned animal masks and animal speech more often than Nietzsche. Reading Nietzsche, as Margo Norris observes, "is like listening to a lion roaring in the wilderness."[31] His philosophy is one of the most radical responses to the Darwinian bridging of the gap between man and animal. The Nietzschean animal is not simply the product of its environment, but roams free.

While Nietzsche accepts the major premises of evolution and the idea of animal vestiges in man and even the whole notion of evolving forms and *becoming*, he rejects the teleological aspect of evolutionary thinking, which focused on progress along a selective continuum toward a perfect endpoint. Nietzsche's unease with evolutionary thinking does not emanate from the prospect that man evolved out of slime, but rather that man positions himself superior to the natural order, proclaiming: "'We have reached the destination, we are the destination, we are the perfection of nature'" (I:267). He corrects man's pompous vision of himself as the ultimate terminus of animal evolution: "He is most certainly not the great culmination of animal evolution. He is certainly not the crown of creation: every creature is next to him on the same level of perfection . . ." (II:1174). Nietzsche favors a more synchronous model, where "the whole animal and plant world develops not from lower to higher . . . but rather everything simultaneously, above, through and against one another" (III:741). Much in Nietzsche's response to Darwin is in fact devolutionary and regressive. "Humanity does not depict a development towards the better, or the stronger or higher. . . . Progress is simply a modern idea, that is to say a wrong idea" (II:1166).[32] The philosopher sees evolutionary thinking as a futile and misguided attempt to create distance from his animal being.

Nietzsche reflects such insights in his *Nachlaß der Achtzigerjahre:*

> When people talk of "humanity" they have a basic idea of something which "separates" and distinguishes Man from nature. But there is no such separation in reality: the "natural" qualities and the ones called really "human" are inseparably intertwined. Man in his highest and noblest powers is wholly nature and bears her uncanny dual character. (III:291)

Nietzsche, who was quite aware of the permeability of the division, saw a need to "consider where the beast ends and the man begins" (V:149) and sought to overturn the theological and metaphysical definition of man in the philosophical tradition. "We no longer deduce mankind from 'spirit' or from 'divinity,' we have put him back amongst the animals . . ." (II:1174). "Now the history of mankind is merely the continuation of the history of animals and plants; indeed in the lowest depths of the sea the universalist historian finds traces of himself in the slime" (I:266).

The prophet Zarathustra tells mankind: "You have travelled the way from worm to man and much in you is still worm. Once you were apes and still now

Man is more ape than any ape" (II:279). Like many of his contemporary vital-
ists, such as Haeckel and Uexküll,[33] Nietzsche rejected the deterministic thrust
in Darwin's argument and assumed that there were processes in living organisms which were "beyond" the observable causalities and mechanisms of the
laws of physics and chemistry. Such Cartesian means of understanding animality produce instead a vitalistically castrated animal. Nietzsche's project on the
other hand was to reawaken man to his primal origin and reacquaint him with
instinct.

Nietzsche posits that man's animality is at the very basis of morality and
culture. Indeed, for him, "the whole moral phenomenon [is] an animal one."
"Everything we refer to as 'Socratic virtues,' is 'animalistic': a consequence of
those drives, which teach one to look for nourishment and to avoid enemies"
(I:1032). Animal survival instincts underlie all human intelligence, psychology, and behavior. Man's "higher" faculties and ambitions, including creative
acts are rooted in physiology, that is, in animal instincts emanating from the
material body. Here Nietzsche forwards one of his most radical formulations
of the animal act when he discusses aesthetics as "applied physiology"
(II:1041). For Nietzsche, it is essentially in the body, in its animal drives and
impulses, that the origins of culture are to be found. "All conscious life, the
spirit, the soul, the heart, goodness and virtue: in whose service are these
things? In . . . basic animal functions: above all the advancement/expansion of
life" (IX:450). Human morality appears here as an unhealthy concealment of
animal functions, which seek their natural release in expressive vitality.

Man has lost consciousness of his animal vigor, his "*Tierverstand*," or animal
sense, yet remains vaguely envious of beasts and nostalgic for their blissful
"forgetfulness," for their animal happiness ("*das Glück des Tieres*"), and their
relief from the burden of conscience and the memory of the past.[34] Unlike
humans, Nietzsche's animals are "*unhistorisch*," tied only "to the tethering post
of the moment" (I:211). Unable to lie or put on airs, the animal cannot help
but be honest, "appearing in every moment only as that which it is" (I:211).
Man, on the other hand, the great sublimator of instinct, has become an
imposter, "*ein vielfaches, verlogenes, künstliches und undurchsichtiges Tier*," a
chameleonlike coward deceiving himself through hypocrisy and self-denial.
This is Man, "*das kranke Tier*," "*das Haustier*," "*das Herdentier*," the sick, bur-
dened, and subjugated animal who "has lost his healthy animal sense" (II:152)
and needs therapy. "Man is something that should be overcome" (IX:279).
And in many ways Nietzsche's is just that protracted attempt to allow Man to
overcome himself and become, as the subtitle to *Ecce Homo* suggests, what he
already is—an animal.

This feat of recovering, of *becoming*, of recuperating implies a series of animal acts, some of which involve embracing animal power, others forging a "pathos of distance," a thwarting of cultural mechanisms. *Becoming*, unlike the normal philosophical exercise of apprehending *being*, is not a matter of ascertaining a "what?," of grasping a notion or concept. *Becoming* is an experience of difference which unites instead of divides, an experience of the line or boundary as a drawing together, a configuring, not a drawing apart. "To become what one is, one must not have the faintest notion of 'what' one is."[35] Both of these acts simultaneously invoke both an ability to remember and to forget—remembering an image of an attractive animal essence, and forgetting or letting go of that which barricades the two spheres, that which is *all too human*.

This premoral vitality of becoming is the source of all human achievements. Great artists learn to embrace and harness their animal natures awakened by competition and the desire for a "victory over *Nebenbuhler*" (I:559). Man's desire for the truth is also to be found in animal instinct. "The struggle of systems, including scruples of theoretical knowledge, is a struggle of particular instincts. The so-called drive for knowledge can be traced back to a drive to adapt and overcome . . ." (III:734). Nietzsche suggests that to take the animal out of the human is to render the human inhuman. "To call the taming of an animal its 'improvement' is for our ears almost a joke. Anyone who knows what goes on in menageries has doubts as to whether the beast is 'improved' there. . . . It is no different with the tamed human being whom the priest has 'improved'" (II:979). To eradicate or pervert the human's animal impulses is to sublimate his creativity. "Man needs what is most evil in him for what is best in him—that whatever is most evil is his best power" (II:464). "Those of his capacities which are terrible and considered inhuman may even be the fruitful soil from which alone all humanity in impulses, deeds and works can grow forth" (III: 291). To remove or pervert man's animality is to eradicate the basis of his creativity, his intelligence, and his higher pursuits. If man denies his instincts, they will become poisonous and make him sick, "until their strength, their will to power turns against itself" and finally kill him. In this, Nietzsche shares Freud's belief that the greatest threat to psychological health is not the immoral impulses of the id, but rather its damming up and turning inward.

We are tempted to believe Nietzsche when he claims that man stands with "every living creature next to him on the same level of perfection" (II:1174). But upon closer inspection, we notice him in *Wille zur Macht* imposing his own heirarchy, one based not on the supposed perfection of animals' biological forms, but rather according to unseen "quanta of power," their degree of wildness and their power to evade domestication.

Nietzsche's *scala naturae* consists of two basic groups: the weaker *"Sklaventiere,"* or domesticated animals in the service of man, and the *"Raubtiere,"* the less slavish animals of prey. Counted among his *"Sklaventiere"* are the ruminants, livestock, and the various beasts of burden, cows, and camels. These are the sick animals bearing the Kantian burden of the "thou shalt," without question or complaint. "Like a camel, he [man] kneels down and lets himself be well loaded." "We are told: 'Yes, life is a grave burden.' But only man is a grave burden for himself." These are the "sick animals" (II:862), "the weak seeking refuge in the herd, a social organ "geared toward standing still and maintaining, there is nothing creative in it" (IX:202). But the herd animal is more than just a sociological type for Nietzsche. Herd behavior actually disproves the claims of evolutionary science. Roaming in herds and flocks is a survival strategy, yet it actually prevents the strong individual from surviving and results instead in "the unavoidable promotion of the average, even below-average types" (III:748).

Predators, on the other hand, exist apart and derive their value not merely from group belonging. Leaders of the herd possess a quite different animal nature, that of "the independent, or the 'animals of prey'" (IX:203), at a distance from the flock, a kind of nomad, evading the codes of the settled.[36] It is as if, with animals as well as humans, all do not submit equally to the dictates of the environment and natural selection: some huddle together in fear and conformity; some strike out on their own; it is useless to invoke a universal law of evolution to explain both the existence of the pigeon and the eagle.

Of all the beasts of prey, Nietzsche felt man to be "the best beast of prey" (IX:456). But in *Genealogy of Morals*, it is the lion, the *blond beast* who, although the most commonly misunderstood of Nietzsche's animals, bears the largest burden of the philosopher's doctrine on culture and morals. The lion is Nietzsche's barbarian: "the beast of prey is unmistakable, the magnificent 'blond beast' lustfully prowling after prey and victory; this hidden basic layer needs a release now and then and must return to the wilderness" (II:786).[37] Cultural renewal requires a "return to wildness," to power, on the part of an exemplary few. The animal *par excellance* in turn-of-the-century Germany, the lion, has become the cultural hero, the philosopher himself, in Nietzsche's antithetical scheme.

In the present climate of technological dogmatism and political disinterest, the extravagant animal acts of Nietzsche and Wedekind hold out their appeal. The wild, animalistic philosophy of Nietzsche could serve as an antidote to the conformism and false security of the oppressive mass culture promised by technology. And in a post-revolutionary, apolitical climate, Wedekind's rollicking *Circus mundi* suggests access to that gratuitous force which bonds people together as animals.

Notes

1. For further discussion of pets in the nineteenth century, see Kathleen Keete, *The Beast in the Boudoir: Petkeeping in Nineteenth-Century Paris* (Berkeley, CA: University of California Press, 1995) and Susan Hamilton, "Pets and Scientific Subjects: Constructions of the Animal Body in Victorian Anti-vivisection Periodicals," in Anthony Purdy, *Literature and the Body* (Atlanta: Rodopi, 1992), 77–89.

2. Martin Heidegger, "Letter on Humanism" in David Farrell Krell, ed., *Basic Writings* (San Francisco: Harper Collins, 1993), 217–265. For further discussion of the end of humanism, see Diana Fuss, ed., *Human, All Too Human* (New York: Routledge, 1996).

3. For a complete discussion of the Renaissance carnival, see M. Bakhtin, *Rabelais and His World* (Bloomington: Indiana University Press, 1987).

4. Michel Foucault, *The Order of Things: An Archeology of the Human Sciences*, trans. A. Sheridan (London: Tavistock, 1989).

5. For further information about the development of zoos see Stephen St. C. Bostock, *Zoos and Animal Rights* (New York: Routledge, 1993); Henri Ellenberger, "The Mental Hospital and the Zoological Garden," in Joseph Klaits, ed., *Animals and Man in Historical Perspective* (New York: Harper and Row, 1974); Carl Hagenbeck, *Von Tieren und Menschen* (Munich: List, 1954); Robert Bendiner, *The Fall of the Wild, the Rise of the Zoo* (New York: Dutton, 1981); Gustave Loisel, *Histoire des menageries de l'antiquité à nos jours* (Paris: O. Doin, 1912); Wilfrid Blunt, *The Ark in the Park: The Zoo in the Nineteenth Century* (London: Hamish Hamilton, 1976).

6. Animal baitings occurred on an even larger scale in the *Hetzgärten* of the Renaissance. See Heinz-Georg Klos, *Berlin und sein Zoo* (Berlin: Haude & Spener, 1978), 15.

7. Lynn Abrams, "The Taming of Popular Entertainment," in *Worker's Culture in Imperial Germany: Leisure and Recreation in the Rhineland and Westphalia* (New York: Routledge, 1992), 96.

8. Several schools of painting evolved out of perceived connections between primitive animality and primal creativity at the turn of the century—for example, the "Fauves," "Die Brücke," and "Der blaue Reiter."

9. Frank Wedekind, *Die Tagebücher: Ein erotisches Leben*, ed. Gerhard Hay (Frankfurt: Athenäum Verlag, 1986), 231. All translations of Wedekind texts are mine unless otherwise stated. (". . . im Zirkus könne man sich bewegen, das sei was anderes.")

10. Frank Wedekind, *Gesammelte Werke*, vol. 2 (Munich: Georg Müller, 1912), 218. ("*Ist es richtig, daß man im Zirkus die freie Verfügung über seine Person behält?*")

11. R. W. Flint, *Marinetti: Selected Writings* (New York: Fararr, Strauss and Giroux, 1972), 120.

12. Rilke also made habitual visits to the *Jardin des Plantes*, which inspired his famous animal poems. For the inspiration this Parisian zoological garden provided him and other turn of the century writers and painters, see Luc Vezin, *Les Artistes au Jardin des Plantes* (Paris: Herscher, 1990).

13. Frank Wedekind, "Middlesex Musikhall" (1894), in *Gesammelte Werke*, vol. 9 (Munich: Georg Müller, 1921), 336.

14. One such flea pantomime was *Die Flöhe oder Der Schmerzentanz*; another, entitled *Bethel*, included a steady stream of exotic animals trained to perform.

15. Frank Wedekind, *Prosa, Dramen, Verse* (Munich: Albert Langen, 1960), 430.

16. David Blackbourn and Geoff Eley, *The Peculiarities of German History: Bourgeois Society and Politics in Nineteenth-Century Germany* (New York: Oxford University Press, 1984), 201.

17. Frank Wedekind, "*Weihnachtsgedanken*" (1912), in *Gesammelte Werke*, vol. 9 (Munich: Georg Müller, 1921), 404.

18. Frank Wedekind, "*Kunst und Sittlichkeit*," in *Gesammelte Werke*, vol. 9 (Munich: Georg Müller, 1921), 379.

19. Frank Wedekind, *Five Tragedies of Sex*, trans. Frances Fawcett and Stephen Spender (London: Vision Press, 1952), 101.

20. Friedrich Nietzsche, *Sämtliche Werke in zwölf Bänden* (Stuttgart: Alfred Kröner Verlag, 1964), 9:270. All translations of Nietzsche's works are my own unless otherwise stated. All subsequent references to Nietzsche's works, noted parenthetically in the text, will be to the volumes abbreviated as follows unless otherwise indicated:

    I: *Werke in drei Bänden*, vol. 1, ed. Karl Schlechta (Munich: Carl Hanser, 1960);
    II: *Werke in drei Bänden*, vol. 2, ed. Karl Schlechta (Munich: Carl Hanser, 1960);
    III: *Werke in drei Bänden*, vol. 3, ed. Karl Schlechta (Munich: Carl Hanser, 1960).

21. Friedrich Nietzsche, *Thus Spoke Zarathustra*, in *The Portable Nietzsche*, ed. and trans. Walter Kaufmann (New York: Viking Press, 1954), 307.

22. Friedrich Nietzsche, *Thus Spoke Zarathustra*, in *The Portable Nietzsche*, ed. and trans. Walter Kaufmann (New York: Viking Press, 1954), 165.

23. Frank Wedekind, *Die Tagebücher: Ein erotisches Leben*, ed. Gerhard Hay (Frankfurt: Athenäum Verlag, 1986), 304.
    "... erschien ich mir wie ein Tierbändiger, der rückwarts den Löwenkäfig verläßt und, um nicht zerissen zu werden, keine der Bestien aus dem Auge lassen darf, bis die Tür sich geschlossen."

24. Frank Wedekind, *Die Tagebücher*, ed. Gerhard Hay (Frankfurt: Athenäum Verlag, 1986), 235.

25. Carl Hagenbeck, *Beast and Men: Carl Hagenbeck's Experiences for Half a Century among Wild Animals*, trans. Hugh S. R. Elliot and A. G. Thacker (London, New York, Bombay, Calcutta: Longmans, Green and Co., 1909), 118.

26. Frank Wedekind, *Prosa, Dramen, Verse* (Munich: Albert Langen, 1960), 324.

27. Frank Wedekind, *Prosa, Dramen, Verse* (Munich: Albert Langen, 1960), 349.

28. Sol Gittleman's translation of Wedekind's *Fritz Schwigerling*, in *Frank Wedekind* (New York: Twayne Publishers, 1969), 54.

29. Max Horkheimer and Theodor W. Adorno, "Man and Animal," in *Dialectic of Enlightenment* (New York: Herder and Herder, 1972), 257.

30. Friedrich Nietzsche, *Gesammelte Werke*, vol. 9 (Munich: Georg Müller, 1921), 294.

31. Margot Norris, *Beasts of the Modern Imagination: Darwin, Nietzsche, Kafka, Ernst, and Lawrence* (Baltimore: Johns Hopkins University Press, 1985), 80.

32. See Uwe Japp's article, "Nietzsches Kritik der Modernität," in Ulrich Fülleborn, *Das Neuzeitliche Ich in der Literatur des 18. und 20. Jahrhunderts* (Munich: W. Fink, 1988), 234–243; and Robert Gooding-Williams, "Nietzsche's Pursuit of Modernism," *New German Critique* 41, Spring/Summer 1987, for a further discussion of Nietzsche's relation to Modernism.

33. The eighteenth-century debate between vitalism, the notion that organisms are controlled by a sensitive soul, and mechanism, which considered organisms as machines to be comprehended in regard to their movements and forces, continued to be hotly debated in Germany in the field of physiology during Nietzsche's era.

34. For a very different "neoanthropomorphic" discussion of "animal happiness" see Vicki Hearne, *Animal Happiness* (New York: Harper Collins, 1995).

35. Friedrich Nietzsche, *Ecce Homo*, in *The Basic Writings of Nietzsche*, trans. Walter Kaufmann, (New York: Random House, 1968), 710.

36. Interesting parallels exist between Nietzsche's depiction of the predatory desire to exist apart from the herd and the kind of "extrinsic and decodifying" thinking which Gilles Deleuze refers to as "nomadic thought." See Gilles Deleuze, "Nomad Thought," in *The New Nietzsche: Contemporary Styles of Interpretation*, ed. David Allison (Cambridge, MA: MIT Press, 1985), 148–149.

37. A lust for destruction, victory, power, and domination are also the traits which constitute the notion of the barbarians, the "noble races" among which Nietzsche counted the Germans. "The profound, icy mistrust that Germans arouse as soon as they come to power, in our times again—is still a late form of that indelible horror with which for centuries Europe looked on at the raging of the blond Germanic beast (although there is hardly a conceptual let alone blood-kinship between the old Germanic race and us Germans)," (II:786). For further discussion of Nietzsche's "blond beast" see Detlef Brennecke, "'*Die blonde Bestie,*'" *Germanisch-romanische Monatsschrift*, 51, 1970.

Bibliography

Abrams, Lynn. "The Taming of Popular Entertainment," in *Worker's Culture in Imperial Germany: Leisure and Recreation in the Rhineland and Westphalia*. New York: Routledge, 1992.

Bendiner, Robert. *The Fall of the Wild, the Rise of the Zoo*. New York: Dutton, 1981.

Blackbourn, David, and Geoff Eley. *The Peculiarities of German History: Bourgeois Society and Politics in Nineteenth-Century Germany*. New York: Oxford University Press, 1984.

Bostock, Stephen St. C. *Zoos and Animal Rights*. New York: Routledge, 1993.

Brennecke, Detlef. "'*Die blonde Bestie,*'" *Germanisch-romanische Monatsschrift*, 51, 1970.

Ellenberger, Henri. "The Mental Hospital and the Zoological Garden," in Joseph Klaits, *Animals and Man in Historical Perspective*, New York: Harper and Row, 1974.

Flint, R. W. *Marinetti: Selected Writings*. New York: Fararr, Strauss and Giroux, 1972.

Gittleman, Sol. *Frank Wedekind*. New York: Twayne Publishers, 1969.

Gooding-Williams, Robert. "Nietzsche's Pursuit of Modernism," *New German Critique*, 41, Spring/Summer 1987.

Hagenbeck, Carl. *Von Tieren und Menschen*. Munich: List, 1954.

Japp, Uwe. "*Nietzsches Kritik der Modernität*," in Ulrich Fülleborn, *Das Neuzeitliche Ich in der Literatur des 18. und 20. Jahrhunderts*, Munich: W. Fink, 1988.

Loisel, Gustave. *Histoire des menageries de l'antiquité à nos jours*. Paris: O. Doin, 1912.

Nietzsche, Friedrich. *Gesammelte Werke*. Munich: Georg Müller, 1921.

———. *The Portable Nietzsche*, ed. and trans. Walter Kaufmann. New York: Viking Press, 1954.

———. *Sämtliche Werke in zwölf Bänden*. 12 vols. Stuttgart: Alfred Kröner Verlag, 1964.

———. *Werke in drei Bänden*. 3 vols., ed. Karl Schlechta. Munich: Carl Hanser, 1960.

Norris, Margot. *Beasts of the Modern Imagination: Darwin, Nietzsche, Kafka, Ernst, and Lawrence*. Baltimore: Johns Hopkins University Press, 1985.

Pasley, Malcolm, ed. *Nietzsche: Imagery and Thought*. Berkeley: University of California Press, 1978.

Wedekind, Frank. *Five Tragedies of Sex*, trans. Frances Fawcett and Stephen Spender. London: Vision Press, 1952.

———. *Gesammelte Werke*. Munich: Georg Müller, 1921.

———. *Prosa, Dramen, Verse*. Munich: Albert Langen, 1960.

———. *Die Tagebücher: Ein erotisches Leben*, ed. Gerhard Hay. Frankfurt: Athenäum Verlag, 1986.

9 🦎

On Being "The Last Kantian in Nazi Germany"
Dwelling with Animals after Levinas

David Clark

for Tilottama Rajan

Apes too have organs that can grasp, but they do not have hands. The hand is infinitely different from all grasping organs—paws, claws, or fangs—*different by an abyss of essence.* Only a being that can speak, that is, think, can have hands.

—Martin Heidegger, *What Is Called Thinking?*

I saw well why the gods do not speak to us openly, nor let us answer. Till that word can be dug out of us, why should they hear the babble that we think we mean? How can they meet us face to face till we have faces?

—C. S. Lewis, *Till We Have Faces*

I. The Butchery of Everyday Life

"The Last Kantian in Nazi Germany": this is how Emmanuel Levinas describes "Bobby," the dog who befriends him during his "long captivity" in a slave labor camp.[1] Thirty years after the fact, Levinas briefly tells the story of his terrible days in Camp 1492, days whose numbing inhumanity is momentarily relieved by the arrival of an animal that offers a semblance of respect. I say "semblance" because Levinas's experience of Bobby is informed by conventional assumptions about animality that make it impossible for him straightforwardly to attribute dutifulness to a creature that is not human. *Mon semblable—mon frère:* Bobby doubles for the human, yet he is not human, and this indeterminacy about his ontological and moral status at once triggers Levinas's most dogmatic claims about nonhuman life and tests the limits of their coherence. The enigma of the animal evokes contradictory thoughts and feelings in Levinas: it is these sentiments, and the axioms by which they are articulated, that form the focus of my remarks in this essay. What is clear is that the dog provides welcome succor to the prisoners, but the fact that he is the last of his kind reminds us that he performs this duty—if duty is what it is—in an ashen world on the brink of extinction. Yet Levinas's essay does not begin with such searing recollections. The first half of it is taken up with a spritely reflection upon Talmudic readings of Exodus 22:31, in which God grants certain eating rights to dogs. How can creatures of "pure nature" be said to possess "rights" (151)? What supreme act of faithfulness to "man" prompted God to consecrate them in this unusual way? Levinas dallies with the "talmudic Doctors" who attempt to resolve these questions, but their "high hermeneutics" and "subtle exegesis" (152) are, finally, not to his liking. As he says, he is always "thinking of Bobby" (151), and that thought unerringly returns him to the singularity and the solitude of the true task at hand, the work that his essay is destined to do: namely, bearing witness. No "allegories," no animal fables of any kind, after Camp 1492.

Levinas sets the scene with the barest of details: "There were seventy of us in a forestry commando unit for Jewish prisoners of war," he recalls; "the French uniform still protected us from Hitlerian violence" (152). As "soldiers" rather than as "civilians"—the difference, we are reminded, lies in the sheer contingency of a piece of cloth—the prisoners are spared extermination in a death camp. But of course there is nothing to shelter them from other acts of brutality, acts whose informing prejudice, Levinas suggests, is as old as Judaism itself. An "archetypal" ruthlessness characterizes his captors, for whom the Jews have never been more than "animals," and for whom bestialization therefore remains the chief means by which to render the Jews humanly unthinkable. Laden with animalistic rhetoric, Levinas's account painfully reproduces the biologism that naturalizes his incarceration. "We were beings entrapped in their species" (153), he recalls, in effect turning the "paradox" that had quickened the minds of the "talmudic Doctors" inside out: once reduced to a creature of "pure nature," the Jew obliges no one, bears no rights. His sentences weighty with the burden of the memory of this humiliation, Levinas glimpses himself through the voracious eyes of his captors, eyes that "stripped us of our human skin":

We were subhuman, a gang of apes. A small inner murmur, the strength and wretchedness of persecuted people, reminded us of our essence as thinking creatures, but we were no longer part of the world. . . . We were . . . beings without language. (153)

Robbing the prisoners of the power to speak, the Nazis cause them to question their ability to reason, language and thinking being the exemplary characteristics by which the human has always been decisively distinguished from the animal. What breaks the binding force of this animalization is an animal, "Bobby." Wandering into the camp, the dog "unwittingly" bears witness to the humanity of Levinas and the other prisoners, remembering what the Nazis, in their unremitting savagery, have effaced. Like some strange, reversed *pharmakos*, Bobby is cast *into* (not out of) the mock-polis of the camp, restoring it—albeit momentarily—to a semblance of ethical "health." Levinas asks: Are we not *men?* In his own way, Bobby answers: yes, and again, yes!

He would appear at morning assembly and was waiting for us as we returned, jumping up and down and barking in delight. For him, there was no doubt that we were men. . . . This dog was the last Kantian in Nazi Germany. . . . (153)

The animal act described in this passage, the focal point of the essay's concluding paragraph, gives us much to think about. Suffice it to say that I will be able here to touch upon only some of its complexities. If humans are capable of treating others like animals, it may also be true that animals are capable of treating others *like humans.* Or like humans *should* be treated, "Kant" here operating as a kind of prosopopoeia for dutifulness, and for the "oughtness" that is ordinarily said only to tug on the conscience of human beings. Is Levinas's figure merely a sentimentalizing anthropomorphism, improperly attributing human qualities to an animal who in turn finds those qualities in the prisoners, that is, grasps that they are "men," not animals? The specter of falling into such pathos haunts Levinas's text; midway through the essay, he stops himself: "But enough of allegories! We have read too many fables and we are still taking the name of a dog in the figurative sense" (152). It could be said that it is Levinas's allergy to animal fables that propels his narrative toward the concluding account of the slave camp, where, he hopes, a dog is just a dog. Even here, though, he must work against the allegorizing resonances of his own story, for Bobby's apparently dutiful behavior unavoidably recalls the scene in Homer's *Odyssey* where Ulysses is greeted by his faithful hound, the last true Greek in Ithaca. Unable *not* to anthropomorphize Bobby,

Levinas nevertheless preemptively attempts to distinguish his account from its epic pretext: "No, no!" he exclaims, Bobby and I are *not* like that dog and his master, for "they were in Ithaca and the Fatherland," but "Here," in Nazi Germany, "we were nowhere." "Nowhere" means a historical moment—the Holocaust—where mawkishness is utterly irrelevant, "beyond pathos," as Levinas says elsewhere.[2] But it also means the dystopia of Camp 1492, where neither human nor animal is at home, the placeless place where the animalization of the Jews makes it *imperative* to (re)think the uses to which the ontotheological distinction between the two realms can be put.[3] "We," who? Who is my neighbor? To whom (or what) are obligations owed? With whom (or what) do I dwell? Levinas's work insistently raises these fundamental questions, the protoethical openings for thought that come before every ontology. What matters above all is thinking rather than dissolving the distinction between the *ethos* of the human and the animal. The "Nazi Germany" that has brought the Kantians to the threshold of extinction is all the evidence that one would ever need to grasp the foolishness and the mortal danger that comes of blurring the boundaries between human and nonhuman life. As Richard Klein points out, the "Nazi *Lebensphilosophie* . . . explicitly assimilated human striving to the impulses of animal instinct."[4] We see at least one reason why Levinas is so nervous about the prospect of anthropomorphizing Bobby: the sentimental humanization of animals and the brutal animalization of humans are two sides of the same assimilating gesture. In humanizing the animal, these fictions risk the tropological reversal by which persons are in turn bestialized, which is to say the biologisms and racisms that naturalize ethnic cleansings and the creation of concentration camps, whether in Nazi Germany or present-day Bosnia.

Those who object to the impropriety of anthropomorphic projections, Heidegger once pointed out, presuppose a punctual knowledge of what it is to be properly human.[5] But the propriety of "humanity" is what is least certain and most vulnerable for Levinas, exposed as it is to the infinite heteronomy of others. Do these others include animal others? Are we not responsible for those nonhuman others, as they sometimes appear to be toward us? But who is "*us*"? If the thought of "the animal" is in question, so too, inevitably, is the thought of "the human" with which it has always been inextricably bound. Bobby's delightful greetings compel Levinas to consider how it is that a "mere" animal could treat him with more dignity than his human captors, captors who could be said to behave like animals[6] and to incarcerate their prisoners like animals—tellingly, fantastically, the "animal" is available as a figure for both master and slave—if it were not for the fact that the question of what constitutes the animal is precisely what Bobby's dutiful behavior raises and complicates. We might also say that, unlike the Nazis, Bobby meets and engages Levinas *face to face*, were it not for the fact that what constitutes a face, and whether animals can be said to possess a face—a question to which I will return—is also implicitly in question here, as it is elsewhere in his work.

What is apparent is that sentimentalizing anthropomorphisms make genuinely ethical thought, whether we understand this in Kantian or Levinasian terms, impossible, for, under the guise of a certain pathos, they peremptorily annihilate differences in the name of the (human) same. We must therefore stop "taking the name of a dog in the figurative sense" (152), Levinas insists: that is the denunciation of rhetoric that acts as the engine of his essay. Figuring animals, we *con*figure the human. But at what cost to the animals? What is more violently exclusionary: that the Jews are animalized by the Nazis, or that the "animal" has for so long been used as a marker by which ferociously to abject the other? Right away, Levinas's essay invites us to think counterintuitively, for how, as is said in good conscience, can we even consider the obligations that are due animals, "the debt," as he says, "that is always open" (152) to them, when it is the obligations to the *human* other that are most cruelly at risk, that most palpably deserve consideration in a Holocaust testimony?

Levinas's essay is remarkable for bringing these two questions into such close proximity, almost suggesting that the two forms of prejudice—one against the Jews, the other against animals—are in some way comparable. The animalization of human beings leads directly to the most horrific consequences, to be sure; but before we hear of this, before Levinas tells us about what it feels like to be incarcerated as a beast by the Nazis, he reminds us that the animalization of animals is in its own way also deadly, and thus worthy of our concern. How are animals animalized by humans? Levinas's answer is at once complex and brutally simple: *we eat meat.* Cloaked in a certain mocking humor, Levinas's opening paragraph circles warily around the "carnivorous virility"[7] of human beings. Like the dogs described in the biblical pretext for his essay, we too consume "flesh that is torn by beasts in the field." We *are* those beasts, devouring each other in "the horrors of war," sublimating our carnivorous desires into "hunting games," and finally, eating meat. This, from his opening paragraph:

> There is enough, there, to make you a vegetarian again. If we are to believe Genesis, Adam, the father of us all, was one! There is, at least, enough there, to make us want to limit, through various interdictions, the butchery that every day claims our "consecrated" mouths! (151)

Remember this, Levinas advises, "as you plunge your fork into your roast." *We are killing animals,* even if the murderousness of that sacrifice is effaced at the dinner table, while our mouths water and our eyes grow big. The consecration of flesh-sharing *is* its erasure, the spiritualization and *denegation* of its gory reality. Derrida: "The putting to death of the animal, says this denegation, is not a murder" (*EW* 283). But this other scene, the every day "butchery" behind the veneer of civilization, competes with yet another. Levinas makes a point of telling us that, all along, he has had something else firmly in mind. While he speaks to us about our carnivorous appetite for the animal other, the memory of another animal intrudes. He has always already intruded: "I am thinking of Bobby," he writes, in the present progressive tense. These two thoughts, then, are *contiguous*, thought together, even if, in the narrative of the essay, they are necessarily unpacked one after the other. It is Levinas's way of narrowing the distance between them without actually saying that they are the same thing. The implications of this contiguity are obvious and troublesome: the "noncriminal" putting to death of the animal is put alongside the "noncriminal" putting to death of the European Jews. About what the two thoughts say to each other, Levinas is pointedly silent: it is enough, for now, in the aftermath of "Hitler's exterminations" (xiii), that they are considered jointly. For a scandalous instant, Levinas acts the part that Bobby will more or less play at the end of the essay, that is, as the one who, in the absence of others and in the absence of a respect for the other, *testifies* to the worthiness of the imprisoned and the murdered. Indeed, he reminds us that these others *are* murdered, butchered so that we may eat well. Here, it is *he*, not Bobby, who witnesses the biologistic, naturalized, and consecrated degradation of the other. The testimonial logic of his essay's narrative could then be expressed in this way: first, human (Levinas) on behalf of animal, then, animal (Bobby) on behalf of human. The momentous implications of this chiasmic ethical exchange are irresistible. As John Llewelyn argues, Levinas here "all but proposes an analogy between the unspeakable human holocaust and the unspoken animal one" (114).[8] For all his perspicuity about Levinas's essay, however, Llewelyn may slightly understate what he sees there. By characterizing the essay as doing everything *but* making such a proposition, we must be careful not to shrink from its double scene of sacrifice. For is this not *exactly* the proposition that Levinas is making, even and especially if he does not literally write it out for us to read? Levinas proposes this analogy between sacrifices by *not* proposing it, in a whispering gesture that is strategically affirmative *and* negative: "yes," because there is no denying the implications of Levinas's opening meditation on what it means, what it really means, to be an eater of flesh; "no," because Levinas does not simply equate the two events, much less call them by the same name, *l'Holocauste*. Perhaps the point is not so much that Levinas makes the analogy between animal sacrifice and human murder, but that this analogy, once made, is so difficult to read. Perhaps it is not that the "unspeakable human holocaust" is so distant from the "unspoken animal one" that it can only be denigrated by the comparison, but that the notion that animals are murdered is elevated, if only provisionally, to the highest thought. In other words, the fact that the question of our obligations to animals is raised in such a maximally important context, indeed, as the opening move in the evocation of that context, puts to us that the thought of the human, no matter how profound—the incarceration and extermination of the Jews standing as the figure *par excellence* for what Jean-Luc Nancy calls "an absolute responsibility"[9]—can never be wholly divorced from the thought of the animal.

To be sure, the lightness of Levinas's touch reminds us that, for him, nonhuman animals cannot make the same morally relevant claims upon us as human ones. Levinas will never be confused with the animal liberationist, for whom allowing "the interests of his own species to override the greater interests of members of other species" is unacceptable.[10] I would argue, in fact, that Levinas's contiguous thoughts about the "butchery" of animals and the murder of Jews resonate strangely *with* and constitute a subtle renunciation *of* Heidegger, who, in a series of lectures given in Bremen on technology in 1949, infamously claimed that the "motorized food industry" was "in essence the same as the manufacturing of corpses in gas chambers and extermination camps."[11] Heidegger's claim will always need to be read very slowly, since its extreme callousness makes it impossible definitively to distinguish between, on the one hand, his long-standing *critique* of the West's technological logic, for which the industrialization of agriculture and the bureaucratization of genocide are identical expressions of the "complete Europeanization of the earth and man,"[12] and, on the other hand, a certain dehumanizing absolutism in Heidegger's own thinking and politics. In this instance, as perhaps in many others, Heidegger may have become what he beheld. For Levinas, however, there is no question about the cruel basis of Heidegger's remarks—nor about its origins far back in Heidegger's work. Levinas readily concedes the critical power of Heidegger's "extraordinary book of 1927," but asks rhetorically if "there was never any echo of Evil in it."[13] It cannot be accidental that evidence of such reverberations are to be found amid Heidegger's most violently dogmatic claims about animality. For example, in the name of more rigorously determining how the being-toward-death of *Dasein* makes it into something that surpasses living creatures (a determination that is not without its Levinasian equivalent, as I shall argue), *Being and Time* distinguishes between the dying [*Sterben*] of *Dasein* and the perishing [*Verenden*] of beings that are merely alive: the human properly dies, whereas the animal simply ceases to live.[14] With this distinction in mind, Heidegger's Bremen assertion takes on utterly chilling consequences: insofar as the Jews perish with and *like* the animals who die in meat-processing plants, that is, as essentially similar "fabrications" of the military-industrial-agricultural complex, *they cannot be human;* which is to say, *because* the military-industrial-agricultural complex fails to distinguish between animals and certain animalized humans, it slaughters them both with impunity. It goes without saying that none of this annihilating logic informs Levinas's comparison. Responding to Heidegger's claim, Levinas says simply: "This stylistic turn of phrase, this analogy, this progression, are beyond commentary."[15] Where Heidegger levels differences in the name of "essence," Levinas bids us, for a moment, to think two distinct thoughts together, and in doing so safely preserves the incalculable differences between feeding people in the industrialized West and murdering them. Levinas's comparison is as unmistakable as it is delicate, dwelling within the interior, apposite spaces of his essay. In this gesture, important as much for *what* it might mean to us as it is for its being made at all, he points to the danger of making pronouncements from the relatively secure vantage point of a fundamental ontology. Instead, he offers an opening and a lure for thought. He risks a question about the (animal) other, where Heidegger carelessly pronounces the death of the difference between their demise and the murder of the European Jews. Levinas quietly, almost inadvertently, allows us to think that there are other horrors capable of making a claim upon our conscience, other forms of "butchery"—Levinas's terrible, savage word so pointedly puts this to us—without for a moment suggesting that they are the *same* horror as the Holocaust. For both thinkers, the blindness of the West culminates in its arrogant faith in an instrumental reason that transforms the planet into so much raw material awaiting assimilation. But in Heidegger's desire to grasp the basis of this inherently rapacious manner of being in the world, and, more important, in his overweening confidence as a *thinker* that he can stand neutrally apart from its actual destructiveness, Heidegger threatens to *overlook* the names and the faces of the others for whom this neutrality means nothing less than annihilation. In Levinas's memorable phrase about Heidegger's failure to remember, the German philosopher proceeds *"as if consenting to horror."* And so he embodies everything Levinas has fought against: namely, the murderous indifference to difference by which alterities are compelled to be *im Wesen dasselbe* ["in essence the same"].

In this, as in so many other ways, Levinas anticipates Derrida, for whom Heidegger's extraordinary statement represents an object lesson in what he calls "the ideology of difference." In attempting to deconstruct this ideology, with its insistence upon "a single limit between white and black, Jewish and non-Jewish," animal and human, Derrida is *not* arguing that difference is irrelevant, especially when we are speaking about "the difference between people and animals, . . . between Auschwitz and battery farms." Derrida says:

> No, no I am not advocating the *blurring* of differences. On the contrary, I am trying to explain how drawing an oppositional limit *itself* blurs the difference, the *différance* and the differences, not only between man and animal, but among animal societies—there are an infinite number of animal societies, and within animal societies and within human society itself, so many differences. (*RH* 183)

Ideologies of difference are, in the end, ideologies of "homogeneity" (*RH* 184), strategies and discourses that suppress uncontainable and irreducible variation in the name of an impossibly pure distinction between the same and the other. Criticizing Heidegger's philosophical and political investment in such purity, his high-minded distaste for mixing it up with more earthly others, Levinas will say that "*Dasein* . . . is never hungry."[16] From this utterly anorexic perspective, Heidegger risks blurring the difference between a meal and a corpse, while at the same moment and in the same gesture ferociously reinscribing the oppositional limit between those who are in a position to practice a fundamental ontology and those who are not. Speaking not from the relative safety of Bremen, but from behind the barbed wire of Camp 1492, Levinas cannot afford to make such sacrifices, dissolving as they do the difference between life and death for people and animals alike.

"But enough of this theology!" (151). With that mock exclamation, Levinas attempts to bring sudden closure to his thoughts on animal sacrifice, making it seem as if it had all been a false start and a strange detour. But a detour from what true path? When, two paragraphs later, he interjects: "But enough of allegories!" (152), we see that he is yet again working the conceit that he is writing in the "wrong" mode. Much of the essay unfolds in this self-consciously dilatory manner, one effect of which is to throw into sharper relief the purposiveness that comes only with the concluding memories of Bobby and the slave camp. And even there, as I have suggested, Levinas continues to feel as if his account could, at any moment, fall into mere fabulation, or worse, sentimentality. Throughout, the thought of the animal is always somehow too anthropomorphic, always vanishing beneath the surface of its humanistic interpretations. In his opening sentence, Levinas acknowledges the problem "of attaching too much importance to what 'goes into a man's mouth,' and not enough to what comes out" (151), but his pretense at embarrassment over succumbing precisely to this hazard puts to us that his flirtation with what he ironically dismisses as mere "theology" was worth the effort. In the apparent absence of an overarching design to the essay, the ensuing analogy between the "butchery that every day claims our 'consecrated' mouths" and the *other* butchery that haunts all of *Difficult Freedom* in effect operates as a kind of ghost narrative, linking the essay's oddly disparate thoughts and tones into a delicate whole. For a moment at least, before his allergy to making too much of animals overtakes his competing concern that we have made too little of them (especially when we sit down at the dinner table), the philosopher almost sounds as though he will abstain from animal flesh, as if he were the last vegetarian in the meat-eating West. Almost. Significantly, he does not in fact call for the end to animal sacrifice, but for its thoughtful restriction. But in the name of what? On what grounds would animals oblige us to treat them in this fashion? Levinas does not say, content instead with evoking images of the feeding frenzy that lies just beyond our sight as creatures of culture. "There is, at least, enough there to make us want to limit, through various interdictions, the butchery" of everyday life. The careful self-distancing of Levinas's syntax is worth remarking upon. It tells us that he is not as much concerned with the letter of dietary laws, as with the more general—but no less pressing—question of what it means to consume animal flesh in the first place, what it says about *us*. Who are *we* for whom the murderous violence of killing the animal other and sharing its flesh "at the family table" is so effortlessly "sublimated by intelligence" (151)?

This is not the first time that Levinas had asked his readers to consider what John Caputo calls "a repressed discourse on eating in philosophy."[17] A decade earlier, in *Totality and Infinity*, eating figures forth the irreducibly excessive relationship that the subject shares with the world:

> Eating . . . is to be sure not reducible to the chemistry of alimentation, [nor] . . . to the set of gustative, olfactory, kinesthetic, and other sensations that would constitute the consciousness of eating. This sinking one's teeth into the *things* which the act of eating involves above all measures the surplus of the reality of the aliment over every represented reality, a surplus that is not quantitative, but is the way the I, the absolute commencement, is suspended on the non-I.[18]

For Levinas, our fleshliness and our utter dependence upon consuming flesh voluptuously exposes and commits the "I" to the other in ways that are "ultimately prior to his ontological relation to himself (egology) or to the totality of things that we call the world."[19] Always before the "I" and the "non-I," and, as the condition of the possibility of their mutual imbrication, there is "nourishment." As Seán Hand remarks, "this conception of earthly enjoyment, whose forgetfulness of self is the first morality, marks a decisive break with *Dasein*."[20]

Enjoyment, nourishment, eating—all are corporeal figures with which Levinas evokes the fundamental responsibility that the self has for the frailty of the other, the other's desires, hungers, thirsts, hurts, and pleasures. In Heidegger, *Dasein* is the virile and resolute entity that ostensibly does without food so as better to fix its sights on the alterity of its own death; in Levinas, *Dasein* suffers the pangs of hunger, and in that suffering it is always already turned towards the face of the others who are also hungry and who will also die. In the slightly later essay on Bobby, however, nourishment and enjoyment suddenly take on darker meanings, for they are phenomena that consistently occur *at the expense of the animal other* whose flesh we consume. To eat, we must eat an other; one creature's nourishment means another gets stripped of its skin: that is the cold logic of us warm-blooded animals that *Totality and Infinity* represses and that Levinas's reflections upon the butchery of everyday life recover for thought. Inasmuch as the earlier text generalizes the consumed others into "things" and "aliment," figuring them as foodstuffs whose craving makes the "I" possible, it remains wholly centered on the needs of "man" and thus caught within the ecology that it critiques. Where in *Totality and Infinity* the animal's sacrifice at the hands (and teeth) of the human goes unnoticed, in "The Name of a Dog" it summons us to an obligation that Levinas almost always reserves for human beings: you *ought* not to kill me.

II. Refusing the Animal Face; or, We Are What We Eat

> There is no such thing as Animality, but only a regime of differences without opposition. The concept of animality, along with the "world poverty" of the animal, are human artifacts, indeed, artifacts that are difficult to wield; and their effect is to *efface* differences, to homogenize.
> —Jacques Derrida, "On Reading Heidegger"

> The animal is the *dreamed* object.
> —Luc Ferry, *The New Ecological Order*

Levinas's disturbing image of a domestic space—the dinner table—forming an alibi for murder recalls questions raised by Derrida in his recent work on what he calls "the carnivorous virility" (*EW* 280) of Western cultures. Why do these cultures leave "a place . . . open . . . for a noncriminal putting to death" (*EW* 276) of living creatures? How is responsibility to the human other also a tacit form of permission to act irresponsibly toward the animal other? How does indifference to the animal configure the human? Significantly, Derrida almost

always raises these questions by rereading the philosophemes and critical positions that are central to Levinas's critique of "traditional humanism" (*EW*
279). In quite different contexts (which itself attests to the fundamental
nature of the problem at hand), Derrida characterizes animal sacrifice as symp-
tomatic of a generalized carnivorous violence, a "carno-phallogocentrism"
modeled upon the "virile strength of the adult male" (*EW* 280; *FL* 953).
According to this "schema," "the subject does not want just to master and possess nature actively. In our cultures, he accepts sacrifice and eats flesh" (*EW*
281). The killing of animals, and the concomitant construction of the "animal"
as that which may be freely put to death for the purposes of consumption, is profoundly related to the constitution of human *Dasein*. For that reason, he
argues, "If we wish to speak of injustice, of violence or of a lack of respect
toward what we still so confusedly call animals, we must reconsider in its
totality the metaphysico-anthropocentric axiomatic that dominates, in the
West, the thought of just and unjust" (*FL* 953).

Needless to say, this reconsideration extends well beyond the question of
what or whether meat should be eaten:

> The question is no longer one of knowing if it is "good" to eat the other or if
> the other is "good" to eat, nor of knowing which other. One eats him regard-
> less and lets oneself be eaten by him. . . . The moral question is thus not, nor
> has it ever been: should one eat or not eat, eat this and not that, . . . man or
> animal, but since *one must* eat in any case and since it is and tastes good to
> eat, and since there is no definition of the good [*du bien*], *how* for goodness'
> sake should one *eat well* [*bien manger*]? And what does this imply? What is
> eating? How is this metonymy of introjection to be regulated? (*EW* 282)

Alluding to this passage, Caputo observes: "We have to eat and we have to
eat something living. That is the law of the flesh."[21] As if cognizant of this
imperative, Levinas does not call for an outright abstention from carnivorous-
ness, but for grasping the significance of the *law of the flesh* that articulates us,
or, in his words, "that every day *claims* our 'consecrated' mouths." If we cannot
not assimilate the other, and if what "we" *are* is irreducible to a complex spec-
trum of incorporation and interiorization (of which animal sacrifice is but one
example), then the need to examine the axioms by which these forms of "eating" are conducted, far from becoming irrelevant, becomes all the more
pressing. (On this point, Derrida differs most profoundly with Heidegger, or at
least the Heidegger for whom the myriad differences between the industrial
consumption of human and animal corpses had ceased to matter.) Briefly, for
Derrida the point is not that we must stop eating meat—as he says, the distinc-

tion between animal and plant "flesh" is itself suspect—but to think critically about how carno-phallogocentric discourses and regimes (i) "install the virile figure at the determinative center of the subject" (*EW* 280); (ii) abject those (others) who are deemed not to have the same brawny "appetites" as "men": women, homosexuals, celibates, and vegetarians (*EW* 281); and (iii) sacrifice animals in such a way that their being put to death is not considered killing (*EW* 283).

As an example of the most profound "ideology of homogeneity," Derrida argues, carno-phallogocentrism requires that strict distinctions be maintained between "symbolic" and "real" objects of sacrifice. This is no more apparent than in the interdiction, "Thou shalt not kill," which Derrida reads after Levinas as:

> Thou shalt not kill thy neighbor. Consequences follow upon one another, and must do so continuously: thou shalt not make him suffer, which is sometimes worse than death, thou shalt not do him harm, thou shalt not eat him, not even a little bit, and so forth. (*EW* 279).

On the other hand, "The putting to death of the animal is not a murder," a "denegation" or repression that Derrida links "to the violent institution of the 'who' as subject" (*EW* 283). The neighbor, the neighborhood of the human, with its attendant determinations of just and unjust action toward the other, is in this way constructed over and against the realm of the nonhuman, generalized and simplified as the "animal," for which the sixth commandment is inapplicable. According to the exclusionary principles of this "sacrificial" logic, humans may consume and be consumed in any number of symbolic ways, but are forbidden to be carnivores of each other, "real" cannibalism figuring forth the animalizing behavior *par excellence,* the very mark distinguishing "advanced" from "primitive" societies. Here, the extraordinary exceptions to the law against anthropophagy prove the rule of culture. Animals and other living creatures, on the other hand, may be put to death at will. "Such are the executions of ingestion, incorporation, or introjection of the corpse," Derrida argues; "An operation as real as it is symbolic when the corpse is 'animal' (and who can be made to believe that our cultures are carnivorous because animal proteins are irreplaceable?)" (*EW* 278). Only animals, *as* animals, "naturally" form real sacrifices to each other (or what Levinas calls "this devouring within species" [151]).

Yet the separation of "symbolic" from "real" operations and objects of ingestion is extremely problematical, since "eating" is at best a metonym for "infinitely different modes of the conception-appropriation-assimilation of the other" (*EW* 281). Moreover, how is one to distinguish decisively between symbolic and nonsymbolic forms of carnivorous violence, when that distinction, in addition to "all symbolic or linguistic appropriations" that involve the capture and consumption of the other, is irreducible to a generalized "eating" that precedes and exceeds the constitution of the "human." As Derrida observes, determining a purely *symbolic* form of sacrifice that would decisively define the "human," "is very difficult, truly impossible to delimit in this case, hence the enormity of the task, its essential excessiveness, a certain unclassifiability or the monstrosity of what *for which* we have to answer here, or *before* which (whom? what?) we have to answer" (*EW* 278). At what point *is* an (animal) corpse "just" a corpse, or eating "simply" eating? What perspective, short of the loftily panoptic one that Heidegger adopts in his 1949 lectures, would enable us to make such absolute determinations? A radical surplus of differences and *différance* will always unsettle the oppositional limit between the human and the animal, and the man-centered determinations of "the just and the unjust" upon which the rigorous purity of this limit rests. To the extent that this excess displaces the thought of the "human" (and thus the "animal"), it is rightly felt to be "monstrous" and "unclassifiable"—and for that reason, entirely useful to the "task" of gaining a point of critical leverage on the humanisms that have always presupposed and policed an essential difference and oppositional limit between human and nonhuman life.

Can we say that Levinas disrupts "the boundaries that institute the human subject (preferably and paradigmatically the adult male, rather than the woman, child, or animal) as the measure of the just and the unjust" (*FL* 953)? In the opening paragraph of his essay, as I have argued, Levinas's disconcerting analogy strikes twice at the heart of a human-centered cosmos: "we" live in a culture that failed catastrophically to grasp the injustice of killing Jews; but "we" also live in a culture for which the justness of putting animals to death is simply not an intelligible consideration. The fact that Levinas is willing to raise the second question alongside the first, which is to say, in such close proximity to "'the' question" and "'the' figure of responsibility" (*EW* 285) characterizing our modernity, suggests the maximal nature of what is at stake here, the radical possibilities that can be opened up when the reach of the ethical question *who is my neighbor?* is widened to include nonhuman acquaintances. If animals are also murdered, if their deaths are no longer denegated as merely being put to death, then to whom or what am I answerable? The unstated analogy between the murder of Jews and the killing of animals in effect creates a *rhetorical* neighborhood in which animals and humans dwell and summon each other into responsibility.

Elsewhere in Levinas's work, including elsewhere in the essay on Bobby, this call goes mostly unheard. For example, Levinas has been asked if animals have faces, and thus if they command the respect that the human face commands. His response is telling:

> One cannot entirely refuse the face of an animal. . . . Yet the priority here is not found in the animal, but in the human face. We understand the animal, the face of an animal, in accordance with *Dasein*. The phenomenon of the face is not in its purest form in the dog. In the dog, in the animal, there are other phenomena. For example, the force of nature is pure vitality. It is more this which characterizes the dog. But it also has a face. . . . The human face is completely different and only afterwards do we discover the face of an animal.[22]

Much could be said about the rich interview of which this response forms a small part, and I can focus on only a few details here. We should note that, from the start, Levinas never questions whether there are "animals" and "humans." Like Heidegger before him, the insistence upon the oppositional limit dividing the two entities presupposes that they exist as such. Even when Levinas disrupts the boundaries constituting the human, as he certainly does when he characterizes the subject as always already being held "hostage" to an absolute Other, he reinscribes the boundaries defining the animal, as if his critique of humanism remained more or less within a certain anthropological space. Levinas's somewhat evasive syntax qualifies any openness to the animal other by casting that muted act of affirmation in the form of a (double) negative: that one cannot *entirely* say "no" to the animal face means saying "yes" is the exceptional rather than the categorically imperative act, supplemental in nature, rather than constitutive. The problem lies not with the human, who cannot or will not see this face, but decisively with the animal, whose face lacks the "purest form" that we are presumed to see with absolute clarity when the *visage* is human. What it is about the animal face that lingers once the human has finished with its refusals remains quite unclear, since it is difficult to conceive of an absolute demand and responsibility—which is what the "face" usually connotes in Levinas's work—that is also somehow partial. Levinas concedes, positively, that there is something about the animal that compels us to face it; but he focuses negatively on the something else which spoils and reduces that duty. All faces *as* faces are irrefutable, but some are less irrefutable than others. The notion that the animal face is not in its "purest form" implies that there is a continuum joining the faceless to the faced, when everything else about Levinas's rhetoric points assertively towards an abyss of essence dividing the two phenomena. The animal face is "completely" other than the human face, yet the human remains the implacable standard against which the "purity" of the animal face is measured. Thus the animal both has and does not have a face; it is characterized in its essence by having (face) without having. In this redoubled and contradictory gesture, strongly reminiscent of the illogicality characterizing Heidegger's description of living creatures as *weltarm* [poor-in-the-world],[23] Levinas insists upon an absolute separation of human and animal while at the same moment reinscribing the animal face in what Derrida would call "a certain anthropocentric or even humanist teleology" (OS 55).

The animal's face cannot be entirely ignored; yet Levinas is scrupulously careful to assert that even this fractional connection vis-à-vis the human must *not* be misinterpreted as placing animals on a developmental path that might lead to the human:

> The widespread thesis that the ethical is biological amounts to saying that, ultimately, the human is only the last stage of the evolution of the animal. I would say, on the contrary, that in relation to the animal, *the human is a new phenomenon.*[24]

Levinas's experience with and reflection upon Nazism makes it imperative that the "ethical" *not* be contaminated by the "biological," lest the destinal thinking of the latter become the means by which to exterminate the obligations of the former. The frankly anthropocentric insistence that the human cannot be reduced to an essence has remained, as Derrida suggests in another context, "*up until now* . . . the price to be paid in the ethico-political denunciation of biologism, racism, naturalism" (OS 56). But this does not preclude us from tracing the axiomatic decisions, not to say the contradictions and elisions, underwriting Levinas's discourse of animality, a discourse whose very attempt to think beyond the ontological reinscribes ancient ontotheological distinctions between the human and animal. For example, one sign that Levinas resorts to the profoundest metaphysical humanism is that he proceeds as if the distinction between the "ethical" and the "biological" was *itself* not consequentially ethical in nature, a sealing off of one neighborhood from another, and a ghettoizing of the animal in the ancient space of the "biological"—for which we may take Levinas to mean something like *Nur-noch-leben*, "just-plain-life."[25] Levinas's move against the "biological" almost exactly reproduces Heidegger's long-standing objection to *Lebensphilosophie*, both ancient and modern. Original thinking, that is, thinking that presupposes the originality—or "newness"—of the human phenomenon, only suffers at the hands of the zoologists.

For that reason, Heidegger was offended by Aristotle, who had failed to set "the *humanitas* of man high enough" by calling the human an animal equipped with language.[26] For both thinkers, the being-human of the human wholly exceeds the thought of the biological in which animality is immured; the heteronomic relation to the other, the being-ethical of the human, is unrelated to the life of the (other) living creatures, whose infinite differences from humans, but also from each other, are erased, and that erasure in turn is *fixed* by the name *par excellence* for natural "rule": the "biological." For Levinas, the animal face is always compromised by competing phenomena, all of them unnamed except for the most pressing, indeed, the very figure of *irrepressibility:* namely, the "pure vitality" of "the force of nature." "The being of animals," Levinas will subsequently say, "is a struggle for life" (172). The animal is imagined to be the creature for which being-alive takes precedence over all other essential characteristics: without remainder, the being-animal of the animal *is* its "vitality." Notwithstanding the radical critique of traditional humanisms that Levinas mobilizes around the notion of the "face," he resorts to the most conventional conceptual schemes when he tries to account for the animal other. According to this configuration, "Man" is exemplarily free from the blind force of nature, whereas animals are immersed in the liveliness that constitutes their animated existence to the precise extent that it deprives them of their liberty, their ability to "question," to anticipate both their "own" death and the death of another, as well as to reason, to speak, to mourn, to have a history, or to possess a soul. Levinas frankly puts to us that he "understand[s] the animal in accordance with *Dasein*": that is, he measures the animal against the "purity" of *Dasein*, "purity" here signifying *Dasein*'s prior, bare, and asymmetrical relation to the Other. The animal enjoys an excess of life over face, even if the means by which one could make, much less weigh, these relative distinctions, remains completely mysterious. *Dasein*, on the other hand, is something more and better than merely being-alive. And if Levinas is also to insist, *contra* Heidegger, that his version of *Dasein* feels the pangs of hunger, then that only proves that he is forced to separate it from the being-alive of animals without making that vitality entirely inaccessible to it.[27]

When Levinas turns his mind to an animal other than a dog, he falters, as if he were at the point of exceeding the conceptual tolerances of his own argument, the place where the "ethical," already overextended into the animal kingdom and thus compromising the putative "newness" of the human "phenomenon," must finally break with the "biological": "I don't know if a snake has a face. I can't answer that question. A more specific analysis is needed" (172). Without a clear or consistent sense of what the proper trait of the animal *is*, Levinas finds himself—squeamishly?—unable to say either "yes" or "no" to the snake. Summarily to deny the snake what was equivocally given to the dog would perhaps betray too clearly how *Dasein*'s point of view is not neutrally indifferent to the "biological," but anthropocentric and even sentimental in its hierarchization of the living creatures. The earlier claim that the dog's face could not be entirely disavowed was positively predicated on the possibility, however partial, of there being something like an animal *Dasein*; but Levinas makes it clear at this point that the same claim also negatively opens the way, in theory, for a continuous gradation of refusals that increases the farther "down" the evolutionary scale one looks. To be fair to Levinas, he does call for additional "analysis" into the question. When considered in the context of his rather dogmatic assertions about human *Dasein*, however, his hesitancy about the snake's face points to the following logic: if the dog's face is mostly denied, and if the snake's face remains unclear, then the notion of the face of, say, the insect, will be more questionable still—perhaps incomprehensible or irrelevant; nothing about Levinas's rhetoric of animality precludes that conclusion and exclusion. Discriminating between animal genera, Levinas never doubts that there is a uniform region—but not quite a neighborhood—called *animality*, for which any particular creature should stand as an example. But how can one animal genus be "more" animalistic than another at the same time that "animality" as an essentializing concept is expected to maintain any kind of meaningful force? Levinas falls into an anthropological discourse which Derrida would say "is all the more peremptory and authoritarian for having to hide a discomfiture" (OS 11)—in this case, the tacit concession that "animality" does not describe the nature of living things but is a variably meaningful figure in service of configuring and consolidating the exemplarity of the human. Working with two different standards of animal exemplarity, Levinas reproduces the oppositional limit between human and animal *within* the realm of the biological. To do so, he relies upon at least two traditional and teleological schema: (i) Evoking a biological hierarchy of relative "complexity" that ranks warm-blooded mammals "over" cold-blooded reptiles, Levinas naturalizes the superiority of the dog vis-à-vis the snake. In other words, he makes the putative "biological" proximity of the dog to the human substitute for a nearness in ethical essence—this, notwithstanding his explicit insistence that thinking *Dasein* is a function of the founding difference between the "ethical" and the "biological." (ii) Levinas is perhaps never more firmly within the grasp of an anthropology than in his choice of exemplary animals. For the "dog" and the "snake" are of course not two living creatures among many, but the very emblems, respectively, of dutifulness and unqualified friendship (this, for Jews, Greeks, and Christians; Levinas evokes all three contexts in his essay), and of irresponsibility, lowliness, and evil bestiality.

"With the appearance of the human—and this is my entire philosophy—there is something more important than my life, and that is the life of the other" (172). By this point we need hardly say that the "other" to which Levinas refers is paradigmatically the other human, whose importance is marked by its ability to stand outside "nature" and the "biological." As Derrida observes: "What is still to come or what remains buried in an almost inaccessible memory is the thinking of a responsibility that does not stop at *this* determination of the neighbor, at the dominant scheme of this determination" (284). For Levinas, only the human is truly subjected to and by the injunction, "Thou shalt not kill." The sixth commandment is the basis for all ethics; it is the "primordial expression," "the first word" that configures the human, summoning it to an asymmetrical locution before it has said or done anything: "to see a face is already to hear: 'thou shalt not kill.'"[28] But Levinas leaves unexplained how the human grasps the importance of "the *life* of the other" and thus comprehends the possibility of its *death*, while at the same time being something completely different from the "vitality" of living things. We might ask Levinas the same question that Derrida asks of Heidegger: "What is death for a *Dasein* that is never defined *essentially* as a living thing?" (OS 120). What can "life" and "death" mean in the discourse of the "ethical" once it is decisively divided from the realm of the merely "biological"? (We might also reverse the terms of the question and ask what an "animal" is if it attaches "importance" to its own life but remains constitutively incapable, which is to say *in all cases*, unable either to intimate "the life of the other" or to bear responsibility for it? But what then is life for the mortal animal that it should be said not to mourn the death of the other life?) If the face of the animal does not confront us, then the "asymmetrical relation with the other" (225) is rendered impossible, and the interdiction that is the basis of ethics has no binding effect.

Of course, within the human neighborhood the sixth commandment can hardly be said to have been scrupulously obeyed; it is, as Levinas says, an "authority . . . without force" (169). The face is a "demand" that remains as the possibility of ethics whether we accept or deny that "demand." But even its refusal is reappropriated to the anthropocentric axioms governing Levinas's discourse. We see this perhaps most clearly in *Totality and Infinity*, where Levinas argues that "violence" and "War . . . presuppose the face and the transcendence of the being appearing in the face" (222). If "Thou shalt not kill" means "Thou shalt not kill—except in certain cases, for example, in battle," then the privilege of this murderous exception also lies entirely with the human. Humans "hunt" animals and "labor" with nature, to be sure, but because the objects of these confrontations lack a face, Levinas claims, it cannot accurately be said that "warfare" or "violence" is carried out against them.

To some extent, this curious and somewhat worrisome claim is informed by the distinction—which we have already encountered—Heidegger makes when he distinguishes between the dying [*Sterben*] of *Dasein* and the perishing [*Verenden*] of beings that are merely alive. In the case of Levinas, the entitlement of pursuing war, and thus of suffering its fatal violence, lies properly with "Man" and is an element of the propriety of "Man." According to this logic, animals are not *bona fide* casualties; they are hunted down and they perish, but they do not die in battle with human beings. (Interestingly, by the time he writes his essay on Bobby, Levinas will recognize this denegation of murder for what it is—making killing into a kind of sport.) By extension, it could be argued, it *is* argued, that the agricultural-industrial-technological complex does not carry out warfare against the natural world; it "develops" and "cultivates"[29] the "wilderness," that is, that which lies outside of the neighborhood of "civilized" "Man." This is not merely a question of semantics, but of the ways in which philosophemes like "warfare" and "violence" are put into the service of configuring the human, and of policing a series of mutually reinforcing boundaries that divide realms, each of which are imagined to be separately homogeneous—"human" and "nonhuman," "Man" and "nature." But if it is not warfare that has been conducted against the buffalo, the Brazilian rain forest, and the animalized human (the terrible epithets "savage" and "Gook" come to mind), to cite only a few examples, then what is it? What is effaced or ignored by restricting "warfare" to mean the systematic violence of humans against humans, as something peculiar to *Dasein*, the sole creature capable of apprehending "the importance of the life of the other"? Inasmuch as Levinas designates the human neighborhood as the "totality" that is exemplarily capable of suffering the violence of war, he saves the global village by destroying it, or at least by exposing it to the possibility of its destruction. But, as always, the perimeter marking the human from the nonhuman, the faced from those without faces, is unstable, disrupted, subjected to differences that cannot be contained by the separating out of the "ethical" from the "biological" (but *not* thereby collapsing one region into the other). If these complications were not always already in place, why would there be any need for the kinds of imperious, insistent moves characterizing Levinas's discourse (but not only his, as we have seen in the case of Heidegger) with respect to the enigma of the animal?

At the risk of being too literal-minded, I might quickly recall—and then only interrogatively—the horrific case of the Vietnam War to throw into relief both the limitations of Levinas's claim, and the need to think of a responsibility that does not stop at his determination of the neighbor. Could one meaningfully describe what the American military did to the human population of Vietnam as *warfare* and not extend that term to describe what it also did, and with equally systematic ferocity, to the Vietnamese countryside using Agent Orange? At what point could one distinguish between the destruction of an agricultural way of life and the people living that life? Perhaps only a so-called First World culture, which is to say a culture that knows nothing of the realities of subsistence farming, could afford to call one form of violence "warfare" and the other, using the jargon of the motorized food industry, the work of "defoliation." What ideology of homogeneity would need to be in place, what oppositional limits would need to be inscribed in the name of the exemplarity of human *Dasein*, in order for one to say that the American military did not *murder* Vietnam, the land, its ways of life, its peoples, its animals? Or that the peoples and the animals and the place in which they all dwelled did not *differently* command a form of absolute respect from America, that they did not *differently* summon the army of occupation to the originary obligation, *Thou shalt not kill?*

Although Levinas does not say it this way, only by projecting a face upon nonhuman others, and thus subjecting them to the rhetorical violence of a prosopopoeia, can they be said to be murdered. But who is to say that one manner of speaking about killing is rhetorically aberrant and the other proper, or that some creatures die and others cease living? *Totality and Infinity* suggests that we can say that we conduct "warfare" against animals only by anthropomorphically confusing that ferocity with what is actually happening, namely "hunting." Similarly, "violence" bears only upon human *Dasein*, whereas bringing force to bear upon the faceless elements "reduce[s] itself to a labor."[30] But he can make this claim only by ignoring how "warfare" and "violence" are themselves figures, figures that carry out the work of *anthropomorphizing* "Man" by differentially positing those qualities that make human living and dying *human*, over and against the nonviolence that is imagined to happen to the faceless animals and elements. In this anthropocentric universe, animals and the elements of the "natural" world are the objects of human action—hunting, labor—rather than entities that oblige us fundamentally. The being-war of war and the being-human of humanity are here openly, deeply complicit with each other, a complicity we might consider when we think of the denegations of murder once the nonhuman is decreed not to have a face, the alibis that always put the human somewhere else, doing something else when it comes to killing animals and dehumanized or animalized humans: the "culling" and "management" of herds, the "euthanization" of laboratory animals, but also the "cleansing" and "pacification" of human populations, the "saving" of villages by their incineration, and the "manufacturing" [*die Fabrikation*] of corpses. Above all, Levinas teaches us *not* to analogize incomparably different deaths, with too little to say or care about their differences, in the manner of Heidegger. In the essay on Bobby, as I have argued, he even obliges us to think of human and animal deaths as capable of illuminating each other in their separate darknesses. For the most part, however, Levinas's neighborhood remains resolutely human. As Derrida argues, "The 'Thou shalt not kill'—with all its consequences, which are limitless—has never been understood within the Judeo-Christian tradition, nor apparently by Levinas, as a 'Thou shalt not put to death the living in general'" (*EW* 279). The sixth commandment has a double force in culture: not only, as Levinas contends, as the interdiction that commands obligation to the human other, but also as tacit *permission* to think the animal others, and all the living things for which the "animal" comes zoomorphically to stand, as lying "outside" the neighborhood of call and response. To this extent, Derrida sees a striking similarity between Heidegger and Levinas: "In spite of the differences separating them, they nonetheless remain profound humanisms *to the extent that they do not sacrifice sacrifice*." For both, the human subject lives "in a world where sacrifice is possible and where it is not forbidden to make an attempt on life in general, but only on human life, on the neighbor's life" (*EW* 279).

III. The Cyborg Kantian

> Animals; difficulty of explaining these.
> —F. W. J. Schelling, *On the History of Modern Philosophy*

> Beneficence toward those in need is a universal duty of man; this is so because they are to be regarded as fellow men, i.e., as needy rational beings, united by nature in one dwelling place for mutual aid.
> —Immanuel Kant, *The Metaphysical Principles of Virtue*

To the extent that Levinas asks us to reconsider the consecrated butchery of everyday life, Derrida's assessment cannot be entirely correct. For a moment, Levinas in fact *does* appear willing to sacrifice sacrifice, or at least to put into question the humanism which is rightly appalled at the murder of Jews but less worried about the killing of animals. But if he is willing to extend the neighborhood encompassed by the sixth commandment to the animals at the beginning of his essay, by its conclusion he decisively returns to the anthropocentric universe in which Derrida finds him dwelling. That return and reinscription of the privilege of the human is most complexly evident in the account of Bobby with which my remarks began, and especially in his characterization as "last Kantian in Nazi Germany." Let us return to the story that is on Levinas's mind from the beginning of his essay, but whose details are relayed only in its closing sentences. For a few weeks, "about halfway through our long captivity," Levinas writes, the Nazi guards allowed "a wandering dog to enter into our lives." The prisoners call him "Bobby, an exotic name, as one does with a cherished dog."

> He would appear at morning assembly and was waiting for us as we returned, jumping up and down and barking in delight. For him, there was no doubt that we were men. (153)

For recognizing the faces of the prisoners as *human* faces, rather than as mere instruments, the *technē* of the Nazi regime, Bobby is called a "Kantian," the last of his kind. What can Levinas's striking anthropomorphism mean in this context? The answer to that question is necessarily difficult, since Levinas's conception of human obligations to the animal other is here mediated both by his complex relationship with Kant[31] and by Kant's own conception of animals. Most obviously, however, it is Bobby's seemingly dutiful behavior towards the prisoners that attracts Levinas's ostensibly well-meaning attribution. We might recall that, according to Kant, human beings elicit respect for each other out of a compelling sense that the other person is a rational agent, that is, an agent who is capable of operating freely and thus in a disinterested fashion under the aegis of the moral law. Bobby behaves in a manner that appears to meet Kant's expectations of an unconditioned goodness, a goodness that refers neither to personal qualities or strengths, such as temperament or character, nor to obedience to the particular customs or laws of a society. Moreover, he grasps this founding quality in the prisoners, which, according to the fundamentally anthropocentric axioms of Kant's discourse, is indistinguishable from perceiving them as "men." As Kant argues, in observing the comportment of the (human) other, we apprehend the sentiment of profound respect—which he calls "something like inclination, something like fear"—that subjects our "animalistic," nonrational interests in maximizing pleasure and minimizing pain to the force of rule.[32] Grasping the freedom in the other to act in a manner that can be universally willed or followed, we necessarily confirm and enact the same freedom in and for ourselves. Until the guards expel him from the slave camp, Bobby is for Levinas a living testament to the survival of this moral life, the life that accedes categorically to the imperative: "Act in such a way that you always treat humanity, whether in your own person or in the person of any other, never simply as means, but always at the same time as end."[33]

Levinas pays Bobby this high compliment, but instantly qualifies it to the point of retraction. For all of the respect that the dog outwardly embodies in his delighted barking, "friendly growling," and wagging tail, and, notwithstanding the palpable way in which Levinas is moved by this show of affection and understanding, Bobby remains inwardly deficient, "without the brains needed to universalize maxims and drives" (153). He is too stupid, "*trop bête*," the French condensing idiocy and animality into one crassly anthropocentric expression. Bobby makes up for the absence of unconditional goodness in the human neighborhood; indeed, he embodies the last stand of that goodness. But because he lacks the know-how and the liberty truly to stop himself from acting in a way that cannot be universalized, he is only a kind of simulation. In a land that is all but devoid of freedom and rationality, Levinas puts to us, Bobby is as good as goodness gets. But his actions are at best a moral addendum to and substitute for true dutifulness. Although he looks like a Kantian and sounds like a Kantian, and has a humanizing effect on the prisoners that is explicitly called Kantian, he is *not* Kantian. How could he be? "[T]he dog is a dog. Literally a dog!" (152). Levinas is adamant that we not misinterpret Bobby, lest we fall into fanciful stories about the faithfulness of animals: this is not Ithaca, and I am not Ulysses, he flatly reminds us. By characterizing the ethical and ontological question that Bobby vividly poses as a hermeneutical problem, however, Levinas deflects attention from the discomfiture that prompts his austere claim that Bobby is a kind of depthless surface, the experience of which should not be confused with the apprehension of the moral law that Kant reserves for humans and humans alone. Because he is immured in his creatureliness, Bobby is putatively not at liberty to behave otherwise than according to his more or less craven interests. As such, he embodies Levinas's conviction that "the being of animals . . . is a struggle for life without ethics."[34] Seen in this light, his reiterated desire to speak as literally and as unsentimentally as possible about animals takes on somewhat less flattering connotations: "the dog is a dog" is not a benignly neutral description, still less a deanthropomorphizing attempt to let the dog be what it is, free from its human configurations, but, quite to the contrary, a disciplinary action whose tautological form captures Levinas's desire to seal Bobby up in the prison of his species, lest he say more or do more than what is anthropocentrically allotted him.

The most telling irony is that, in qualifying his claim that Bobby is the "last Kantian in Nazi Germany" on the grounds that he lacks "the brains needed to universalize maxims and drives," Levinas almost exactly reproduces Kant's estimation of animals.[35] As Kant argues, animals are not morally relevant creatures as such, since they lack reason:

> To judge by reason alone, man has no duties except to men (himself or others), for his duty to any subject at all is the moral constraint by his will. Accordingly, a subject who constrains (obligates) must, first, be a person; and he must, secondly, be given as an object of experience, because he is to influ-

ence the purpose of a man's will; and such an influence can occur only in the relationship of two existing beings (for a mere creation of thought cannot become the cause of any purposive achievement).[36]

Without the *logos*, animals cannot directly oblige us, and, without obliging us, we are not bound to respect them in return. "In all our experience we are acquainted with no being which might be capable of obligation except man," Kant contends: "[M]an therefore can have no duty to any being other than man."[37] Knowing full well how animals evoke warm sentiments in us and clearly concerned that we not purchase this pathos too cheaply, too uncritically, while we gaze into the eyes of our favourite horse or dog, Kant insists that we reflect more carefully on what it is we are actually doing when we show kindness to animals. If it appears that I have responsibilities to animals, he suggests, this is because I have failed to distinguish between two distinct kinds of duties: direct duties *toward* [*gegen*] an entity regarded as an end in itself; and indirect duties *with regard to* [*in Ansehung*] an entity regarded as a means to an end. According to this schema, Bobby cannot be "Kantian" except by a conceptual and rhetorical confusion that transposes what is properly due to the human *onto* the nonhuman. Kant calls this impropriety "amphiboly," but we might recognize it as the trope of prosopopoeia—the giving of a face to that which is faceless. As creatures of nature, Kant argues, animals are not ends in themselves, and, as such, are closer to the category of things rather than persons. This does not mean that we are free to be unkind towards them, but the argument for abstaining from cruelty is that it debases human beings, who remain the rule against which to measure all forms of respect. (Kant thus applauds the English for excluding butchers from jury duty; it was thought that their profession would induce a bloody-mindedness towards their human peers![38]) Insofar as animals are thinglike, they do not oblige us directly; but insofar as they are *alive*, and in that quickness capable of mimicking the freedom that is the essential trait of humanity, animals do oblige us in an *in*direct fashion:

> Animal nature has analogies to human nature, and by doing our duties to animals in respect of manifestations which correspond to manifestations of human nature, we indirectly do our duty towards humanity. Thus, if a dog has served his master long and faithfully, his service, on the analogy of human service, deserves reward . . .[39]

Like Kant, Levinas readily concedes that we have duties not to treat animals cruelly. But he is just as resolute in keeping these obligations from unsettling either a certain hierarchical order of life or the boundaries that institute the human subject. This, from the same interview in which he questions the face of the dog:

> It is clear that, without considering animals as human beings, the ethical extends to all living beings. We do not want to make an animal suffer needlessly and so on. But the prototype of this is human ethics.[40]

Without ethics and, for the most part, without a face, it is unclear whether animals can be entities for which humans can have any sort of underived responsibilities, which is to say, responsibilities that would throw into question the primacy of the human neighborhood. Bobby may be too preoccupied with his "struggle for life" to warrant the sort of obligations that are reserved for those creatures who think and have a "face" that one could turn *toward* rather than merely *regard*. As Llewelyn has brilliantly demonstrated, "in the metaphysical ethics of Levinas I can have direct responsibilities only toward beings that can speak, and this means beings that have a rationality that is presupposed by the universalizing reason that is fundamental in the metaphysics of ethics of Kant."[41]

Like the biblical exemplar to which Levinas compares him, Bobby has "neither ethics nor *logos*" (152), and these absences have the curious effect of rendering him lifeless while still somehow remaining "alive." Signaling dutifulness without actually knowing or speaking this obligation, without phenomenologically experiencing respect in the manner that Kant describes it, as "something like fear, something like inclination," Bobby is thus closer to a cyborg than a sentient creature; he is not unlike an empty machine of the sort Descartes hallucinated when he looked at animals—but such a strangely attractive machine, fond thoughts of which haunt Levinas's darkest recollections. "I am thinking of Bobby" means, after all, "Witless creature though he is, I cannot forget him." The dog's declared moral status as a kind of animal-robot is strikingly at odds with the richly evocative details of his encounter with the prisoners, details which invite us—albeit against the grain of Levinas's anthropocentrism—to think *otherwise* about the nature of responding and responsibility, and thus to unsettle the oppositional limit that would confine what are confusedly called "language," "rationality," and "ethics" solely to the human sphere. Perhaps in dismissing the dog as *trop bête*, Levinas denies intellectually what he is compelled to acknowledge at an affective level. He may well disqualify Bobby as a *bona fide* Kantian on "technical" grounds, but the brusqueness of his name-calling comes across as a defensive gesture made in the face of a danger it inadvertently reveals. For what *is* Bobby doing when, by Levinas's own moving account, he so gaily greets the prisoners and recognizes them as "other," that is, as "men"? More: what is "language" if it is not the wagging of a tail, and "ethics" if it is not the ability to greet one other and to dwell together *as* others? Levinas says Bobby is brainless, as if he were absent from his own actions, yet this claim only throws into relief the forceful and articulate enigma of the dog's *presence* in the camp, the ways in which he obliges us to reconsider what we think we mean by *logos*, "animal," and, of course, "we." Notwithstanding Levinas's desire to say "no" to the animal, Bobby's face cannot be entirely refused, not because there is something residually "human" or "prehuman" about it, but precisely because of its nonhuman excess, because that face, screened though it is through Levinas's axiomatic discourse, constitutes a "yes" that is not a "yes," a "yes" belonging uniquely to the animal, to *this* animal, and given freely to the human prisoners. It goes without saying that "gift" and "freedom," like "animal" and "human," are all figures put in question by the call of this enigmatic communication, always before us and beyond us. What then is the *logos* that it cannot account for Bobby's languages, and for the multiplication of languages and the differences between languages across the oppositional limit dividing human from animal? Language is the implacable human standard against which the animal is measured and always found wanting; but what if the "animal" were to become the site of an excess against which one might measure the prescriptive, exclusionary force of the *logos*, the ways in which the truth of the rational word muffles, strangles, and finally silences the animal?

These questions are worth asking, it seems to me, because of the "audible" gap between what Bobby says and what Levinas hears him say. To his ears, the dog's language sounds like silence, albeit a silence with an illustrious pedigree. As the essay's concluding sentence confidently informs us, Bobby's "friendly growling, his animal faith, was born from the silence of his forefathers on the banks of the Nile" (153). In Exodus 11:7, to which Levinas is here referring, the dogs fall silent as mute witnesses to the righteousness of those who belong to the living God of Israel. While death moves across Egypt to claim all of its firstborn and an unprecedented outpouring of grief is heard across the land, Israel remains tranquil and safe. Even the witless dogs are compelled to recognize that fact:

> A rabble of slaves will celebrate this high mystery of man, and "not a dog shall growl." At the supreme hour of his institution, with neither ethics nor *logos*, the dog will attest to the dignity of its person. *This* is what the friend of man means. There is a transcendence in the animal! (152; emphasis mine)

Levinas's exclamation has several connotations here. It recalls the Talmudic scholars who are wondrously struck by the phenomenon of a creature who finds itself out of its place in the order of things: "the paradox of a pure nature leading to rights" (152). "Transcendence" also reminds us of Bobby's function as a silent and surrogate witness. As Shoshana Felman argues, for Levinas the "witness's speech is one which, by its very definition, transcends the witness who is but its medium, the medium of the realization of the testimony."[42] This transcendence would seem literally and even parodically to be the case with the dog, who involuntarily attests to the dignity of "man" without grasping the significance of what it has done. But where the lacuna between the witness and the witness's speech (or, we could say, between the performative and constative functions of the testimonial act) exposes the human to "the absolutely other," to whom it is held "hostage,"[43] in the animal this transcendent convocation serves the sole function of confirming the exemplarity of the human: it is the animal's privilege not only unwittingly to be held hostage by the human other, but also never to be *autrui* for "man." According to an authoritarian logic that informs almost all of Levinas's essay, by which the animal has in the mode of not-having, the dog is granted the power to be more than itself only insofar as it rigorously remains itself—*dans l'animal*—vis-à-vis "Man." The terms of this paradoxical, and, as it were, one-sided responsibility are corroborated by Levinas's uncertain pronoun reference—"This"—which makes it impossible to determine whether the dog is "the friend of man" in spite of or *because* it lacks "ethics" and "*logos*." It may well be that as long as animals are quiet, as long as they remain speechless and stupid, they will be allowed into the neighborhood of the human—but always under the threat of deportation—to perform a certain supplemental witnessing work. If the animal speaks, it will speak only silence, in deference to those who truly possess language and ethics.

What is important here, however, is the way in which the muteness of the animal resonates with Levinas's account of his treatment by his captors. In this silence, which is decidedly *not* a silence at all, but articulate gestures and sounds peremptorily *figured* and denegated as silence, it is impossible not to hear an echo of the muteness to which Levinas is reduced by the Nazis. For Levinas, nothing captures the violence of anti-Semitism more powerfully than the Nazis' unwillingness to hear the suffering voices of their prisoners. The unspeakable Holocaust begins with an assault on the language of its victims, and, for that reason, Levinas's account of life in Camp 1492 is rich with semiotic metaphors and turns upon a series of thwarted, interned, and strangled speech acts. "The strength and wretchedness of persecuted people" resounds through the camp, yet is reduced to "a small inner murmur" (153), heard only in the heart of the prisoners. Their richly diverse languages—written, gestural, affective—go perversely unnoticed, held in a kind of suspended animation: "our sorrow and laughter, illnesses and distractions, the work of our hands and

the anguish of our eyes, the letters we received from France and those accepted for our families—all passed in parenthesis" (153).

So important is the connection between language and responsibility that
Levinas can only describe the heartless abrogation of the latter in semiotic
terms as the sundering of significance itself. For him, Nazi racism "shuts people
away in a class, deprives them of expression and condemns them to being 'signifiers without a signified'" (153). Summing up the experience of these
silencings, Levinas asks: "How can we deliver a message about our humanity
which, from behind the bars of quotation marks, will come across as anything
other than monkey talk?" (153) Monkey talk? For the Nazis a languageless
human is nothing more than an animal; but what is "animality" that it not only
names the incoherence to which the Nazis reduce the Jews but also represents
the figure that comes most readily to hand to describe what it feels like to live
and survive that degradation? Reading this bestializing figure, I am thinking of
Bobby's barking and of the ancient assumption, against all intuitive evidence,
that animal sounds are merely *phonē asēmos*, "signifiers without a signified."
When we are told that Levinas and his fellow prisoners "were beings entrapped
in their species . . . beings without language," we might be forgiven for recalling what this essay so matter-of-factly says about Bobby in almost exactly the
same words. For a disconcerting moment, the prisoners and the dog threaten
to exchange their differently silenced spaces—a crossing made all the more
troublesome in an essay that begins, as I have argued, by asking us to consider
the butchery of animals against the backdrop of the extermination of the Jews.
Can we find the words to answer for the contiguity of these silences? How *not*
to speak of it? How to read the Nazi subjection of the Jews and Levinas's subjection of the animal *slowly enough?*

Levinas naturalizes his anthropocentric projections on Bobby by seeing
them from the reverse angle: the prisoner watches the dog watching the prisoners, and in watching, ostensibly witnessing the truth of their humanity.
Simultaneously welcomed, regulated, and expelled, Bobby traces and retraces
the oppositional limits that configure the human and the animal. Surviving "in
some wild patch in the region of the camp" (153), he is the subaltern who, for
a time, moves freely from the untamed margins of Camp 1492 into its closely
surveilled and policed interior. He is the outsider who accidentally befalls
Levinas's world, yet the very fact that he instantly recognizes the men *as* men
reminds us that he is a domesticated creature, and thus already a dweller
inside, with and among humans. As befits the savagely dystopic conditions of
the slave camp, the dog reverses the function of the scapegoat and is received
into the polis to perform a certain purifying work, only to be cast out by the

guards after "a few short weeks," thereby returning the camp to its savage "integrity." The introjection of Bobby's (simulated) goodness restores a minimal health to the camp, yet his inclusion is also inseparable from his summary exclusion from the neighborhood of human freedom and rationality. Beneficial inasmuch as he augurs the last remnants of a Kantian dutifulness—and for that, named and cherished—risky insofar as he provisionally substitutes for the human, speaking out of turn—and for that, carefully treated with unsentimental caution. He is the good medicine whose salutary effects are powerful enough to reach far forward into Levinas's future; but his impact is finally only a placebo effect, or perhaps a form of animal triage in a time of terrible need. Bobby performs a limited testimonial function, speaking for the other without the *logos*; but this role is a temporary measure, in earnest of the true human witness whose account—in the form of Levinas's essay—has always already usurped Bobby's place in our reading of it.

Notes

Versions and portions of this paper were presented at the meetings of the Modern Language Association (San Diego, 1994), the North American Society for the Study of Romanticism (Durham, 1995), and the Kentucky Foreign Language Association (Lexington, 1996). Charles Rzepka encouraged me to write this paper; for that, much thanks. I am very grateful to Peter Babiak, Stephen Barber, Rebecca Gagan, Jennifer Ham, Alice Kuzniar, Matthew Senior, and Tracy Wynne for listening to and commenting upon this paper. Research for this project was partially funded by the Social Sciences and Humanities Research Council of Canada and by the Arts Research Board of McMaster University.

1. "The Name of a Dog, or Natural Rights," in *Difficult Freedom*, trans. Seán Hand (London: The Athlone Press, 1990), 153. The original French version appears in *Celui qui ne peut pas se servir des mots* (Montpellier: Fata Morgana, 1976). Unless otherwise indicated, all subsequent references to Levinas will be to this essay and will be parenthetically cited by page number in the body of the essay.

2. "Beyond Pathos" is the title of the opening section of *Difficult Freedom*.

3. The homelessness of this "home" is brought out by Levinas, who remarks upon the "extraordinary coincidence" of the "fact that the camp bore the number 1492, the year of the expulsion of the Jews from Spain under the Catholic Ferdinand V" (152).

4. "The Power of Pets," *The New Republic*, July 10, 1995, 23.

5. See Heidegger's *Schelling's Treatise on the Essence of Human Freedom*, trans. Joan Stambaugh (Athens, OH: Ohio University Press, 1985), 124.

6. Matthew Senior has reminded me that Eugène Ionesco "animalizes" the Nazis in *Rhinocéros*.

7. The phrase is from Jacques Derrida and is discussed at length later in the essay. See "'Eating Well', or the Calculation of the Subject," trans. Avital Ronell, in

Points: Interviews, 1974–1994, ed. Elisabeth Weber (Stanford: Stanford University Press, 1995), 280.

    All subsequent references to Derrida will be cited parenthetically in the text and keyed to the following abbreviations: *A: Aporias,* trans. Thomas Dutoit (Stanford: Stanford University Press, 1995); *EW:* "'Eating Well', or the Calculation of the Subject," trans. Avital Ronell, in *Points: Interviews, 1974–1994,* ed. Elisabeth Weber (Stanford: Stanford University Press, 1995), 255–287; *FL:* "Force of Law: The 'Mystical Foundation of Authority'," trans. Mary Quaintance, *Cardoza Law Review* 11.5–6 (July/August 1990), 919–1039; *OS: Of Spirit: Heidegger and the Question,* trans. Geoffrey Bennington and Rachel Bowlby (Chicago: University of Chicago Press, 1989); *RH:* "On Reading Heidegger: An Outline of Remarks to the Essex Colloquium," *Research in Phenomenology* 17 (1987), 171–188.

8.   "Am I Obsessed by Bobby? (Humanism of the Other Animal)," in *Re-reading Levinas,* eds. Robert Bernasconi and Simon Critchley (Bloomington and Indianapolis: Indiana University Press, 1991), 235.

9.   Nancy uses this phrase in one of his questions to Derrida (*EW* 285).

10. I cite Peter Singer, *Animal Liberation: Towards an End to Man's Inhumanity to Animals* (London: Jonathan Cape, 1976), 9.

11. I follow the translation of Thomas Sheehan, "Heidegger and the Nazis," *The New York Review of Books* (June 16, 1988), 41–43. Part of the German text is found in Wolfgang Schirmacher, *Technik und Gelassenheit* (Freiburg: Alber, 1983), 25.

12. Martin Heidegger, *On the Way to Language,* trans. Peter D. Hertz (New York: Harper & Row, 1971), 15–16.

13. "As If Consenting to Horror," trans. Paula Wissing, *Critical Inquiry* (1989), 15 (Winter 1989), 488.

14. *Sein und Zeit* (Tübingen: M. Niemeyer, 1972), 240.

15. "As If Consenting to Horror," 487.

16. *Totality and Infinity: An Essay on Exteriority,* trans. Alphonso Lingis (Pittsburgh: Duquesne University Press, 1969), 134.

17. *Against Ethics: Contributions to a Poetics of Obligation with Constant Reference to Deconstruction* (Bloomington and Indianapolis: Indiana University Press, 1993), 197.

18. *Totality and Infinity: An Essay on Exteriority,* 128–129, emphasis mine.

19. "Dialogue with Emmanuel Levinas," trans. Richard Kearney, in *Face to Face with Levinas* (Albany, NY: State University of New York Press, 1986), 21.

20. "Time and the Other," in *The Levinas Reader,* ed. Seán Hand (Oxford: Basil Blackwell, 1989), 37.

21. *Against Ethics: Contributions to a Poetics of Obligation with Constant Reference to Deconstruction,* 198.

22. "The Paradox of Morality," trans. Andrew Benjamin and Tamra Wright, in *The Provocation of Levinas: Rethinking the Other,* eds. Robert Bernasconi and David Wood (London and New York: Routledge, 1988), 169.

23. Derrida discusses the "contradictory and impossible" logic underwriting

Heidegger's claim (in *Sein und Zeit*) that "the animal has a world in the mode of not-having" (*OS* 47–57).

24. "The Paradox of Morality," 172, emphasis mine.

25. I am thinking here of Heidegger's use of this phrase in *Being and Time*. See *Sein und Zeit*, 50.

26. Martin Heidegger, "Letter on Humanism," in *Basic Writings*, ed. and trans. David Farrell Krell (San Fransisco: Harper Collins, 1993), 234.

27. I borrow and modify David Farrell Krell's insight into Heidegger's vexed view of animal life: "Unfortunately, the clear division of ontic from ontological, and biological from existential, depends upon a scission in being that ostensibly would divide *Dasein* from just-plain-life without making such life absolutely inaccessible to it." See Krell's *Daimon Life: Heidegger and Life Philosophy* (Bloomington and Indianapolis: Indiana University Press, 1992), 94.

28. *Difficult Freedom*, 8.

29. William Spanos, whose work on Heidegger and on the technological perspective of the West *after* Heidegger powerfully informs this section of my essay, points out that "to cultivate and bring to fruition" mean "'to colonize' in the Roman sense of the word." See *Heidegger and Criticism: Retrieving the Cultural Politics of Destruction* (Minneapolis: University of Minnesota Press, 1993), 196.

30. *Totality and Infinity*, 142.

31. Space prevents me from addressing the important question of how Levinas's critique of Kant colors the argument of "The Name of a Dog, or Natural Rights." We should recall that for Levinas, Kant's understanding of "obligation" is insufficiently scandalous. As Jean-François Lyotard argues:

> If I am obligated by the other, it is not because the other has some right to obligate me which I would have directly or mediately granted him or her. My freedom is not the source of his or her authority: one is not obligated because one is free, and because your law is my law, but because your request is not my law, because we are liable for the other. Obligation through freedom or consent is secondary. (See *The Differend: Phrases in Dispute*, trans. Georges Van Den Abbeele [Minneapolis: University of Minnesota Press, 1988], 112.)

Perhaps one way in which Levinas signals the "secondariness" of Kantian obligation is by ambivalently attributing it to an *animal*, indeed, an animal whose kind is on the verge of extinction. The fact that respect has, as it were, gone to the dogs, may say as much about the inherent limitations of Kant's conception of obligation as it does about the exterminating violence of "Nazi Germany."

32. *The Metaphysical Principles of Virtue* (part 2 of *The Metaphysics of Morals*), trans. James Ellington (New York: Bobbs-Merrill, 1964), 105.

33. *The Moral Law*, trans. H. J. Paton (London: Hutchinson, 1966), 91.

34. "The Paradox of Morality," 172.

35. For a useful summary of Kant's position with respect to animals, see Alexander Broadie and Elizabeth M. Pybus, "Kant's Treatment of Animals," *Philosophy* 49 (1974), 375–383.

36. *The Metaphysical Principles of Virtue*, 105.

37. *The Metaphysical Principles of Virtue*, 105.

38. *Lectures on Ethics*, trans. L. Infield (New York: Harper Torchbooks, 1963), 240.

39. *Lectures on Ethics*, 239–240.

40. "The Paradox of Morality," 172.

41. *The Middle Voice of Ecological Conscience: A Chiasmic Reading of Responsibility in the Neighbourhood of Levinas, Heidegger, and Others* (London: Macmillan, 1991), 57.

42. "Education and Crisis, or the Vicissitudes of Teaching," in *Testimony: Crises of Witnessing in Literature, Psychoanalysis, and History*, by Shoshana Felman and Dori Laub (London: Routledge, 1992), 3.

43. Levinas: "The responsibility for another, an unlimited responsibility which the strict book-keeping of the free and non-free does not measure, requires subjectivity as an irreplaceable hostage." See "Substitution," in *The Levinas Reader*, 113.

Bibliography

Broadie, Alexander and Elizabeth M. Pybus. "Kant's Treatment of Animals" *Philosophy* 49 (1974), 375–383.

Caputo, John D. *Against Ethics: Contributions to a Poetics of Obligation with Constant Reference to Deconstruction.* Bloomington and Indianapolis: Indiana University Press, 1993.

Derrida, Jacques. *Aporias*, trans. Thomas Dutoit. Stanford: Stanford University Press, 1995.

———. "'Eating Well', or the Calculation of the Subject," trans. Avital Ronell, in *Points: Interviews, 1974–1994*, ed. Elisabeth Weber. Stanford: Stanford University Press, 1995. 255–287.

———. "Force of Law: The 'Mystical Foundation of Authority'," trans. Mary Quaintance. *Cardoza Law Review* 11.5–6 (July/August 1990), 919–1039.

———. *Of Spirit: Heidegger and the Question*, trans. Geoffrey Bennington and Rachel Bowlby. Chicago: University of Chicago Press, 1989.

———. "On Reading Heidegger: An Outline of Remarks to the Essex Colloquium." *Research in Phenomenology* 17 (1987), 171–188.

Felman, Shoshana. "Education and Crisis, or the Vicissitudes of Teaching," in *Testimony: Crises of Witnessing in Literature, Psychoanalysis, and History*, by Shoshana Felman and Dori Laub. London: Routledge, 1992. 1–56.

Hand, Seán. "Time and the Other," in *The Levinas Reader*, ed. Seán Hand. Oxford: Basil Blackwell, 1989. 37–38.

Heidegger, Martin. "Letter on Humanism," in *Basic Writings*, ed. and trans. David Farrell Krell. San Francisco: Harper Collins, 1993.

———. *Schelling's Treatise on the Essence of Human Freedom*, trans. Joan Stambaugh. Athens, OH: Ohio University Press, 1985.

———. *On the Way to Language*, trans. Peter D. Hertz. New York: Harper & Row, 1971.

———. *What Is Called Thinking*, trans. J. Glenn Gray. New York: Harper & Row, 1968.

Kant, Immanuel. *Lectures on Ethics*, trans. L. Infield. New York: Harper Torchbooks, 1963.

———. *The Metaphysical Principles of Virtue* (part 2 of *The Metaphysics of Morals*), trans. James Ellington. New York: Bobbs-Merrill, 1964.

———. *The Moral Law*, trans. H. J. Paton. London: Hutchinson, 1966.

Klein, Richard. "The Power of Pets." *The New Republic*. July 10, 1995, 18–23.

Krell, David Farrell. *Daimon Life: Heidegger and Life-Philosophy*. Bloomington and Indianapolis: Indiana University Press, 1992.

Levinas, Emmanuel. "As If Consenting to Horror," trans. Paula Wissing. *Critical Inquiry* 15 (Winter 1989), 485–488.

———. "Dialogue with Emmanuel Levinas," trans. Richard Kearney, in *Face to Face with Levinas*. Albany, NY: State University of New York Press, 1986. 13–33.

———. "The Name of a Dog, or Natural Rights," in *Difficult Freedom: Essays on Judaism*, trans. Seán Hand. London: The Athlone Press, 1990. 151–153. Published originally in *Celui qui ne peut pas se servir des mots* (Montpellier: Fata Morgana, 1976).

———. "The Paradox of Morality," trans. Andrew Benjamin and Tamra Wright, in *The Provocation of Levinas: Rethinking the Other*, eds. Robert Bernasconi and David Wood. London and New York: Routledge, 1988. 168–80.

———. *Totality and Infinity: An Essay on Exteriority*, trans. Alphonso Lingis. Pittsburgh: Duquesne University Press, 1969.

Lewis, C. S. *Till We Have Faces: A Myth Retold*. Glasgow: William Collins Sons & Co., 1956.

Llewelyn, John. "Am I Obsessed by Bobby? (Humanism of the Other Animal)," in *Re-Reading Levinas*, eds. Robert Bernasconi and Simon Critchley. Bloomington and Indianapolis: Indiana University Press, 1991. 234–245.

———. *Emmanuel Levinas: The Genealogy of Ethics*. London and New York: Routledge, 1995.

———. *The Middle Voice of Ecological Conscience: A Chiasmic Reading of Responsibility in the Neighbourhood of Levinas, Heidegger and Others*. London: Macmillan, 1991.

Lyotard, Jean-François. *The Differend: Phrases in Dispute*, trans. Georges Van Den Abbeele. Minneapolis: University of Minnesota Press, 1988.

Schirmacher, Wolfgang. *Technik und Gelassenheit*. Freiburg: Alber, 1983.

Sheehan, Thomas. "Heidegger and the Nazis." *The New York Review of Books*, June 16, 1988, 38–47.

Singer, Peter. *Animal Liberation: Towards an End to Man's Inhumanity to Animals*. London: Jonathan Cape, 1976.

Spanos, William V. *Heidegger and Criticism Retrieving the Cultural Politics of Destruction*. Minneapolis: University of Minnesota Press, 1993.

10 🙣

Animal Speech, Active Verbs, and Material Being in E. B. White

Paul H. Fry

Ordinarily it is not zoomorphism but anthropomorphism that gets discussed in essays on talking animals, as of course it would. The tradition of Aesop and La Fontaine continues unabated in modern children's literature, and I should say right away, echoing Edward Hoagland, that E. B. White sometimes takes a calculated Orwellian delight in the humanity of his animals.[1] To me the most wonderful of all his animal creations is also the most human: White's real-life dachshund Fred, the officious, libidinous pharisee of the *One Man's Meat* period.[2]

Because all three of White's children's books are indeed beast fables among other things, on some other MLA panel[3] one might explain how they intermingle the motives of parable and satire. In *Stuart Little*, for instance, we are never allowed to decide whether Stuart is a mouse or a person,[4] but in either case he is a Lilliputian in whom we see ourselves reflected. Although Stuart's birth from a human mother and amorous attachment to a bird seemed so shocking to an influential children's librarian that she begged White not to publish the book, White's little zoomorph is still considered by townspersons to be a suitable escort for the two-inch human being, Harriet Ames, of Ames' Crossing. So pervasive is the mild springtime eroticism of White's evocation of youth that when the town named for Harriet's family appears in the bold print of a chapter title the word "crossing" seems to recall Mendel's sweet peas.

The student of anthropomorphism would then go on to remark—on that other panel—that in both *Charlotte's Web* and *The Trumpet of the Swan*, the gradual shift from human to animal perspectives as the plots go forward by no means entails a retreat from human concerns: with the geese as Aristophanic chorus, Charlotte, Wilbur, Templeton, and the old sheep together clearly comprise, and are meant to comprise, a human typology. And perhaps the least motivated—hence most fascinating—part of *The Trumpet of the Swan* is its analysis of a speechifying, morally troubled patriarchalism. Not just the old cob modeled on White's father, but Sam's father Mr. Beaver, Mr. Brickle the camp director, Lucky Lucas the booking agent, and the Head Man at the zoo are guilty at times of the bombast, the suspiciously evasive purple prose habit, from which Strunk and White's *Elements of Style* is meant to wean the reader.

Talking too much, viewed the more ironically when it is talking animals who talk too much, is itself the anthropomorphic key to White's zoomorphism. Perhaps in the long run, all I shall succeed in saying, despite having talked too much, is that White uses talking animals to show that animals do not talk. Louis the swan, with his speech defect, is the first talking animal in history who is born unable to talk. He shows by example that, in the register of animal being, one need not communicate, or better, express the community of being, through the medium of language exchange. Of course animals are people too, as all the research on chimp and dolphin language has proven, and that is why all the other swans talk to each other—and why elsewhere White transcribes report after report of humanoid bird behavior from a book about Massachusetts birds.[5] But Louis shows that animal expressiveness has a nonhuman, or at least not characteristically human, dimension: his utterances are confined to the opposite extremes, respectively, of pure sound—the sound of his trumpet—and of a telegram-style *writing*, not talk, that is compressed even more vigorously than the concise prose recommended by Strunk and White.

The windy proser is an American type, and White follows his patron saint Thoreau in finding an American smugness about Manifest Destiny in the very habit of anthropocentrism itself, which is after all nothing but estrangement from the natural world. Driving his car to Walden Pond, White asks: "Am I not partly leaves and vegetable mold myself?—a man of infinite horsepower, yet partly leaves."[6] Even the word "horsepower" sabotages human visions of grandeur and restores the primacy of somatic being. When the doctor in *Stuart Little* says that "it is very unusual for an American family to have a mouse,"[7] he performs the surgical task to which I shall return in concluding, the task that lays bare in zoomorphism the absurdity of nationalism and the basis for White's favorite political cause: world federalism. "To be free, in a planetary sense," wrote White in a *Harper's* essay before the Americans entered the war, "is to feel that you belong to the earth. To be free, in a social sense, is to feel at home in a democratic framework" (*One Man's Meat*, 138). Here exhorting us to distinguish ourselves from Hitler by joining the fight against him, in general White pursues his vocation as a writer in order to reveal the common ground of planetary and social freedom. "I would like to be Chairman of the World myself," says Stuart in his brief role as schoolteacher. "'You're too small,' said Mary Bendix. 'Oh, fish feathers,' said Stuart. 'Size has nothing to do with it'" (92). Binding all the orders of animal being together (fish, birds, mammals), a talking rodent rejects inessentials in an oath of federation.

Our true commonality is our animal being, and White's children's stories anti-pedagogically and anti-intellectually teach the intelligence how to recover this state of being. Nothing more clearly shows the gentleness of his teaching than the odd fact that all his fictive human beings are no better than grown-ups usually are, yet are still in a state of much greater readiness for zoomorphic thinking than we readers are. Different children's writers handle the tricky business of human responsiveness to animal speech in different ways, but none so exuberantly return to the problem as White. Whereas all his animals always understand human speech, his people respond to animal speech in completely unpredictable ways. In *Stuart Little*, everyone understands Stuart, but his family may not understand Margala the bird and probably does not understand Snowbell the cat. More remarkable and more typical of White is the response of strangers to Stuart. Ranging from perfect equanimity to considerable surprise, each response nevertheless belongs in common to an entirely different register of cognitive expectation from the dizzying, life-transforming astonishment we readers would feel on hearing a mouse talk. Yet White prevents the principle of willingly suspended disbelief from suppressing the issue by insisting on the very range of responses—each is a new study in surprise—and on the amusement that each occasions.

Matters become even more complex in the next two books. We are only gradually made aware that Fern Arable understands the speech of the barnyard animals in *Charlotte's Web* as speech. At first she seems only to be responding sympathetically to grunts and squeals: "'They're going to *what?*' screamed Wilbur. Fern grew rigid on her stool."[8] No preternatural knowledge need be inferred here. But in the next chapter, Fern gives the correct names of the spider and the rat and accurately paraphrases Charlotte's bedtime stories. Even here, though, we need only switch into the mode of A. A. Milne and see Fern as Christopher Robin conferring humanity on his playthings. Every rationale falls away, finally, when Charlotte's writing appears for all to see. Yet even though it's called a miracle and attracts the curious from far and near,

Charlotte's web is not really an ontological violation of barnyard life but exists for the Arables, the Zuckermans, and all the visitors to the Fair alike at the extreme verge of rural normalcy yet still within it. In *The Trumpet of the Swan*, lastly, we are made to feel at first that superhuman yet still credible powers of zoological observation help Sam Beaver gradually to learn the language of swans, but as the plot develops, the world at large needs no such special knowledge and becomes more and more comfortable, absurdly comfortable, with a swan that works for a salary, stays at the Ritz, writes on a slate, and plays the trumpet.

The point seems to be that the problem of communication is not really a problem at all, but serves rather to displace a real problem: establishing community of being. Louis the swan is again the paradigm. He communicates with human beings only because he does human things, not swanlike things, and the absurdity of this humanizing leads to the frustration White briefly touches on when Louis returns to his family and realizes that they cannot read his writing. Despite enjoying his music and admiring his ability to write (not to mention swim, dive, and fly), the other swans, who talk to each other and sometimes talk too much, cannot share any kind of intelligible sign system with Louis except the semiosis of feeling. He can be talked *to* in English, or rather talked at, especially by his father; but his bride Serena never says a word to him, and we accordingly take their blissful happiness to be the happiness of living without disembodied signification.

People define themselves as language users, which is to say, with Dr. Dorian in *Charlotte's Web*, a talker himself: "People are incessant talkers—I can give you my word on that" (110). "Why does a bird need to read and write?" asks the teacher in *The Trumpet of the Swan*. "Only *people* need to communicate with one another."[9] They also apparently need to jabber. Despite the pointed exception of White's loquacious geese, animals are very different, as he suggested in 1930 when describing the efforts of a scientist recording animal sounds in a zoo: "A major difficulty is getting the animal to make any sound at all, animals having a penchant for absolute silence."[10] This is so often not the case that one suspects White of meaning something a little inobvious. Not silence so much as a Wordsworthian quietness is in any case the state of human readiness for understanding, for community of being. Posing as exemplars of this readiness, Fern is raptly attentive on her milkstool in *Charlotte's Web*, and Sam Beaver sits motionless at the pond's edge watching the swan's eggs hatch in *The Trumpet of the Swan*.

This state of receptiveness to the *infans* and the nonhuman is a recurrent theme in White's essays and poems:

Hold a baby to your ear
  As you would a shell:
Sounds of centuries you hear
  New centuries foretell.[11]

"Who can break a baby's code?" this poem continues, suggesting as White always does that prelinguistic forms of organization are the bedrock of planetary freedom. When he wants to make this point explicit, he modestly quotes an expert:

> Dr. Vannevar Bush, who is in a far better position to discuss science and progress than I am, once said, "Man may, indeed, have evolved from the primordial ooze, and this may be accepted as good if we assume that it is good to have complex life on earth, but this again is an arbitrary assumption." (*Essays of E. B. White*, 40)

To illustrate Strunk's insistence on vivid writing in *The Elements of Style*, White quotes at surprising length from a story by Jean Stafford about a drunkard who keeps monkeys, a talking bird, and other animals, and is beloved of children—a holy idiot leveling modes of being, in other words, who is also White's comment in miniature on the mission of Will Strunk: the redemption of writing from prolixity. In his memoir of his old teacher, White says that Strunk, when speaking, would pare down his sentences so zealously that he was often left with too little to say, and would flesh out his lectures by repeating everything three times: "Rule Seventeen. Omit needless words! Omit needless words! Omit needless words!" The rule itself points toward the distilled writing of Charlotte and the telegram style of Louis, but the repetition of the rule is like the gabbling of geese in *Charlotte's Web*. "'Thank you, thank you, thank you,' said the goose. 'Certainly-ertainly-ertainly,' said the gander" (44–45). Strunk's Rule Eleven, "Make definite assertions"—scorning, as White puts it, "the tame, the colorless, the irresolute"[12]—inculcates a bustling agency that it would perhaps be a mistake to call human. The animal, too, is definite. Keats's field mouse that has a purpose, its eyes bright with it, is the forerunner of all White's animals. Just as concision borders on the eclipse of meaning, syntax giving way to sheer repetition,[13] so Strunk's key words—vigor, definiteness, force—bespeak the intensity, the total absorption, of unself-consciousness. The dialectic thus hidden within the doctrine of straightforwardness arrives finally at death, as Strunk and White seem to concede in their metalingual illustration of joining two independent clauses with a colon: "But even so," they write, "there was a directness and dispatch about animal burial: there was no stopover in the undertaker's foul parlor, no wreath or spray" (8).

Charlotte redeems writing from the shuffling volubility of human talk by spinning the word "humble" in the vicinity of birth and death: the egg sac she weaves and the spinning out of her life's thread are both parts of Charlotte's seamless web. As she points out, "humble" means "'not proud' and it also means 'near the ground'. That's Wilbur all over" (140). Indeed it is, but the humus in this word appears also in the word "human," while its sound is the very hum of existence itself. When it is no longer near the ground, writing is linked to advertising—White's career for a year in the twenties—from which Templeton in the dump had earlier torn out the words "terrific" and "radiant"—fine words also, the latter being soft soap from a soap ad, but still hyperbolic signs of Charlotte's con-artistry. "Pitchman's jargon" is what Strunk and White call adjectival excess (45).[14]

Even the expression that starts it all, "Some Pig," simple, colloquial and non-derivative though it is, has that element of falseness about it that belongs to any language designed for conferring aura on an object—which is to say, in Fregean terms but in reversal of Fregean values, to confer meaning rather than to make sense. That everyone except Mrs. Zuckerman thinks the pig is the miracle and not the writing—they are all sold on Wilbur—quite neatly exposes the false transparency of language. Granted, semiosis is a miracle ("We have received a sign, Edith" (80)), but it is also the medium of error: "I got the plan for it out of a book, fool-fashion," says one of White's Maine neighbors in *One Man's Meat* (245). Like the people in one of his parables who "by witlessness and improvidence, escape many of the errors of accomplishment" (*The Second Tree from the Corner*, 70), but also like the Henry James, whose mind was too fine for an idea to slip through, White and his New Yorker colleagues cultivated stylistic refinement in order to avoid the purposefulness of error: White's wife Katharine at the fiction desk disapproved of plot in short stories, and the editor Harold Ross made the magazine what it was because he was "suspicious of 'thinking'" (he always wrote "thinking" in quotes).

Writing that is humble, near the ground even if perhaps somewhat proud, has a great deal to do not with animal speech, but with animal sounds; and the meeting point of these extremes is the place where style, for which one has an "ear," and the onomatopoetic noises of the world intersect: the ko-hoh of the trumpeter swan, the thrice-repeated ontic apiary of the goslings in *Charlotte's Web*—"bee-bee-bee" (86)—and the four birds earlier in *Charlotte's Web* who name everything in life there is to name: society—"Peabody, Peabody, Peabody"—self-existence—"Phoebe, Phoe-bee"—existence itself—"Sweet,

sweet, sweet interlude"—and the critical perspective: "Cheeky, cheeky!" (43). It is reserved for the crickets, rewriting Keats with their "Summer is over and gone," to name death. The moments, then, when the animals either return to their own languages, languages that sound like English near the ground, or else write English near the ground—these are the moments in which White seems to be venturing on something like a writer's credo. Even though authorial self-consciousness can never be suspended, writing does serve its turn when it seems continuous, like Charlotte's web, with the process world; or when it is an expression of fellow feeling, as when the pigeon writes a note warning Margala of the cats' plot in *Stuart Little*. As the mute swan Louis, with his chalk and slateboard, seems finally meant to show, writing replaces human talk with animal speech.

White thought of himself as an environmentalist; and even though the dump on the Maine farm, where Fred the dachshund is buried among the tin cans and where Templeton the rat browses through last month's magazines, would be the object of an indignant recycling campaign today, White certainly did write of "planetary freedom" as an ecological issue. I think that even for White, though, or perhaps especially for him, there is a difference between the epistemological concerns of the ecologist—knowing how things fit together in a vast scheme, a sign system or code—and the ontological concerns of the writer, for whom the naming of being, Keats's "greeting of the spirit," is what is important. In response to a waiter who claimed to owe his health to eating the skin of fish, White says in *The New Yorker* that he prefers to hold the fish "firmly in mind," not in his stomach: "the protein remembrance of the cool fish-in-being" is what matters to him. That the fish is "perfectly adapted to its environment" is also exciting, but it can be a source of energy only when it remains unknown, unconsumed in any sense of the term, including that form of objectification which differentiates it ecologically: "It is a mistake to under-estimate the sustaining power of a thing in its natural, or undigested form" (*The Second Tree from the Corner*, 220). A broad, radical, libertarian streak coexisted uneasily with White's liberalism (I am speaking chiefly of the essays, but it could be shown in the children's books as well), and there is accordingly a tension between global concern and *laissez-faire* in his sense of the human place in the natural world. World federalism for White is the community of existence without local regulation, "planetary freedom"; and his writing attempts to name this freedom, following the precepts of Strunk and White, in the concise, vigorous language of undigested animal being. If there is some sense in which he is not an environmentalist, it is the sense in which animals are not environmentalists.

Notes

1. See Hoagland, "The Voice of the *New Yorker*," in *Critical Essays on E. B. White*, ed. Robert L. Root, Jr. (New York: G. K. Hall & Co., 1994), 60.
2. White's biographer Scott Elledge thinks that Fred "may have encouraged him to create other animal characters" (*E. B. White: A Biography* (New York: Norton, 1984), 278).
3. This essay was originally presented at the MLA Conference in San Diego, California, December, 1994.
4. See White's amusing letter about this in *Letters of E. B. White*, ed. Dorothy Lobrano Guth (New York: Harper & Row, 1976), 270.
5. "Mr. Forbush's Friends" (on *Birds of Massachusetts and Other New England States* by Edward Howe Forbush), *Essays of E. B. White* (New York: Harper Colophon, 1977), 268–276.
6. White, *One Man's Meat* (New York: Harper & Row, rpt. 1982), 66.
7. White, *Stuart Little* (New York: Harper Trophy, 1945), 3 (henceforth cited parenthetically by page).
8. White, *Charlotte's Web* (Columbus, OH: Weekly Reader Books, 1952), 49 (henceforth cited parenthetically by page). When Charlotte speaks up a moment later, White very uncharacteristically resorts to the passive voice in order to make it unclear whether Fern hears her: "Fern was just about to jump up [in response to Wilbur's screams] when a voice was heard" (50).
9. White, *The Trumpet of the Swan* (New York: Harper Trophy, 1970), 58.
10. White, *Writings from the "New Yorker" 1927–1976*, ed. Rebecca M. Dale (New York: Harper Collins, 1990), 164.
11. White, "Conch," *The Second Tree from the Corner* (New York: Harper & Row, rpt. 1984), 195.
12. William Strunk, Jr. and E. B. White, *The Elements of Style*, 3rd ed. (New York: Macmillan, 1979), xvi (henceforth cited parenthetically by page).
13. In a parable called "Irtnog," White reflects with surprising ambivalence on the condensation of books into digests and digests into meaningless code words: "With the dwindling of reading, writing fell off. Forests, which had been plundered for newsprint, grew tall again; droughts were unheard of; and people dwelt in slow comfort, in a green world." *Quo Vadimus? or the Case for the Bicycle* (New York: Harper and Brothers, 1938), 49.
14. For another view of advertising in *Charlotte's Web*, see Helene Solheim, "Magic in the Web," in *Critical Essays*, ed. Robert L. Root, 156–157n. Puffed-up writing appears also to be taken from what White, in *The Elements of Style* (83), calls "the world of criticism," which supplies, for example, the all-too-radiant word "luminous."

Bibliography

Elledge, Edward. *E. B. White: A Biography*. New York: Norton, 1984.

Hoagland. "The Voice of the *New Yorker*," in *Critical Essays on E. B. White*, ed. Robert L. Root, Jr. New York: G. K. Hall and Co., 1994.

Solheim, Helene. "Magic in the Web," in *Critical Essays on E. B. White*, ed. Robert L. Root, Jr. New York: G. K. Hall and Co., 1994.

Strunk, William, Jr., and E. B. White. *The Elements of Style*. 3rd ed. New York: Macmillan, 1979.

White, E. B. *Charlotte's Web*. Colombus, OH: Weekly Reader Books, 1952.

———. "Irtnog," in *Quo Vadimus? Or the Case for the Bicycle*. New York: Harper and Brothers, 1938.

———. *Letters of E. B. White*, ed. Dorothy Lobrano Guth. New York: Harper and Row, 1976.

———. "Mr. Forbush's Friends," in *Essays of E. B. White*. New York: Harper Colophon, 1977.

———. *One Man's Meat*. New York: Harper and Row, 1982.

———. *Stuart Little*. New York: Harper Trophy, 1945.

11

"Surely, God, These Are My Kin"
The Dynamics of Identity and Advocacy in the Life and Works of Dian Fossey

Karla Armbruster

> The dividing line between nations may well be invisible; but it is no less real. How does one cross that line to travel in the nation of animals? Having traveled in their nation, where lies your allegiance? What do you become?
> —Sy Montgomery (1991, 267)

In December of 1966, Dian Fossey traveled to Africa to study the endangered mountain gorilla in its native habitat: the rain forests of the Virunga Mountains, which straddle the border between Zaire and Uganda to the north and Rwanda to the south. Sponsored by Dr. Louis Leakey and aided by a grant from the National Geographic Society, Fossey began her research in what is now Zaire (then the Belgian Congo). Soon, however, political disturbances prompted her to move her study area to the Rwandan Parc des Volcans, where she founded the Karisoke Research Center in mid-1967. The center, which Fossey ran until she was murdered in 1984, served not only as her base of operations but also as a site for a variety of other scientists to study the gorillas. While Karisoke was founded for the purpose of scientific research, and the work Fossey and other scientists conducted there added substantially to knowledge of gorilla biology and behavior, today Fossey is primarily known not as a scientist but rather, in the words of Vera Norwood, as "the American woman most famed for her advocacy of the rights of African wildlife to autonomy" (1993,

245). Fossey's own writings indicate that advocacy, rather than pure research, was her priority all along. As early as 1970, in an article in *National Geographic*, Fossey stressed the threats that the gorillas faced from poachers and cattle herders "trespassing" in their habitat, and she characterized her own research as part of an effort to help save the gorillas by learning more about them.[1]

Her desire to act as an advocate for the gorillas grew out of a lifelong tendency to defend and aid those she viewed as in need of her help and protection: the disabled children with whom she worked as an occupational therapist in Louisville, Kentucky; the chickens given to her as food that she promptly turned into pets; her dog, Cindy, whom she went to great lengths to rescue after she had been kidnapped by Rwandan poachers. However, from the first time Fossey saw the mountain gorillas, she felt an especially strong and immediate affinity for them, an affinity she characterized as a bond of kinship. This bond, modified and strengthened as she learned about and interacted with the gorillas over the years, would inspire her to spend the rest of her life speaking and acting on the gorillas' behalf. Central to Fossey's advocacy was her profound sense that the gorillas had an inherent right to live in their native habitat unharmed by humans. This notion, along with Fossey's own relationship to the gorillas, constituted a fundamental challenge to dominant Western ideologies that perceive human culture as separate from and superior to animals like the gorillas.[2] However, Fossey enjoyed a great deal of popular interest and approval early in her career, suggesting that her culture initially interpreted her act of reaching out across the species boundary as nonthreatening. Eventually, though, her uncompromising advocacy of the gorillas came into conflict with the political, economic, and ideological needs and priorities of groups including the American public, the scientific and conservation communities, and the Rwandan and United States governments, and she and her work were transformed into a site of intense cultural anxiety. This anxiety suggests that her actions and discourse may have destabilized the nature/culture boundary in ways that were subversive of the dominant cultural ideologies of separation and superiority that she saw as working against the survival of the gorillas.

However, as cultural theorists who have explored the complex issues involved in the act of speaking for others have pointed out, advocacy that seeks to subvert any aspect of the dominant culture is not a straightforward task; the ideologies that ground domination of all kinds are pervasive forces that work to construct human subjectivity and conceptions of nature within Western culture, and cannot easily be escaped.[3] And so it is important to examine the constructions of human and (nonhuman) animal identity and the relationship between them at work in Fossey's life and writings, and to ask how those constructions may have both subverted and reinforced the dominant ideologies she set out to challenge. Ultimately, by asking the question that Fossey herself might have been most interested in—what difference did her controversial relationship with the gorillas make to their chances for survival?—I seek to suggest ways in which we might construct our relationships with animals that will foster the liberation and welfare of both humans and other animals.

Fossey's Kinship with the Mountain Gorillas

Dian Fossey saw mountain gorillas in their native habitat for the first time in 1963. In her journal, she conveyed her reaction by quoting the words of an African boy who had accompanied her expedition as a cook:

> "*Kweli nudugu yanga!*" These words in Swahili, whispered by the awestruck Manual, who was also seeing his first gorilla, summed up exactly what I was feeling. "Surely, God, these are my kin." (Mowat 1987, 14)

While Fossey did not begin to forge a truly intimate relationship with mountain gorillas until she began her study of them in 1967, her immediate sense of kinship with these animals helps to explain the somewhat unorthodox approach she took in her work with them. This approach was characterized by Fossey's desire to adapt "herself to gorillas' perceptions of how animals should behave in the forest" (Norwood 1993, 245). "Open contacts," Fossey writes,

> . . . slowly helped me win the animals' acceptance. This was especially true when I learned that imitation of some of their ordinary activities such as scratching and feeding or copying their contentment vocalizations tended to put the animals at ease more rapidly than if I simply looked at them through binoculars while taking notes. (1983, 11)

Because of this willingness to adapt her behavior in response to the gorillas, Fossey gained access to their daily activities in a way that allowed her significantly to add to scientific and popular knowledge of the species. For example, as Sy Montgomery notes, her discoveries included how females transfer between family groups, how a raiding silverback (the male leader of a family group) will sometimes kill the infant of a female he has kidnapped so she will come into heat, and how gorillas sometimes eat their own excrement in order to recycle nutrients (1991, 149).

While Fossey claimed that her willingness to "act like a gorilla" violated textbook instructions "merely to sit and observe" when conducting animal behavioral studies, Norwood asserts that Fossey's techniques matched "widely accepted practices" for such studies (Fossey 1970, 51; Norwood 1993, 246). However, what was unquestionably unique about Fossey's approach was the attitude underlying it: a sense of deep respect for the gorillas as well as a willingness to regard them as individual subjects rather than merely the objects of her study. For example, Fossey's resolution never to follow a gorilla group once it chose to leave grew not only out of her practical need to win the gorillas' trust, but also out of a sense that she was an "intruder" in the gorillas' domain (1983, 14). In addition, her sense of the complexity of the "character and depth of the gorillas' lives" led her to refuse to use standard tools of animal behavior studies, such as predetermined sampling schedules and check sheets of typical behaviors (Montgomery 1991, 147). Although such indications of her respect and admiration for the gorillas provoked some criticism from her doctoral thesis advisor, she persisted in conducting her research on her own terms. Fossey's strong regard for the inherent dignity and rights of the animals she studied was rooted in her sense of the animals as subjects, as living beings with whom she had much in common, such as the capacity to feel pain and fear. Despite indications in *Gorillas in the Mist* that she was concerned about accusations of anthropomorphism or lack of objectivity, she also acknowledges and empathizes with the suffering of gorillas wounded by poachers and with the terror they feel when unknown humans intrude upon their territory.[4] When she describes how Digit, one of her favorite gorillas, was killed and mutilated by poachers, she conveys a sense of an almost overwhelming empathy: she tells the reader, "I tried not to allow myself to think of Digit's anguish, pain, and the total comprehension he must have suffered in knowing what humans were doing to him" (1983, 206).

A number of writers and scholars have speculated that Fossey's gender in some way influenced her unusual approach to the gorillas she studied.[5] And in fact, one of the reasons Louis Leakey originally chose Fossey to study the gorillas was that she was a woman. Leakey, who was also responsible for initiating Jane Goodall's research on chimpanzees in Tanzania and Biruté Galdikas' work with orangutans in Indonesia, deliberately chose women for long-term primate behavior studies because he believed they possessed a special talent for observation, a biological and cultural predisposition to make long-term commitments (usually demonstrated by raising children), and a sensitivity to interpersonal relations that would help them establish a rapport with the animals they studied (Norwood 1993, 250; Montgomery 1991, 71, 81). While Leakey's broad assumptions about women's inherent natures conjure up the specter of essentialism, there is evidence that Fossey's approach to the animals she studied fits into a strong tradition of women's interaction with wildlife.[6]

Norwood places Fossey in a tradition of women, including Delia Akeley and Lois Crisler, whose stories demonstrate the conflict female researchers often feel between a desire for connection with wild animals and a sense of responsibility for negative consequences to the animals resulting from that connection. As Norwood explains:

> Women have been taught that, as females, their strengths lie in empathy with and concern for other individuals. They have entered the habitats of wolves, gorillas, and elephants expecting to immerse themselves in a network of relationships requiring reciprocity and ethical responsibility. (1993, 211)[7]

True to this pattern, Fossey developed relationships with mountain gorillas—both as individuals and as family groups—that became far more important to her than the progress of her own research or the goals of the institutions that funded her work. For example, in describing an encounter initiated by a gorilla named Macho, Fossey writes: "On perceiving the softness, tranquillity, and trust conveyed by Macho's eyes, I was overwhelmed by the extraordinary depth of our rapport. The poignancy of her gift will never diminish" (1983, 201). In response to the trust and acceptance she sensed from gorillas like Macho, Fossey took on the responsibility of protecting their welfare. As Norwood notes, what was most remarkable about Fossey's work with the gorillas was her unshakable ethical commitment to the animals themselves (1993, 245–246). Her book is filled with passages which reveal her deep sense of responsibility for them: not only does she condemn the poachers who threaten the gorillas' safety and the spreading agricultural development encroaching on their already diminished rain forest habitat, but she also anxiously speculates that human contact, even with researchers, could be spreading diseases to the gorillas. But the most dramatic manifestation of her commitment to the gorillas' welfare was her uncompromising practice of what she called "active conservation," which meant vigorously and regularly patrolling the gorillas' habitat to keep it empty of poachers and their traps. In fact, Fossey had little use for graduate students whose only interest in coming to Karisoke was their own research; she approved only of students who "cherished the animals of the forest above their personal interests" and expected all her students to participate in active conservation (1983, 162).

Ultimately, Fossey's positioning of herself as the gorillas' protector and advocate grew out of her profound sense of kinship with them, a bond she to some extent learned to develop by watching the gorillas themselves interact within their family groups. The characteristic of the gorillas that she most often described with admiration was their loyalty to these groups, which are typically composed of two to twenty animals (ten, on average) and are led by a silverback, a sexually mature male over the age of fifteen years (1983, 10). The gorillas' commitment to protecting the members of their family group is graphically illustrated by Fossey's descriptions of several instances when all the adults in a family fought to the death in an attempt to prevent poachers from capturing an infant member of the group. In addition, she tended to judge individual gorillas based on their contribution to the harmony and stability within family groups. In particular, she admired the leader of Study Group 5, a male silverback whom she called Beethoven, writing that "the members of Group 5 have taught me how the strong bonds of kinship contribute to the cohesiveness of a gorilla family unit over time. The success of Group 5 remains a behavioral example for human society, a legacy bequeathed to us by Beethoven" (1983, 105). And Fossey herself followed that example, behaving with as much courage and single-mindedness in her defense of the gorillas as they did in their defense of each other.[8] In a very real sense, Fossey transgressed the species boundary to claim these gorillas as her family. Both Fossey and those who knew her seemed to sense this transgression, sometimes speaking of her as having "become" a gorilla.[9]

A Touch across the Boundary of Difference

In her relationship of kinship with the gorillas, Fossey reached across the boundary of difference and superiority that Western culture had constructed between itself and the rest of nature. While Western society at first managed to interpret Fossey in a way that reconciled her relationship with the gorillas with cultural norms and desires, eventually the uncompromising advocacy that grew out of that relationship made such an interpretation impossible to support, and Fossey's career became the site of cultural anxiety, controversy, and, potentially, subversion. The changing cultural constructions of Fossey's relationship with the gorillas can be illustrated through the interpretive possibilities of a very well known photo of Fossey originally published in a 1971 issue of *National Geographic* (Figure 1). This photo captures Fossey in the moment of experiencing "the first intimate touch between any human and a mountain gorilla" (Norwood 1993, 210). In the photo, Fossey is lying down, almost hidden in the vegetation of the rain forest, with only her head and forearms visible; her right arm is stretched out towards Peanuts, a young adult male gorilla, who appears to be reaching out to touch her hand with his.[10] Fossey's left hand is touched to her lips, and her face registers what Farley Mowat, one of her biographers, has described as "pure ecstasy" (1987, 85).

Figure 1. Dian Fossey and Peanuts in Rwanda, 1970. Photo by Robert M. Campbell © National Geographic Society.

As Norwood explains, this representation of a peaceful, beatific woman receiving the touch offered by a wild animal became one of the most popular and culturally iconized images of Fossey in American society.[11] Both Norwood and Donna Haraway discuss how the popularity of this image of a "touch across Difference" between gorilla and female human reflects a deep-seated desire within Western industrialized society to bridge the chasm between human culture and nature.[12] However, as Haraway emphasizes, the cultural embrace of this image was predicated on a particular reading of the "touch across Difference" as "the spontaneous touch of the other, the bridge between 'animal' and 'man' built *by the animal* as a spontaneous and supremely meaningful gift" (1989, 148). Only by reading the touch as a gift from nature can the reader or viewer feel absolved "of unspoken transgressions [and relieved of] anxieties of separation and solitary isolation on a threatened planet and for a culture threatened by the consequences of its own history" (156). Haraway shows that Western culture is able to view white women primatologists like Fossey as mediating between culture and nature in such a nonthreatening way because of a "triple code" of gender, race, and science; their positioning at the intersection of complex political and historical forces allows the films and articles that represent them to:

> rigorously exclude the contextualizing politics of decolonization and exploitation of the emergent Third World, obligatory and normative heterosexuality, masculine dominance of a progressively war-based scientific enterprise in industrial civilization, and the racial symbolic and institutional organization of scientific research. Instead, the dramas of communication, origins, extinction, and reproduction are played out in a nature that seems innocent of history. If history is what hurts, nature is what heals. (1989, 156)

While such a reading of the image of "touch across Difference" explains Fossey's early popular appeal, an alternative reading can also be detected in the 1971 photo and in Fossey's written accounts of the incident, the roots of the controversies which would swirl around her later in her career and persist even after her death.

The sequence of events that led up to the photo began when Fossey sensed the attention of Peanuts and responded by pretending to feed on vegetation in order to entertain him and assure him that she meant him no harm.[13] She then began to scratch her scalp to further entertain him, and he scratched his own in response. According to Fossey, "It was not clear who was aping whom" (Fossey 1971, 577; Mowat 1987, 85). Building on this pattern, Fossey extended her hand to Peanuts, and her description of this gesture suggests she did so in the hopes that he would continue to mimic her actions: "I held it palm up at first, as the palms of an ape and a human hand are more similar than the backs of the hand" (Fossey 1971, 577; Mowat 1987, 85). In response, she writes in *Gorillas in the Mist*, "After looking intently at my hand, Peanuts stood up and extended his hand to touch his fingers against my own for a brief instant" (1983, 141–142).

Fossey's texts indicate this interaction, which she described as "among the most memorable of my life among the gorillas," went far beyond the passive receptivity to his touch that can be read into the photo (1983, 142). In the same way, her relationship with the gorillas she studied did not correspond to the popular, culturally nonthreatening image that Norwood suggests she possessed in the early years of her work: a passive "nun of nature whose presence signified a pacified green world" (1993, 210). Instead, Fossey *actively* constructed a relationship between herself and the gorillas that transgressed the socially constructed boundary between human culture and nature. Fossey's apparent willingness to immerse herself in the world of the gorillas and function as a mediator between Western culture and nature may have initially held a strong appeal for the people of that culture, as Haraway describes; however, that same relationship of connection to the gorillas ultimately led her to behave in ways that profoundly violated dominant cultural expectations in several significant ways.

Her sense of kinship with the gorillas, while initially fitting into an American tradition of women's relationships with wildlife (Norwood 1993), grew to exceed radically the level of commitment that Western society deemed acceptable for a woman. As Norwood notes, the Hollywood film *Gorillas in the Mist* "implies that the arc of Fossey's life began its downward slide into violence and death when she rejected a marriage proposal from a National Geographic photographer" (1993, 210). In this way, the film both helped to create and drew on the "popular image of Dian Fossey as a woman lost to the bounds of civilization" due to her choice of a family of gorillas rather than a conventional human family (Norwood 1993, 211). Even many of the graduate students who worked with Fossey were disappointed that all her energies went to protecting the gorillas rather than towards creating a nurturing atmosphere in the research camp; as Harold Hayes explains in *The Dark Romance of Dian Fossey*, "The students expected a camaraderie that never developed. They expected to get to know her, but she never broke out of her role as leader, as the toughest soldier of the troop" (1990, 281).

Fossey's unwillingness to compromise on the gorillas' immediate safety also transgressed the bounds of behavior considered appropriate by the scientific and conservation communities. She frequently challenged the management of the Rwandan national park within which she worked, insisting that their desire to protect the gorillas' habitat through tourism would only familiarize the gorillas with humans and make them more vulnerable to poachers.[14] Her radical opposition to tourism even took the form of tactics such as firing a gun "in response to an unannounced visit by a tourist group from Chicago" (Hayes 1990, 309). Such public relations disasters made her so unpopular with the Rwandan government that by 1978, according to Harold Hayes (1990), the U.S. State Department was actively trying to persuade Fossey to leave Rwanda temporarily to ease tensions.[15] Clearly, Fossey's attachment to the gorillas and her commitment to protecting them defied the norms of traditional science as well; as Vera Norwood explains, Fossey's

> radical intervention in the park management structure led to much tension with scientific and conservation groups like the National Geographic Society, which ultimately withdrew its support from her project, declaring that her approach was not scientific enough and that she was too emotionally involved with the gorillas. (1993, 249)

While the extent to which Fossey defied societal norms for the behavior of a woman and a scientist created a great deal of anxiety within mainstream Western culture during the later stages of her career, biographers and supporters such as Mowat (1987) and Montgomery (1991) have had little trouble celebrating these aspects of her relationship with the gorillas as subversive of dominant ideologies that foster oppression in general and the destruction of nature in particular. However, more difficult to recuperate is the criticism that Fossey's career is more likely to provoke in recent years: that her methods of protecting and speaking for the gorillas often demonstrated a serious disregard for the rights and needs of the native Rwandans, rights and needs she often saw as diametrically opposed to those of the gorillas. As Harold Hayes describes in *The Dark Romance of Dian Fossey:*

> In pursuit of her singular goal, the protection of the endangered mountain gorilla, Fossey had shot her enemies, kidnapped their children, whipped them about the genitals, smeared them with ape dung, killed their cattle, burned their property, and sent them to jail. (1990, 33)[16]

She also viewed the native population as fundamentally unable to appreciate the gorillas in the way that she and other Westerners could, blaming the species' endangered status on "the encroachment of native man upon its habitat—and neglect by civilized man" (1970, 67). Such behavior and attitudes on the part of a white Westerner in postcolonial Africa can only be interpreted as an oppressive reinscription of ethnic and racial hierarchies, a clear message that Fossey saw native Rwandans not only as inferior to "civilized" Westerners in matters of conservation, but also as less important to her than her chosen family of gorillas.[17]

The Complex Dynamics of Identity and Advocacy

While there are significant distinctions between Fossey's defiance of dominant conceptions of appropriate behavior for a woman and a scientist and her troubling behavior as a white Westerner in postcolonial Africa, her disregard for any of these types of criticism has helped to create her reputation as the mountain gorillas' most zealous and radical advocate, challenging dominant conceptions of nature by testifying to these animals' inherent dignity and right to life and habitat. The degree of anxiety which she has produced within white, Western culture suggests that her actions and discourse were potentially subversive of dominant ideologies, including those that construct animals like the gorillas as separate from and inferior to human culture. And yet, because of the complex intersection of cultural and political forces at which her relationship with the gorillas lay, it was difficult for her—or anyone else—to know or predict whether her words or actions would ultimately help the gorillas or hurt them.

As theorists like Linda Alcoff and Gayatri Spivak have discussed, the practice of speaking for others is fraught with difficulties. Because the position of being able to speak and be heard within the realms of human culture is usually one of privilege, the act of speaking for those with less privilege is implicated in a web of "power relations of domination, exploitation, and subordination" (Alcoff 1991, 15). Consequently, as Linda Alcoff explains in "The Problem of Speaking for Others," "the practice of privileged persons speaking for or on behalf of less privileged persons has actually resulted (in many cases) in increasing or reinforcing the oppression of the group spoken for" (1991, 7). Like the white, upper-middle-class women who often find themselves in a position to speak for less privileged women, humans who wish to act as advocates for nonhuman nature find themselves almost inextricably embedded in dominant ideologies that separate and privilege not only humans over nature, but men over women, whites over other races, Western culture over other cultures, and heterosexuality over homosexuality and bisexuality.

A particular danger for women who speak for nature, as exemplified by certain cultural ecofeminists, is a tendency to "cast women, along with nature, as an oppressed class that did not participate in the masculine agenda of domination" (Norwood 1993, 276–277). By aligning women with nature in a way that elevates both over the male-dominated society blamed for environmental degradation and women's oppression, such ecofeminist writers merely reverse dominant cultural hierarchies, rather than questioning and destabilizing ideologies of dualism and hierarchy overall. As Haraway has pointed out, "The positionings of the subjugated are not exempt from critical reexamination, decoding, deconstruction, and interpretation" (1988, 584).

Significantly, Fossey never attempted to evade responsibility for any part she might play in endangering the gorillas. While her gender may have been one factor in creating this strong sense of responsibility, her scientific training and role may have contributed as well. Her discussion of the gorillas' behavior suggests that she was constantly tempering her desire to see the connections and similarities between herself and the gorillas with a scientifically grounded awareness of their important differences from her. For example, she frequently attributes actions, such as the movement of females among family groups, to the gorillas' tendency to seek out opportunities for reproduction, and she matter-of-factly accepts their habit of eating their own dung, speculating that it might "allow vitamins synthesized in the hindgut to be assimilated in the foregut" (1983, 46). Her sense of the gorillas' significant differences from her comes into play even more strongly when she must struggle to accept and explain behavior such as one female gorilla killing and eating another's infant (1983, 77–78). By confronting such aspects of gorilla behavior as well as aspects she can more easily identify with, Fossey complicates the culture/nature boundary in a way that allows her to make connections across difference without denying that differences exist.

In addition to this strong sense of the biological differences between herself and the gorillas, Fossey was also very much aware of the cultural privilege she, as a member of human culture, held in relation to them; it was this cultural privilege that made her able to act as their advocate. However, her strong sense of difference also made her constantly and painfully aware that she might unwittingly contribute to the forces threatening to harm them. In particular, Fossey's experiences with the complex, unpredictable forces of public opinion and national and park politics raised her awareness of the danger that her intended advocacy could hold for the gorillas. An especially crucial decision involved whether or not to publicize the death of Digit, a young male gorilla whom Fossey came to love and admire more than perhaps any other. While Fossey knew that publicizing his death at the hands of poachers could be used to gain financial support for her active conservation measures, she realized that the administration of the Parc des Volcans would also profit from the publicity. She feared that, as a consequence, Digit would be "the first sacrificial victim [of a series] from the study groups if monetary rewards were to follow the news of his slaughter" (1983, 207). In the end, she decided to publicize the killing, unwilling to let Digit's death be in vain. When other gorillas were killed approximately six months later, she was haunted by doubts: "Since Digit's killing had proved so profitable to the Rwandese park officials, could there possibly be a connection between the first tragedy and the latest timely slaughters?" (1983, 216).

While Fossey's deliberations over decisions involving the gorillas reflect a sense of the complexity of the practice of advocacy, what she seems to have been less aware of was the possibility that the very way she constructed her own identity and her relationship to the gorillas could undermine her attempts to challenge dominant perceptions of their importance in relation to human culture. In particular, in most of her work, Fossey consistently opposed the welfare and interests of native Rwandans to her own priority: the advocacy and protection of the gorillas. For example, in *Gorillas in the Mist*, she points out that the gorillas' jungle habitat is in danger of being converted to fields for growing pyrethrum, a flower used to make natural insecticides. She does so with an understanding that "the average Rwandan living near the boundaries of the Parc des Volcans and raising pyrethrum for the equivalent of four cents a pound" cannot be expected to make the welfare of the gorillas a priority above his or her own survival (1983, 239). However, Fossey's understanding of the situation led her only to position herself with the gorillas against any humans whose needs might come into conflict with theirs; she believed that attempts to impose on Rwandans "the notion of wildlife as a treasured legacy [overlooked] the reality that to most of a local impoverished and inert populace wildlife is considered an obstacle" (1983, 241). Even tourism, which might persuade people to look at the gorillas as a resource rather than an obstacle to economic progress, to her seemed inadequate "compared with more expedient actions that could be taken on [the gorillas'] behalf" (1983, 242). As Haraway points out, the economic and political realities of Rwanda "enter Fossey's book only as a disrupting force in the Garden, through murderous poachers, selfish graduate students, and mendacious politicians" (1989, 147) rather than as the products of a history of racism and colonialism that have shaped the fate of both the native Rwandans and the gorillas.

Ultimately, Fossey's construction of her connection with the gorillas across the culture/nature boundary is one that excluded the possibility of any *other* connections. Rather than seeing herself as radically destabilizing the boundary which divides humans from animals like the gorillas, Fossey questioned this boundary only enough to cross over it and step out of the painful complexities of human culture and history into what Haraway describes as "her culture's dream of an original and timeless nature" (1989, 267). This escapism is graphically illustrated in the second chapter of *Gorillas in the Mist*, which begins with a discussion of the economic and political situation in Rwanda. Fossey emphasizes the country's extreme poverty and ethnic divisions, and explains how these conditions affect the gorillas through threats of habitat loss and poaching. However, her description soon leads away from these troubling issues, through a stone tunnel which she describes as creating "a dramatic entrance into the world of the gorilla. It served as a passageway *between civilization and the silent world of the forest*" (1983, 22, emphasis added).

By insisting on her need to choose between the poles of nature and culture, Fossey constructed her own identity in a one-dimensional way that served to reinforce dominant ideologies that radically separate the two, the same ideologies she attempted to challenge with her message of the gorillas' inherent rights and dignity. However, identity need not be conceived as static and one-dimensional; as Teresa de Lauretis explains in "Eccentric Subjects," feminist theory has reconceptualized the subject as "shifting and multiply organized across variable axes of difference" (1990, 116), axes which can include not

only nature/culture, but also gender, race, class, ethnicity, and sexual orienta-
tion. Such a conception of subjectivity sees the individual subject at the
convergence of multiple, interrelated discursive and social practices: "not a single system of power dominating the powerless but a tangle of distinct and
variable relations of power and points of resistance" (1990, 131). In other
words, identity is constantly being shaped by multiple and sometimes contest-
ing forces, forces related to various axes of difference. As Donna Haraway has
pointed out, a conception of the self as constantly changing, as "split and contradictory," opens up the possibility that such a self can make multiple
connections and thus sustain "the possibility of webs of connections called solidarity in politics and shared conversations in epistemology" (1988, 584).

Because Fossey saw herself as able to connect only with the gorillas, she
failed to see the many interconnections between the oppression of the gorillas
and of the people with whom they shared the country. Thus, she largely failed
to see how she could extend a sense of kinship not only to the gorillas but also
to the humans living in Rwanda by looking for the forces working against the
survival of both. As ecofeminists in particular have taken pains to point out,
the same ideologies of dualism and hierarchy that ground the domination of
nature serve to construct and reinforce the domination of marginalized groups
within human culture.[18] Sadly, Fossey's conceptions of identity and advocacy
served to protect the gorillas only while she was alive, leaving the cultural and
political roots of the threats to the gorillas unaddressed after she died. As
Haraway explains in describing Alison Jolly's work with lemurs in Madagascar,
a more effective goal would be to challenge the nature/culture dualism fully
by "participating in negotiating the terms on which love of nature could be
part of the solution to, rather than part of the imposition of, colonial domination and environmental destruction" (1989, 275).

Since Fossey's death, a program known as the Mountain Gorilla Project
(MGP) has made progress in protecting the gorillas by acknowledging and
building on the ways the welfare of the country's people is connected to that
of the gorillas.[19] In a recent article in National Geographic, noted primatolo-
gist George Schaller reports that the MGP's program of protecting the
gorillas through the combined strategies of anti-poaching, tourism, and education has dramatically increased Rwandans' knowledge of the importance of
the Virungas as a watershed, not just as gorilla habitat, thus stressing the ecological ways that the fates of gorillas and native Rwandans are intertwined. In
addition, by the late 1980s, the MGP's efforts had turned gorilla tourism into
the third largest income-generating activity in Rwanda, and had advanced a
sense that the gorillas were part of Rwanda's national identity (Schaller
1995, 68).

However, in the past few years, Rwanda has been torn by civil war. The war began in late 1990, when the Tutsi-led Rwandan Patriotic Front (RPF) rebelled against the Hutu-dominated government that had been in power since Rwanda's independence from Belgium in 1962. In response, the Hutus carried out a genocidal campaign that left 75 percent of the country's Tutsis dead by mid-July 1994, when the RPF gained control of the government. The roots of this conflict have been traced to legends that the agricultural Hutu people were conquered by warrior-herdsmen Tutsi who invaded the region from Ethiopia centuries ago (Salopek 1995). However, a shared language and religion as well as centuries of intermarriage erased most physical and many cultural differences between the two ethnic groups over the centuries; today's conflict can be traced much more directly to nineteenth- and twentieth-century colonial policies that reinscribed divisions and hierarchies among native Rwandans. For example, the Belgian government which controlled Rwanda from 1920 to 1962 issued ethnic identity cards to the native population, using the ownership of ten or more cattle as the criterion for labeling someone Tutsi. After reestablishing ethnic and class divisions between the majority Hutu and minority Tutsi in this way, the Belgians then capitalized on these divisions by ruling through the Tutsi minority.[20]

Unfortunately, the media discourse concerning the effects of this conflict on the country's gorillas suggests that we have yet to fully recognize the similar, interconnected forces at work in the oppression of people and the domination of nature and to accept the interdependence of nature and culture. In an article entitled "Guerrillas in the Mist," Ken Silverstein offers a scathing critique of the media for covering the gorillas rather than the uprising. Perhaps in response to critiques like Silverstein's, a short, unsigned article on the ecological impact of the Rwandan refugee crisis in *Choices* is careful to stress "the unspeakable human tragedy" as a greater concern than the ecological one.[21] In the title of his October 1995 *National Geographic* article on the situation of the gorillas, Paul Salopek characterizes the relationship between gorillas and humans as "An Uneasy Truce."

Although only one gorilla is known to have died as a result of the conflict, it is important to recognize that such discourse fails to challenge the ideologies of separation and domination responsible not only for the colonial oppression of native Rwandans and the resulting hate and fear that persist between Tutsis and Hutus today, but also for the harm caused to the gorillas by people of many nationalities and ethnicities. Ironically, Fossey's journals indicate one way she might have moved towards more substantively challenging such ideologies—had she lived—by a program that would have addressed the intertwined fate of nature and oppressed peoples. In late 1983, she wrote of an entirely new idea for the protection of the remaining mountain gorillas; one that, hopefully, will eliminate once and for all the barriers that continue to divide native blacks from white expatriates, pit one country against another (Zaire/Uganda/Rwanda), and one organization against the other. (Mowat 1987, 297–298)

Her idea was to make use of conservation funds to sponsor a guardian group for each family of gorillas; the guardian groups, consisting of Rwandan park guards, their families, and assistants, would be responsible for contacting their gorilla groups every few days to maintain a constant record of each gorilla's location and status. Unfortunately, Fossey did not live long enough to put her plan into action; however, her characterization of the need to end barriers and divisions by linking the fate of the Rwandan people with that of the gorillas suggests that she was beginning to visualize and construct connections not just across the human/nature boundary, but across other boundaries, including those of race and nationality, as well.

While Fossey's challenge to the ideology of boundaries was limited, serving to blur only the boundaries between herself and the gorillas rather than questioning the larger division between human culture and nature, in the courage and determination she showed in transgressing cultural boundaries between herself and the gorillas Fossey gives us a place to start. As Alexander Wilson explains in *The Culture of Nature:*

> Western cultural history is full of examples of a desire to live in a world of nature uncontaminated by human presence. Yet this quest for paradise—which in the history of colonialism has placed aboriginal peoples in an impossible position—is not just a negation of modern civilization. It is also a positive reaching out to embrace the other animals that inhabit this Earth. (1991, 126)

By combining Fossey's example of how to reach out across boundaries in kinship with a profound sense of the complex and shifting nature of human identity, it may become possible to cross many boundaries, boundaries between different groups of people as well as those between humans and nature, ultimately destabilizing the worldwide forces of domination and oppression that confine and damage us all.

Notes

1. As Fossey explains in this same article, most poachers were not in search of the gorillas; rather, their presence terrified the gorillas and disrupted their family

groups and activities, and the snares they set for duiker (a type of antelope) could nevertheless catch and harm the gorillas. However, as Fossey learned, occasionally poachers would be employed to capture infant gorillas to sell to zoos and other customers (see Fossey 1983, Gordon 1993, and Mowat 1987). This type of poaching was especially destructive because entire family groups of gorillas will fight to the death to protect their infant members.

2. For discussions of the history of the nature/culture dualism within Western culture, (see Berman 1984, Bookchin 1982, Merchant 1981, Ritvo 1995, White 1967, and Wilson 1992).

3. For feminist/postcolonial discussions of the problems of speaking for others, see Alcoff 1991 and Spivak 1987, 1988, and 1989.

4. For a discussion of the history of the taboo against anthropomorphism in Western culture and particularly in science, (see Lockwood 1989). In *Gorillas in the Mist*, Fossey often reveals her awareness of the cultural expectation that she be an "objective" scientist by qualifying her desire to ascribe human motivations and feelings to the gorillas. As I explain, though, Fossey did violate the anthropomorphism taboo to the degree necessary to connect with the gorillas as subjects.

5. Another factor in Fossey's willingness to see similarities between herself and the gorillas may have been a tendency among social scientists of her era to use primatological data to hypothesize about human behavior in reconstructions of human evolution (Sperling 1988, 158). In fact, one of the primary reasons Leakey initiated primate studies (including Fossey's) was his hope that they might provide insight into the behavior of early humans that would aid him in his research in paleoanthropology (Montgomery 1991, 74).

6. According to Diana Fuss, "Essentialism is classically defined as a belief in true essence—that which is most irreducible, unchanging, and therefore constitutive of a given person or thing" (1989, 2). For feminists, however, ". . . essentialism can be located [more specifically] in appeals to a pure or original femininity, a female essence, outside the boundaries of the social and thereby untainted (though perhaps repressed) by a patriarchal order" (Fuss, 2). Statements which explicitly or implicitly claim that women have certain inherent characteristics concern antiessentialist feminists. Such critics point out that male-dominated society has used the idea that women possess innate characteristics, such as a tendency for self-sacrifice, to justify women's subjugation and oppression. Even approaches like Leakey's that attempt to valorize women for possessing these qualities do not challenge the underlying ideologies responsible for women's oppression. As Linda Alcoff points out, such responses do "not criticize the fundamental mechanism of oppressive power used to perpetuate sexism and in fact [reinvoke] that mechanism in its supposed solution" (1988, 415). In addition to perpetuating the dualism between men and women, essentialism conceives of the individual subject as unitary and unchanging, a conception which, as Diana Fuss points out, sees the subject as standing "outside the sphere of cultural influence and historical change" (Fuss 1989, 3).

7. While Norwood suggests that women's tendencies to empathize with and feel responsibility toward wild animals that they study arise from their gender socialization, Evelyn Fox Keller has specifically examined the cultural processes by which such a socialization occurs in *A Feeling for the Organism* (1983) and *Reflections on Gender and Science* (1985).

8. Fossey's tendency to see the gorillas as behavioral examples for humans fits into a pattern that Susan Sperling identifies in the popularized primate studies of the 1960s and 1970s, which she sees as sharing "a marked prescriptive attitude—that to understand and cure human social ills we must look at primate biological roots and attempt to align our own behavior more closely with our primate nature" (1988, 180).

9. See Montgomery 1991, 271–272.

10. The photo's caption, however, reveals that Peanuts is actually drawing back his hand after having made contact with Fossey's.

11. This image was echoed in National Geographic's 1975 documentary, *Search for the Great Apes*, which includes a scene in which Fossey is touched by another young male gorilla, Digit, who thus symbolically "ends Fossey's solitude, bringing her into the community of nature" (Haraway 1989, 149).

12. Haraway discusses this moment of touch between primate and white, female researcher in great depth, focusing on images of Jane Goodall and Biruté Galdikas as well as of Dian Fossey in "Apes in Eden, Apes in Space: Mothering as a Scientist for National Geographic," the seventh chapter in *Primate Visions* (1989). She returns to this image in relation to Jane Goodall in particular in "The Promises of Monsters: A Regenerative Politics for Inappropriate/d Others," 1992. The phrase "touch across Difference" is Haraway's (1989, 149).

13. My account of this moment comes from Fossey's descriptions of it in (1) her 1971 *National Geographic* article; (2) *Gorillas in the Mist*; and (3) entries from her journals (as reprinted in Farley Mowat's 1987 biography of Fossey, *Woman in the Mist*). The *National Geographic* article also contextualizes the photograph with two other photos; the first shows Peanuts approaching Fossey, and the second shows Fossey scratching her head as a mischievous smile plays across her face.

14. It is important to note that Fossey sometimes made official statements condoning certain types of tourism, especially as it became clear to her that tourism was impossible to avoid. However, it is also clear that she never overcame her fears that tourism would spread disease to the gorillas and habituate them to people to the extent that they would not fear poachers. In her day-to-day activities, she did little to promote tourism and sometimes actively resisted it.

15. There are some indications that Fossey's outspoken opposition to poaching and tourism may have led to her 1985 murder. The Rwandan government charged Wayne McGuire, an American graduate student who was working with Fossey, and Emmanual Rwelekana, a Rwandan tracker who had worked for Fossey up until several months before her death, with the murder. However, most accounts of Fossey's murder express skepticism that either of these two were responsible, focusing instead on the difficulties Fossey created for the Rwandan tourism industry and the black market trade in gorillas for zoos and other collectors. (See Gordon 1993, Hayes 1990, Mowat 1987, and Shoumatoff 1986.)

16. Although Fossey's unrelenting advocacy of the mountain gorillas inspired antagonism in a wide variety of people in different countries and organizations, here Hayes is primarily referring to Rwandan poachers and cattle herders who lived in the vicinity of Karisoke Research Center.

17. First held as a colony as part of German East Africa, Rwanda was then "administered" by Belgium through a League of Nations mandate between 1920 and 1962 (Bonner 1994).

18. For ecofeminist and other discussions of the ideological interconnections among the domination of nature and the oppression of human beings based on factors such as race and gender, (see Gaard 1993, Griffin 1978, Haraway 1988, 1992, Murphy 1991, 1994, Quinby 1990, and Ritvo 1995).

19. Ironically, Fossey objected to the MGP's approach to gorilla conservation during her lifetime. Her objections stemmed in part from her opposition to the type of gorilla tourism that the MGP supported, but she also had a history of personal difficulties with Amy Vedder and Bill Webber, who had worked with her as graduate students and went on to found the MGP in 1978.

20. For histories of the Rwandan conflict, (see Bonner 1994 and, especially, Gourevitch 1995).

21. See "Rwandan Refugee Crisis Triggers Ecological Disaster" (1995).

Bibliography

Alcoff, Linda. "Cultural Feminism versus Poststructuralism: The Identity Crisis in Feminist Theory." *Signs: Journal of Women in Culture and Society* 13.3 (Spring 1988), 405–436.

———. "The Problem of Speaking for Others." *Cultural Critique* (Winter 1991), 5–32.

Berman, Morris. *The Reenchantment of the World.* New York: Bantam, 1984.

Bonner, Raymond. "A Once-Peaceful Village Shows the Roots of Rwanda's Violence." *New York Times,* July 11, 1994.

Bookchin, Murray. *The Ecology of Freedom: the Emergence and Dissolution of Hierarchy.* Palo Alto, CA: Cheshire Books, 1982.

de Lauretis, Teresa. "Eccentric Subjects: Feminist Theory and Historical Consciousness." *Feminist Studies* 16 (Spring 1990), 115–150.

Fossey, Dian. "Making Friends with Mountain Gorillas." *National Geographic* 137 (January 1970), 48–67.

———. "More Years with the Mountain Gorillas." *National Geographic* 140 (October 1971), 574–585.

———. *Gorillas in the Mist.* Boston: Houghton Mifflin, 1983.

Fuss, Diana. *Essentially Speaking: Feminism, Nature and Difference.* New York: Routledge, 1989.

Gaard, Greta, ed. *Ecofeminism: Women, Animals, Nature.* Philadelphia: Temple University Press, 1993.

Gordon, Nicholas. *Murders in the Mist: Who Killed Dian Fossey?* London: Hodder and Stoughton, 1993.

Gourevitch, Philip. "After the Genocide." *The New Yorker* LXXI (December 18, 1995), 78–95.

Griffin, Susan. *Woman and Nature: The Roaring Inside Her.* New York: Harper and Row, 1978.

Haraway, Donna. "Situated Knowledges: The Science Question in Feminism and the Privilege of Partial Perspective." *Feminist Studies* 14 (Fall 1988), 575–599.

———. *Primate Visions: Gender, Race, and Nature in the World of Modern Science.* New York: Routledge, 1989.

———. "The Promises of Monsters: A Regenerative Politics for Inappropriate/d Others," in *Cultural Studies*, eds. Lawrence Grossberg, Cary Nelson, and Paula A. Treichler. New York: Routledge, 1992, 295–337.

Hayes, Harold T. P. *The Dark Romance of Dian Fossey.* New York: Simon and Schuster, 1990.

Keller, Evelyn Fox. *A Feeling for the Organism: The Life and Work of Barbara McClintock.* San Francisco: W. H. Freeman and Company, 1983.

———. *Reflections on Gender and Science.* New Haven: Yale University Press, 1985.

Lockwood, R. "Anthropomorphism Is Not a Four Letter Word," in *Perceptions of Animals in American Culture*, ed. R. Hoage. Washington: Smithsonian Publications, 1989, 41–56.

Merchant, Carolyn. *The Death of Nature: Women, Ecology, and the Scientific Revolution.* San Francisco: Harper and Row, 1981.

Montgomery, Sy. *Walking with the Great Apes: Jane Goodall, Dian Fossey, Biruté Galdikas.* Boston: Houghton Mifflin, 1991.

Mowat, Farley. *Woman in the Mists: The Story of Dian Fossey and the Mountain Gorillas of Africa.* New York: Warner Books, 1987.

Murphy, Patrick. "Ground, Pivot, Motion: Ecofeminist Theory, Dialogics, and Literary Practice." *Hypatia* 6 (Spring 1991), 146–161.

———. "Voicing Another Nature," in *A Dialogue of Voices: Feminist Theory and Bakhtin*, eds. Karen Hohne and Helen Wussow. Minneapolis: University of Minnesota Press, 1994, 59–82.

Norwood, Vera. *Made from this Earth: American Women and Nature.* Chapel Hill: University of North Carolina Press, 1993.

Quinby, Lee. "Ecofeminism and the Politics of Resistance," in *Reweaving the World: The Emergence of Ecofeminism*, eds. Irene Diamond and Gloria Feman Orenstein. San Francisco: Sierra Club Books, 1990, 122–127.

Reed, Susan. "Survivors in the Mist." *People* (March 6, 1995), 40–45.

Ritvo, Harriet. "Border Trouble: Shifting Lines of Demarcation Between Animals and Humans." *Social Research.* Special Issue: In the Company of Animals 62 (Fall 1995), 481–500.

"Rwandan Refugee Crisis Triggers an Ecological Disaster." *Choices: The Human Development Magazine* (April 1995), 31.

Salopek, Paul F. "Gorillas and Humans: An Uneasy Truce." *National Geographic* (October 1995), 72–83.

Schaller, George B. "Gentle Gorillas, Turbulent Times." *National Geographic* (October 1995), 65–68.

Shoumatoff, Alex. "The Fatal Obsession of Dian Fossey." *Vanity Fair* 49 (September 1986), 84–90, 130–138.

Silverstein, Ken. "Guerrillas in the Mist." *The Washington Monthly* (September 1994), 21–23.

Sperling, Susan. *Animal Liberators: Research and Morality*. Berkeley: University of California Press, 1988.

Spivak, Gayatri. *In Other Worlds: Essays in Cultural Politics*. New York: Methuen, 1987.

———. "Can the Subaltern Speak?" in *Marxism and the Interpretation of Culture*, eds. Cary Nelson and Lawrence Grossberg. Urbana: University of Illinois Press, 1988, 271–313.

———. "The Political Economy of Women as Seen by a Literary Critic," in *Coming to Terms: Feminism, Theory, Politics*, ed. Elizabeth Weed. New York: Routledge, 1989, 218–229.

White, Lynn, Jr. "The Historical Roots of Our Ecologic Crisis." *Science* 155 (10 March 1967), 1203–1207.

Wilson, Alexander. "Looking at the Non-Human: Nature Movies and TV," in *The Culture of Nature: North American Landscape from Disney to the Exxon Valdez*. New York: Blackwell, 1992.

12 ✢

Humanimals and Anihumans in Gary Larson's Gallery of the Absurd

Charles D. Minahen

In Memoriam Pierre Astier

Break on through to the other side.

—J. D. Morrison[1]

In spite of Stephen King's exhortation not to "explain" or "explicate" but simply to "enjoy"[2] Gary Larson, it seemed only a matter of time before the bold author/illustrator of *The Far Side*, who has had such fun depicting genius-scholar wonks in lab coats so deeply ensconced in their arcane research as to be stupidly oblivious to everything else in the world, would himself be laid out on the dissecting slab for scrutiny under the microscope of academe. Chalk this up to his own success as one of the most original contemporary American cari-caturists, whose universal appeal is immediately clear to the casual observer not the least bit fazed to find "favorite Far Sides" taped to the wall in an ento-mology lab *and* to the closet door of the janitor who sweeps it. Like his art, Larson's audience runs the entire gamut (in fact, if things could read and talk, and of course they can in his world, one would not be surprised to find car-toons stuck to plant stalks, rhinos' backs, or spider webs).

Certainly much of the appeal is attributable to the way Larson seems to "take the side of things," much as the French poet Francis Ponge does in his most famous work, *Le Parti pris des choses*. This title, as Beth Archer notes, is ambiguous, connoting both the side taken "*for* things" (the artist's advocacy or

231

bias in support of them) and the side taken "*of* things" ("the will expressed by the things themselves").[3] In the case of Ponge, I have argued elsewhere that he "takes the side of a thing by lending it his own subjectivity, in order to reveal something about substance or essence, its own primarily but indirectly that too of the human subjectivity it reflects."[4] This lending of subjectivity accounts for how the side is taken *for* things by means of an identification with them (and their cause), but also how the side is taken *of* them, since such a transfer of human subjectivity is required to give voice to, to provide a language for the expression of the will of things that can be understood by humans, who are the true targets of the poet's aesthetic intention.

To compare Larson to Ponge, one must first confront the important generic difference that separates two very different media: the primarily visual art graphic (often with brief word text)[5] of the cartoon, and the exclusively textual prose poem (with only indirectly imagined or limited calligrammatic visual effects). One consequence of this essential difference is the way each form attempts to achieve its intended effect. The hyperbole of caricature and satire in Larson, which is apt to provoke a loud guffaw, is much more concentrated, focused, and direct than the subtle and complex irony and playful humor of a Pongian poem, which may inspire only a silent, internalized—if nonetheless intensely enjoyed—chuckle. This complexity is related in Ponge to the tendency of the prose poem to move between several frames or several takes of a particular scene or state of affairs, which allows the meaning to unfold and develop through many phases, producing ultimately a deeply layered signification. In Larson, by contrast, each cartoon is typically a single framed space[6] with, as it were, one shot to make its point, however subtle and polyvalent that point may be (and often is). A layering effect, however, is created by the many reprises of a given subject and the successive variations produced, which accumulate and add depth to the artist's portrayal of the subject across his total work.

Crossing Over / Breaking Through

With these peculiar qualities of the Larson graphic in mind, I propose first to consider a cartoon that is particularly pertinent to this discussion (and one I have always been amused and intrigued by). A chicken on the near side of a two-lane road is staring at a sign on the far side, which reads "THE OTHER SIDE" (and below) "Why do you need a reason?" (G4:79) [Figure 1]. This is an obvious parody of the question-answer joke: Why did the chicken cross the road? . . . To get to the other side; which is itself a parody of the human obses-

THE FAR SIDE   By GARY LARSON

Figure 1. "The other side," Gary Larson (G4:79).

sion with cause and effect and with deep psychological explanations of motivations. But from a Pongian-Larsonian perspective of "taking sides/sides taken," it depicts the line separating humanity from animality (a legally crossable *broken* line at that!). The chicken stands on the edge of animality facing the sign on the human other side. We readers, significantly, share the view of the chicken from what, for us, would be the far side of animality, which has suddenly become the near side. The artist has already transferred his and our subjectivity to the other side, effectively inviting us to *take that side* along with him as advocates for it. But in order to manifest the *side taken* of the chicken, the bird must reciprocate by crossing over into humanity and break through into the zone of subjective self-consciousness. Only then can it find a comprehensible means of expression for its side by becoming a hybrid humanized animal or *humanimal*. I say "it" because animals (the particular focus of this essay) are generally considered "things" by humans, who feel entitled to hunt or capture or kill or use or buy or sell them as they please.

But the chicken has not yet crossed over and stands there penultimately on the threshold of breakthrough, staring in bewildered incomprehension at a sign that bombastically imposes itself on the scene. Like the ugly American tourist of legend, who expected every foreigner to speak English and was rudely con-

descending when they could not, humanity blares out its message to the rest of
the world in its own language and arrogantly expects the rest of the world's
inhabitants to understand and comply.[7] But the question "Why do you need a
reason?" is not only meaningless but ridiculous if intended for the chicken, who
does not *need a reason* to cross beyond its desire, guided by instinct, "to get to
the other side." Only the other "you" sharing the chicken's space, human readers, are capable of receiving the message, which spoofs the absurdity of needing
to have a reason for everything—a uniquely human teleological obsession.

Humanimal Mimicry, Wordplay, and Reversal

Although this chicken has not yet crossed the road and metamorphosed into a
humanimal, another one clearly has in a cartoon that illustrates what humanimality is all about, namely, the reenacting of human situations by animals to
set those situations in relief and, by recontextualizing them, expose their
essential absurdity.[8] The case in point: a farm wife walking up the path from
the chicken coop to her house, with a basket of eggs on her arm, meets a
chicken walking from the house to the coop, cradling a baby in its wings
(G1:75). Here a very recognizable and mundane human activity, when trans-
posed reciprocally into its equivalent in humanimal terms, is revealed to be
utterly barbaric: humans routinely and without a second thought steal and eat
the unborn offspring of other species. In this particular case, human and
humanimal meet in what might be termed a neutral zone, halfway between
farmhouse and chicken coop.

In other instances, the intrusion of one species into the other's space pro-
duces a glaring incongruity that further heightens the comic effect. A bird
sipping tea with a friend in a nest and looking up at an enormous piano poised
beside them on the branch states, "Oh, my word, Helen! You play, *too*? . . .
And here I always thought you were just a song bird" (G5:142). The insertion
of the human into animal space is already evident in the humanized activity of
the birds, but the piano plopped onto the branch in defiance of the basic laws
of physics adds an element of the ludicrous that greatly increases the sense of
contradiction between natural (animal) and artificial (human) modes of being.
Conversely, a Tarzan-Jane couple are entertaining monkeys and an elephant in
their human space when suddenly the elephant, flinging its martini glass, rears
up on hind legs in front of the piano; the undertext reads: "The party had been
going splendidly—and then Tantor saw the ivory keyboard" (G4:67) [Figure
2]. The sheer size of the elephant, which fills over a quarter of the frame, as
does the piano on the branch in the preceding cartoon, underscores the incon-

THE FAR SIDE   By GARY LARSON

Figure 2. "Tantor's rampage," Gary Larson (G4:67).

THE FAR SIDE   By GARY LARSON

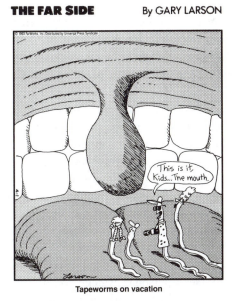

Figure 3. "Tapeworms on vacation," Gary Larson (G5:14).

gruity of the animal in the human setting, further magnifying his[9] humanimal recognition of human treachery. An organ-grinder's monkey holding a cup on top of the piano embodies a clever reverberation of the theme, since the cup it extends for begging contrasts with the drinking glasses held by the other guest monkeys. The hypocritical humans thus feign friendliness toward the animals by inviting them over for cocktails, but the keyboard and little beggar monkey betray their true callous and exploitative attitudes and intentions.

The juxtaposition of disparate sizes is a form of exaggeration that Larson exploits to demonstrate the relativity of the concept of "world" (microcosm versus macrocosm) among various animal species, with the familiar human scale always the implied reference point of mimicry. In some instances, the human is the macrocosmic setting for the microcosmic situation of the humanimal, as when a spider invites her friend to come to see her eggs, adding, "The address is: Doris Griswold, 5 feet 4 inches, 160 pounds, brown eyes—I'm in her hair" (G4:126) or when "Tapeworms on vacation" behold "The mouth" from the vantage of the back of the tongue just under the strange hanging mass of the uvula, opposite a double row of clenched teeth that loom like stone blocks of a walled city in the background (G5:14) [Figure 3]. Other macrocosmic worlds are, progressively by size, a dog, a rhinoceros, and a beached whale. On the dog, a flea-artist microcosmically paints a "dogscape" at sunset (G4:148); a bird-capitalist poised on the rhino's back tells his son, "Someday . . . this will all be yours" (G4:24); and an insect-seducer impresses his dinner date by reserving a romantic table "near the blow-hole" (G3:115). In these last three, the macro/micro disparities serve to intensify, through hyperbole, the aesthetic, economic, and social human behaviors being mocked.

What one might term "the human plastered on the animal," to adapt Bergson's famous definition of laughter,[10] is indeed the essence of humanimality, which always intends, in Larson, a comic effect. Most frequently, this involves a straightforward case of animals mimicking human behavior *in their terms:* for example, a kangaroo with broken bones using a pogo stick instead of crutches (G3:26); a canine talk show featuring "Dogs that drink from the toilet bowl" (G5:155); a male dog complimenting his date on how she stinks (G3:37); flies enjoying a travelogue on "Dumps of the World" (G4:165). As it happens, these are rather exceptional examples of humanimality in which the parodic effect seems to cut both ways, poking fun simultaneously at both human and animal behaviors: the silly awkwardness of humans on crutches and kangaroos hopping; the contradictory human obsession with talk-show dirt and compulsively clean personal hygiene compared to the indiscriminate earthiness of animals; the absurdly arbitrary qualitative value of smells for humans and animals, the former repulsed by what attracts the latter; human filmmaking and watching as a kind of voyeuristic narcissism completely at odds with the mindless unself-consciousness of other species, and so forth.

Notwithstanding these and other examples outside the scope of this study, it is nevertheless the human who is more often than not the unmistakable butt of the joke in Larson's depiction of humanimals. Although the examples are legion, focusing on a few predominant themes can give a good idea of the kinds of parody involved. Human eating habits are a recurrent theme: an adolescent snake complaining about "hamsters again" (G1:9); birds protesting that they did not order "stink bugs" on their pizza (G1:72); a dog hostess bragging to her dinner guests that the roast cat she is serving is "*not* from the market—Rusty caught it himself" (G2:72); a cat picking from a candy box of mixed mice, hamsters, and gerbils (G2:159); a mother anteater at the dinner table agreeing that it is Randy's turn "to eat the queen" (G5:62). Obviously the finicky, complicated, and at times silly human food rituals are exposed by having them acted out by animals, whose relationship with food is survival-oriented and simple. Moreover, the substitution of hamsters for hamburgers, stink bugs for anchovies, roast cat for roast duck, rodents for chocolates, and queen ant for drumstick points up the absurdly relative and arbitrary nature of "taste."

Another theme is human vice and addiction: dinosaurs are shown lighting up, and puffing on cigarettes is "the real reason [they] became extinct" (G1:91); carnivores confess their killing addiction at a meeting of "Maneaters Anonymous" (G2:63); a bull standing by in eager anticipation watches another bull blow up an inflatable cow (G3:14). Not only do these examples satirize self-destructive or ridiculously kinky human behaviors, but the animals in all three cases mimic human poses by standing on two legs or sitting in chairs, a clear indication they are really humanimals. In an interesting twist on this idea, animals are often seen hiding their humanimality from humans, pretending to be just dumb animals, as humans expect them to be. Thus, in a three-frame panel, bipedal cows in a field are warned by a lookout of an approaching car; the car passes as they feign grazing on all fours; once the car has gone, they return to their preferred bipedal stance (G1:26). Or, in a rare six-frame panel, a cow is seen grazing in front of a house; she looks over at the door, approaches it, rings the doorbell, then mischievously prances back to the lawn; in the last frame a bewildered farmer standing in the doorway sees nothing but a grazing cow (G1:21). It is as if animals, in a conspiracy of silence, do not want humans to know they are humanimals, that they are "aware" of what is going on in the world, and that they are subversively planning something—a theme I shall return to and develop later.

A third type of animal mimicry ridicules human concerns with deep or controversial issues. A gorilla in one cartoon literally apes human behavior by confiding to his friend that, although he likes bananas like everyone else, for him, "it goes much more beyond that" (G1:98). (Even the most amateur Freudian would recognize the latent homosexual tendencies in his obsession with such obvious phallic symbols!) In another, a committee of fish listens to an apparently incensed mother fish at a meeting to decide "whether spawning should be taught in school" (G3:155). That fish swim in schools makes them, of course, the perfect species for this parody of a controversial education issue, but the wordplay on "school" is also an example of a favorite Larsonian technique, which may be a secondary factor that in effect doubles the dose of humor, as in this case or the case of Vera the chicken, who finds herself a lone fowl surrounded by bovines and suddenly realizes she is in "a hay bar" (G5:23). Here, the primary parody of the "like with like" syndrome of groups—there may also be a further implied parody of the phrase "birds of a feather flock together"—is extended by the homonymic pun "hay bar"/"gay bar" to include human segregationist practices resulting from prejudice.

In many cases, however, the wordplay is the primary focus and may be based, as in the preceding example, on a form of homonymic punning—a buck receives a "John deer" letter (G3:34), polar bears buy "eskimo thighs" from a vendor on an ice floe (G5:52), Edgar, whose dog is exaggerating his exploits in a dream, is told to "let sleeping dogs lie" (G5:85)—or the play may derive from the recontextualizing of a common expression, such as the depiction of a shark in a print dress with necklace who is "dressed to kill" (G2:17) or the sheep reporter who announces, "And this report just in. . . . Apparently, the grass *is* greener on the other side" (G4:162). Still other versions of wordplay may adapt or distort such expressions: a frog sings "the greens" (G4:31); a zebra in bed is "catching a few Y's" (G5:105); tapeworms are "trying to put the kids through the small intestine" (G5:145); a flea carries a sign amid giant shoots of hair that reads "the end of the dog is coming" (G2:50). In this last example, the pun is coupled with the micro/macro parody of relative worlds, discussed earlier, which doubles the comedic charge. Two further examples of the exact same type of doubling are the depictions of a fly seated at a table amid sprouts of hair responding to a query with "It's a free dead cow" (G5:107), and flea bicyclists rounding the tip of a sleeping man's huge nose in "the grueling Tour de Frank" (G5:25). A final category of wordplay spoofs language itself, that most human of human behaviors: in one scene, dogs watch a human film with subtitles in dog ("Grrrrr haruff! Arfa rawrg. . . .") (G3:110); in another a duck-teacher shows how to diagram the sentence "Quack que quack quack" in "Beginning duck" (G3:144). These are, in fact, examples that cut both ways, reducing human language, through analogy, to a series of absurd verbal noises *à la* Beckett or Ionesco,[11] but also demonstrating that the dumbness associated

with animals is an inference of stupidity derived from their inability to produce coherent speech.

One last type of animal mimicry of human behavior in Larson is based upon
a principle of direct reversal in which humans and animals switch roles. A typical example would be the depiction of bovines driving through town in a
camouflaged panel truck painted with stupidly grinning people (G3:116)
[Figure 4]. Obviously, it is humans who usually camouflage themselves from
animals in order to hunt or entrap them. In Larson's reversal of the situation,
the animals' intention seems more parodic than sinister, since in representing
all the camouflage figures with obnoxious grins, the bovines have allowed their
true opinion of humans to override a more effective realistic depiction, with
the result that the truck does not completely blend in with the crowd of
human passersby. Here, the French word "*bête*" comes to mind, which means
both "beast" and "stupid." Ironically, it is the bovines that consider the humans
"*bêtes*" (beastly stupid). Often, as in this case, the reversal of roles also involves
a reversal of subject and object, with the animal-subject viewing the human-
object as Other. Additional simple examples would be: bemused fish gawking
at humans trapped in a sunken glass bottom boat as if on display in an aquari-
um (where there is also a reversal of wet and dry) (G1:82);[12] bear engineers
piping animal waste into a man's front room (G4:80); a cow at the barn door
telling another cow there is no room, she'll have to sleep in the house (G1:80);
young farm animals furtively smoking behind the house (G3:153); trick-or-
treating young deer dressed as "scary little hunters" (G4:54).

Sometimes "value" is added to the reversal, such as a judgment, which is
usually negative, as in the above camouflage example and in the depictions
both of a scorpion attacked by a "hideous thing with five heads" (a human
foot) (G1:125), and bear voyeurs losing their appetite at the sight of human
nudists (G3:24). But the judgment may also be ironically positive, as when a
squirrel condescendingly thinks the human squatting down to feed it is acting
"so CUTE" (G1:132), or a dog proudly shows off a stuffed trophy of "the hand
that fed me" (G3:47). In other examples, a kind of equal justice value (tit for
tat) is implied. We have already caught a glimpse of this in the picture of the
farm wife and chicken crossing paths carrying, respectively, eggs and a baby,
which exposes humans' callous exploitation of animals. Two parallel cartoons
can be found in early, pre–Far Side Larson, when he published under the title
Nature's Way: in the first, a rabbit wears a human foot around its neck "for
good luck" (P:28); in the second, a scuba diver with a sack of fish runs into a
fish with a sack of divers (P:33). The reversal may also involve a shift of value
due to an unexpected shift of focus: a bird TV reporter at the scene of a flaming plane wreck reports on "the bird sucked into the jet's engines" (G2:181);

Figure 4. "Animal camouflage," Gary Larson (G3:116).

Figure 5. "Horse parliament," Gary Larson (G5:107).

an ugly boy trying to scare an ugly girl with a snake resulted in the reptile suffering "deep emotional scars" (G4:102).

Finally, the value of a trait or activity may itself be reversed: a beaver is ridiculed by other beavers for not having buck teeth (G3:148); snakes hiss with approval a snake speaker (G4:38); for the first time anyone in the horse parliament could remember "one of the members voted 'aye'" (G5:107) [Figure 5]. In addition to the aye/"neigh" value reversal, this last example not only satirizes the herd mentality of politicians who unthinkingly vote the party line, but does so in a way that emphasizes the ludicrous, a common byproduct of humanimal mimicry. The depiction of tiered rows of horses seated in the gallery whinnying in unison before bipedally standing horse leaders suddenly dispels the reverential aura of dignity and decorum that surrounds the concept of parliament, revealing it to be, in reality, a forum for meaningless howling and horseplay. In other related examples, the extremely ludicrous nature of the very concept is itself the primary source of parody, as in the depiction of a wolf "addicted" to "Carol's sheep dip" plunging a full-grown sheep head first into a bowl (G2:141), where the absurdity of the graphic is the source of ridiculousness; or the portrayal of alligators "Bobbing for poodles" (G3:15), where the ludicrous is primarily a function of the text and specifically of the word "poodle," a silly-sounding signifier that signifies a silly-looking dog.[13]

Barnyard Conspiracies

We have already seen, in the images of animals hiding their humanimality from humans, the suggestion of a conspiracy of the former against the latter. It stands to reason that humanimality would pose a threat to humans who are used to using and abusing animals without concern for retaliation, since animals are presumed to be too stupid to know any better. The cruelty and treachery of humans toward animals is all too vividly apparent in the portrayal of a stump-legged elephant on a crutch, crammed into a phone booth in the middle of the savannah, who is shocked to learn that "They turned it into a WASTEbasket" (G1:105) and, as well, of a cowardly hunter who shoots a bear as it peacefully drinks from a pond and then has it stuffed and mounted in a ferocious, reared-up stance (G1:110). Such viciousness and deceit would be criminal if directed toward other humans. But even when not so intentionally destructive, humans are selfishly indifferent and insensitive, as the following examples illustrate: a man orders ham and eggs in a restaurant full of pigs and chickens (G2:134); a deer boyfriend sits with his human date's father in a room full of deer-head trophies (G3:52); a game warden explains to a deer widow standing over the body of her just-killed spouse that the hunter's "license does check out and, after all, your husband *was* in season" (G3:180). The tension in these satirical encounters between humans and animals is high, and it is clear that animals, as self-aware and comprehending humanimals, would have every reason to resent human oppression and seek to overthrow it.

That trouble is brewing is confirmed when Farmer Brown catches his cows studying a meat chart of the human anatomy (G2:54). On another farm, a bovine rebel leader rehearsing the ambush of Farmer Bob is suddenly annoyed by Muriel's rude and distracting cud-chewing (G2:103). Meanwhile, out in a pasture, a sheep rises up from the flock and proclaims, "We don't HAVE to be just sheep!" (G1:144). Dissidence is in the air. Somewhere in a room, a cow-poet, in an eloquent appeal for freedom and an end to the tyranny of human control, stirs up the cow-masses: "The distant hills call to me. / Their rolling waves seduce my heart. / Oh, how I want to graze in their lush valleys. / Oh, how I want to run down their green slopes. / Alas, I cannot. / Damn the electric fence! / Damn the electric fence!" (G4:122). In a last attempt to settle the issue amicably, a dog tells its master, "Stan, I'd like a place of my own" (G5:127).

Still, the situation heats up. Reports of random acts of defiance, disobedience, and sabotage filter in. In a standoff between a dog and a man brandishing weapons, the dog says, "I'll put *my* magazine down when you put yours down" (G2:186). Another dog, gun in hand, confronts its owner at the dinner table, declaring, "Hey, bucko . . . I'm *through* begging" (G3:14). Still another dog seated at a typewriter in the basement threatens its owner with the riposte, "I wouldn't laugh, Jack . . . I know things about you."[14] From an incongruous telephone booth in the barnyard, mischievous livestock make an anonymous prank call to Farmer Bob, telling him his "barn door's open" (G4:132). A sadistic chicken terrorist in a dog suit strips off its disguise and taunts a family of humans as they chomp on drumsticks: "No, I'm *not* your little dog Fifi! I'm the chicken you *thought* you fixed for dinner! Would you like to know where your little Fifi is?" (G4:110). Finally, a flashback to an illustrious past act of sabotage (the Great Chicago Fire) testifies to the nobility of the animal cause, as the successful mission of "agent 6373" (Mrs. O'Leary's cow?) is proudly recalled (G1:41).

Collaborators and cowards, however, threaten the cause. Cattle shun a fellow bovine who has taken a job driving a meat truck (G2:8). A steer traitor squeals on the herd in exchange for a promise not to be slaughtered (G3:129). As for the chicken mob armed with clubs and pitchforks, they balk again at the steps of the farmer's front door, leaving their leader to wonder, "Why is it that the revolution always gets this far and then everyone just chickens out?"

(G4:71) [Figure 6]. Notwithstanding these setbacks, there are a few modest successes. Dogs make a clean getaway in "Master's" car and relish the thought of his reading a letter that mockingly commands him to "Stay!!" (G3:165). A bird not only successfully escapes from its cage but is somehow able to entrap and lock its lady owner in it (G1:34). The message is clear. Humans beware! Humanimals are organizing. The revolution is spreading. It is payback time.

La Bête Humaine

Having up to now viewed the world through more or less exclusively humanimal eyes (and continuing to follow the reverse logic of Larsonism), a radical shift of perspective might at this point seem appropriate, even overdue. We might thus expect that, in a manner inversely parallel to the way he imagines humanized animals evolving "up" into humanimals, Larson would also conceive of animalized humans devolving "down" into *anihumans*. And indeed such beings do inhabit and roam the far side, although they are a rarer breed than their humanimal counterparts. But there is an intermittent transitional creature that first must be considered—the "human beast"—human enough to outwit and dominate simple beasts but bestial enough to kill and torture and commit the most inhuman atrocities without the slightest pang of pity or guilt. The quintessential embodiment of this link in the *Far Side*'s not-so-great chain of being is a character I call "the beast boy," who regularly enters and exits the scene. The most telling depiction of him, in my view, can be found in *Gallery 4* (54), where his huge, looming, ugly, blindly cruel, flat-topped head and bloated torso literally fill the frame, a hyperbole of flesh, a veritable oxymoron of cunning and stupidity [Figure 7]. In this particular situation, he has become a *cause célèbre* of insects, friends of whom he has captured and imprisoned (and no doubt sadistically maimed and tortured) with remorseless pleasure and, until now, impunity.

He is a boy of many names, identities, penchants, and activities. As Billy, he swings obliviously on a rope under the anvil tree (G1:62), plays unawares in the backyard under the watchful, hungry gaze of alligator neighbors (G1:76), ignores the pleas of an adult buried in the sand while gleefully watching the tide come in (G1:192), or receives a wickedly threatening letter from the Tooth Fairy (G2:13). He is also Bobby, who brings for show and tell "something he found on the beach last summer" (a pickled head in a jar) (G1:58), or whose mother scolds him for roughhousing under the hornet's nest suspended over his bed (G2:49). As Danny, he is told by his mother to ignore the monsters moving in next door, since "The more you believe in them, the more

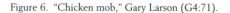

Figure 6. "Chicken mob," Gary Larson (G4:71).

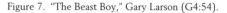

Figure 7. "The Beast Boy," Gary Larson (G4:54).

they'll try to get you" (G2:16), or is frightened into obedience by his father's contrived threat of a monster in the basement (G3:50). Given such parenting, it is no wonder that he becomes a little monster himself.

He is Johnny, who ruins his silly-faced family's portrait by making a silly face (G2:102), Dennis, who has a "rhino tube-farm" in his bedroom (G2:175), Robby, who enjoys burning a brand "R" on the ants of his ant farm (G4:77), Cory, who must prove to his parents he can take good care of cockroaches to get a puppy (G4:97), Todd, who must overcome his fear of alligators downstairs at night to raid the cookie jar (G5:11). Sometimes he is unnamed: the student who best exemplifies the classroom affliction "Basic stupidity" (G3:105), a kid trying to teach a turtle to jump through a flaming hoop (G1:12), a shadowy figure burning ants with a magnifying glass (G1:63), a sadistic son who, delighted with the jars containing his shrunken "mom" and "dad," is told by a genie he still has a third wish (G2:153). Cruelty, stupidity (or just plain ignorance) due in part at least to incompetent and abusive parenting—these are the common threads, but also curiosity about the world and a brutally direct and unaffected involvement in it. The beast boy is, in this sense, the potentially unspoiled human beast, a Nietzschean protosuperman, who has not yet fully degenerated into an all-too-human human or inferior anihuman. But, to finish the list, he is also the youthful incarnation—and here Larson is having fun—of some famous people: Buffalo Bill (G3:136) and Stephen King (G4:49) as decidedly weird children, the young Pablo Picasso (who got an F in art) (G5:109), Santa Ana's son, Juan, whose dad gave him the original Davy Crockett hat for Christmas (G5:128) and, yes, one other beastly child we discover on the cover of *The PreHistory of the Far Side*, "middle row, second from the right," in the picture of "Mrs. Ferguson's first-grade class, 1957." His name is Gary.

The Anihuman Condition

1957 indeed. The entire cast of animate characters in Larson's theater of the absurd—animals, humanimals, anihumans, humans, human beasts—all seem to have been caught in the "twilight zone" of an eternally recurring 1957, caricaturally endowed with all the excesses of that time: beehive hairdos, buns, crewcuts, glasses with fins (like the cars of the period), flower-print mu-mus; and of course just about everyone is—and these are universal traits of modern American bourgeois culture—unremarkably plain or remarkably ugly because everyone is so fat, hugely fat, and lazy (with the advent of TV in the fifties, the couch-potato syndrome is already in evidence long before it had a name).

The humans, in particular, seem dull, dim-witted, gullible, not the least bit clever, although they may think they are: a hunter father teaching his son points to a spot in the woods where there is a pillow, the picture of a deer, and an open book on "How to Win a Doe," and determines that a deer has bedded down there, adding, "After a while, you'll develop an eye for these things yourself" (G2:28). Unlike animals, these pathetically deprived and ill-equipped humans do not even have a survival instinct or the ability, let alone the motivation, to distinguish what is good or bad for them: a man stranded at sea on a crowded rubber raft reaches for a box floating by and says, "Well, we might as well put it on board—although I'm not sure what use we'll have for a box of rusty nails, broken glass, and throwing darts" (G2:126); Doreen, bending down to sit in a chair with a bear trap, spikes, and a snake suspended overhead by a thread, is told not to sit there since "That chair's just not safe" (G4:95).

Nor do these fools have any sense of humor about themselves, even though they are so amusing and funny. They never laugh at or seem to get the jokes they enact, because they are so completely self-unaware. In this respect, they are like animals, but not animals with something extra—humanimals—rather humans with something missing—anihumans. If animals are stupid, it is because they are born that way. Human stupidity, by contrast, often seems to be an acquired way of life. Thinking takes too much effort, it's easier not to; and gradually one winds up a mindless zombie walking about aimlessly in an unself-conscious daze.

A human is truly and unmistakably an anihuman in Larson when perceived by a humanimal like an animal is usually perceived by a human, namely as an inferior objective other. And just as there are degrees of humanimality, so too are there levels of anihumanity. The beast boy, as we have seen, is only at the threshold and has not yet completely "broken through" (although his sheer enormity suggests he is on his way). At the opposite extreme are anihumans who are thoroughly reified things, such as the ones who find themselves hapless prey-objects of a hungry predator's appetite: bears regarding campers in sleeping bags as "Sandwiches!" (G1:55); alligators enjoying the tasty tenderness of a human snack ("That was incredible. No fur, claws, horns, antlers, or nothin' . . . Just soft and pink") (G1:78); polar bears feasting on igloos like candy ("Crunchy on the outside and a chewy center") (G1:160); spiders relishing the thought of trapping a child in a web at the bottom of a slide ("If we pull this off, we'll eat like kings") (G1:140). Sometimes an anihuman is just a pesky little thing that gets squashed, as when an elephant soils himself by accidentally sitting on a man (G1:120).

Slightly higher on the anihuman scale are humans not simply eaten or squashed but treated or considered as animals by humanimals, just as animals are treated or considered by humans: spiders scare another spider by dangling a man (G1:56); a frog sprouting beast-boy warts had been handled by a kid (G3:22); a dog warns another dog not to take table scraps from a man, since "Everyone knows their mouths are dirtier than our own!" (G4:124); a bird stuffs worms all day into an insatiable human baby (G1:106). And still higher are anihumans who, in a role reversal, act like animals: a human shakes his leg as a dog scratches his belly (G1:10); a dog drives a car while a human passenger leans out of the window with his tongue hanging out (G1:137); a man abandons his dog on a leash to go and chase birds (G5:156); a scientist in a lab coat follows a mother duck he has imprinted on (G2:165); a male and female ornithologist attracted to each another flap their arms and shake their heads in a bird mating dance (G3:119).

But the anihumans who best put in perspective the way humans arrogantly and callously use and abuse animals are not ones who exchange roles with animals but rather those who find themselves in a position of inferiority, as a species, to a superior alien species. Here the parody is particularly cogent and effective: three-eyed aliens will punch holes this time in a jar filled with human kids plucked from their bicycles (G1:113); planet-dwelling aliens with spacemen in a jar want to shake it to "see if they'll fight" (G4:26); a one-eyed green alien tells Zorak he has "mixed incompatible species in the earth terrarium!" (G4:134); Hal and Ruby groggily return to their yard work "unknowingly wearing the radio collars and ear tags of alien biologists" (G4:13); a professor is forced to write calculus equations in the center ring of an alien circus, as a one-eyed, four-armed, four-footed alien cracks a whip (G5:74); a car with human skeleton passengers and the skeleton of a deer strapped to it is itself strapped to the top of an alien spaceship (G5:148) [Figure 8]. This last drawing is a rare example of *mise en abyme*, which very vividly illustrates the Larsonian chain of being (here in reverse order from bottom up), with humans unceremoniously dethroned from preeminence and trapped ignominiously in the middle.

By creating all these hybrids, though, like some latter-day Frankenstein holed up in his laboratory, Larson is not proposing that animals be more human, because, as we have seen, humanimals usually end up mimicking corrupt human behaviors and are better off remaining the happy beasts they were born. Nor is he suggesting that humans become more animal-like. *The Far Side* is not Vigny's "*La Mort du loup*" ["The Wolf's Death"], in which the nobly silent and stoic wolf accepts his fate with heroic dignity and sets an example for humanity. A moral such as that may edify, but it simply is not funny, and Larson is a comic artist, not a moralist.[15] In fact, *Far Side* animals often are, in their own way, just as stupid as humans. The problem is that humans should not be, with that large, intricate brain of theirs that has catapulted them to the top of the hierarchy.

THE FAR SIDE   By GARY LARSON

Figure 8. "Skeletons on spaceship," Gary Larson (G5:148).

Why, then, does Larson espouse "taking the side/the side taken" of animals? Is not such a project, as Sartre claims in his critique of Ponge, really just an "effort to see oneself through the eyes of a foreign species, in order finally to rest from the painful duty of being a subject?"[16] By so dehumanizing themselves, are not humans simply seeking relief from the anxiety of for-itself being and the burden of its total freedom and concomitant total responsibility, in order to flee into the blissful unself-consciousness of the in-itself being of things? Perhaps that is in fact what Larson's anihumans are doing. They have chosen bad faith, the course of least resistence, over the arduous, steep path of authenticity. But anihumans are not so much contemptible for their weakness, as absurd. If there is a "message" in Larson, it is simple: life, experience, the world, the micro- and macrocosms, and all that they entail are just there, and their being there is just as absurd as the nonbeing of what should be there. Because, though we become so readily inured to that absurdity, we soon cease to notice it and even begin to believe in the meaningfulness of comfortable routines. By switching and mixing modalities, by grafting the human on the animal, the animal on the human, what a moment ago seemed so normal and full of sense now appears senseless, ridiculous, laughable. Simply put, Larson's comic project, like Ionesco's and Beckett's, seeks to break through the concealing familiarity of habit in order to expose the absurdity of what is and is not there.

Notes

1. *The Doors: The Complete Lyrics*, compiled by Danny Sugerman (New York: Bantam Doubleday Dell, 1992), 170.

2. "On the Far Side," Foreword by Stephen King (G2:6). All references to Larson's works will be to the six large-format volumes abbreviated as follows:

   G1: *The Far Side Gallery* (Kansas City: Andrews and McMeel, 1995, First Printing 1984);

   G2: *The Far Side Gallery 2* (Kansas City: Andrews and McMeel, 1995, First Printing 1986);

   G3: *The Far Side Gallery 3* (Kansas City: Andrews and McMeel, 1994, First Printing 1988);

   P: *The PreHistory of the Far Side* (Kansas City: Andrews and McMeel, 1989);

   G4: *The Far Side Gallery 4* (Kansas City: Andrews and McMeel, 1994, First Printing 1993);

   G5: *The Far Side Gallery 5* (Kansas City: Andrews and McMeel, 1995). The choice of the word "gallery" to describe the collections of Larson's works strikes me as cleverly appropriate. Common to the definitions offered by several dictionaries are two types of space, one for placing things on view and another from which to view things. A museum would be a typical example of the first type, and moving through Larson's books is much like wandering through a museum of natural history, popular art, and culture, or (more accurately) a bizarre hybrid of the two. In effect, the Gallery books are like subgalleries of a grand gallery, in which exhibits are grouped chronologically by period. A curator (critic) might, however, rearrange the collection along thematic lines, with a gallery devoted to, as is the case in this "catalogue," depictions of, specifically, humanimals and anihumans. An example of the second type of viewing space would be the upper level of a theater where the cheapest seats are. Here, the word gallery implicates ironically Larson's audience, who not only see themselves reflected in the caricatures of the gallery's exhibits, but also, like very common spectators occupying the cheap gallery seats to view his theater of the absurd, exemplify, as one dictionary puts it, "a lack of artistic discrimination or sophistication." In the end, then, the joke is (probably not unintentionally) on Larson himself, who is "playing to the gallery," i.e., trying "to gain the favor or applause of the general public, especially by crude or obvious means" [!]

3. "Introduction" to Francis Ponge, *The Voice of Things*, ed. and trans. Beth Archer (New York: McGraw-Hill, 1972), 10–11.

4. Charles D. Minahen, "Char and Ponge **Figuring** Ponge and Char," in *Figuring Things: Char, Ponge, and Poetry in the Twentieth Century*, ed. Charles D. Minahen (Lexington, KY: French Forum Monographs, 1994), 237.

5. The accompanying text is specifically an "undertext" that may function as a narrative expressed by an anonymous narrator who comments upon the graphic, as a title that labels the graphic, as direct dialogue emanating from figures depicted in

the graphic, or as a combination of any of these. I am reluctant to use the term "caption," which has been employed indiscriminately to describe any and all types of accompanying text, except as a synonym for "title," in accordance with its dictionary definition.

6. Rarely the space is subdivided into two or more frames, but the number and incidence of these is low, since, when the standard newspaper rectangle is subdivided, the subdivisions become progressively smaller and harder to assimilate and thus can be deployed effectively only in certain very particular situations.

7. Another example of this expectation is a two-panel frame that depicts "What we say to dogs" ("Okay, Ginger! I've had it! You stay out of the garbage! . . .") and "What they hear" ("blah blah Ginger blah blah blah blah blah. . . .") (G1:30). As is often the case in Larson, however, a theme may cut both ways. Thus, in contradiction to the above, animals are also expected to be stupid, as when cows and chickens debating theoretical physics are heard by a farmer to be mooing and clucking (G1:154); or, more threateningly, two men on safari locked in their Land Rover nervously watch a lion inserting a coat hanger through a crack in the front window (G3:53).

8. In some cases the absurdity of animal behavior is exposed, but my intention is to focus primarily upon the human/animal interface.

9. I am assuming Tantor is a male name. Larson's practice of giving human names to many of the animals in his drawings is a contributing factor to their transformation into humanimals. More often than not they are identifiable hims or hers, although they can also be unspecifically gendered its.

10. See Henri Bergson, *Le Rire: essai sur la signification du comique* (Paris: Presses Universitaires de France, 1975), 29. The exact phrase reads, "*du mécanique plaqué sur du vivant*" ["the mechanical plastered on the living"].

11. See, for example, "Lucky's speech," in Samuel Beckett, *Waiting for Godot* (New York: Grove Press, 1954), 28–29; or the "Bobby Watson" episode (end of Scene I) and the absurd wordplay at the end of the last scene (XI) in Eugène Ionesco, *La Cantatrice chauve* [*The Bald Soprano*], *Théâtre* I (Paris: Gallimard, 1954), 22–24, 53–56.

12. Further examples of this particular reversal theme are: a young goldfish who has "dried his bed again" (G2:12) and fish poking through water from above who are alarmed to discover that "The entire basement looks dry!" (G4:117).

13. With regard to cows, Larson notes that, in addition to finding them to be "the quintessentially absurd animal," "the name 'cow'" itself strikes him as "intrinsically funny" (P:156). I think one could quite justifiably extrapolate a similar attitude on his part toward poodles. Unlike "naturally" absurd cows, though, the absurdity of poodles derives from their artificiality, as is clearly the point of the cartoon "Poodles of the Serengeti" (G3:130), which shows a pack of poodles, sporting the typical bouffant-style ruffs of hair and shaved bald patches, resting under a tree, as a pair of bemused or bewildered giraffes looks on. The incongruity of dog and scene is fully attributable to the effects of human vanity and exploitation, which have stripped these animals of their natural dignity and transformed them into silly, defenseless playthings. Poodles represent, in effect, the very excess of bourgeois indulgence and affectation, as is clear in two other cartoons: in the first, a poodle mother, wearing the telltale winged glasses of a bourgeois maven, says to

her daughter's junkyard-dog boyfriend, "So, Raymond . . . Linda tells us you work in the security division of an automobile wreckage site" (G3:154); in the second, a trio of poodles plotting the murder of their owner realize that "the pampering will end" (G5:80).

14. Clipped from a newspaper but not located in any of the Gallery volumes.

15. Whereas the concept of comedy, from Aristophanes through Molière and beyond into the nineteenth century (e.g., Balzac's *Human Comedy*), used to imply, among other things, the correction of vice, and thus incorporated a moral aim, it seems to me that comedy in the twentieth century has tended to view vice more as just another absurd aspect of the human condition that centuries of moral censure have failed to eliminate.

16. Jean-Paul Sartre, *"L'Homme et les choses," Situations*, I (Paris: Gallimard, 1947, newer repaginated edition), 266. Translation mine.

Bibliography

Beckett, Samuel. *Waiting for Godot*. New York: Grove Press, 1954.

Bergson, Henri. *Le Rire: essai sur la signification du comique*. Paris: Presses Universitaires de France, 1975.

Ionesco, Eugène. *La Cantatrice chauve* [*The Bald Soprano*]. *Théâtre* I. Paris: Gallimard, 1954.

Larson, Gary. *The Far Side Gallery*. Kansas City: Andrews and McMeel, 1995. First Printing 1984.

———. *The Far Side Gallery 2*. Kansas City: Andrews and McMeel, 1995. First Printing 1986.

———. *The Far Side Gallery 3*. Kansas City: Andrews and McMeel, 1994. First Printing 1988.

———. *The Far Side Gallery 4*. Kansas City: Andrews and McMeel, 1994. First Printing 1993.

———. *The Far Side Gallery 5*. Kansas City: Andrews and McMeel, 1995.

———. *The PreHistory of the Far Side*. Kansas City: Andrews and McMeel, 1989.

Minahen, Charles D. "Char and Ponge **Figuring** Ponge and Char," in *Figuring Things: Char, Ponge, and Poetry in the Twentieth Century*, ed. Charles D. Minahen. Lexington, KY: French Forum Monographs, 1994. 233–251.

Morrison, James D. *The Doors: The Complete Lyrics*. Compiled by Danny Sugerman. New York: Bantam Doubleday Dell, 1992.

Ponge, Francis. *The Voice of Things*, ed. and trans. Beth Archer. New York: McGraw-Hill, 1972.

Sartre, Jean-Paul. *"L'Homme et les choses." Situations*, I. Paris: Gallimard, 1947 (newer repaginated edition). 226–270.

Index